Charlotte O. Marshall

Mullings and Musings

A Journey from Grace to Grace

For Pierre —

    Cousin Billy was a favorite cousin. We share these wild relatives.

    May every blessing be yours.

        Charlotte Marshall

Unless otherwise noted, all scripture quotations are from the New Revised Standard Version or the King James Version of the Bible.

Published under the auspices of *Trinity Episcopal Church*, 317 Franklin Street, Clarksville, Tennessee 37040.

10 9 8 7 6 5 4 3 2

Cover: *(Clockwise from upper right)* Mary Marshall (The Bishop of Rossview") with grandchildren; the author's childhood home at Kirkwood; the author standing in a field of tobacco with older son in 1955; Grace Chapel at Rossview, Kirkwood's adjoining community; and Grandma Wickham's son's concrete statue of Andrew Jackson, photographed in mid-1960s prior to its destruction by vandals.

To my husband Jack,

who, on May 15, 1997, has faithfully
mulled and mused with me for fifty years.

And as we have borne the image of the earthy, we shall also bear the image of the heavenly.

I Cor 15:49

CONTENTS

PREFACE

In 1982 I became editor of the *Trinity Trumpet*, the monthly publication of Trinity Episcopal Church, Clarksville, Tennessee. As editor I have written most months a personal cogitation with the title, *Mullings and Musings*. These musings grew out of my everyday experiences, ponderings, and remembrances as I struggled to understand myself— my fears and my guilts—and the world of fundamentalism from which I came.

As I have compiled these random musings and reread them from 1983 to 1996, I am struck by the repetition of my main theme: the all-encompassing gift of Grace. Some new revelation, some doubt given up, some hope rekindled—all have brought me back to the square of unconditional love. If I be repetitive, it is the amazing grace that has been revealed to me again and again as the years of my life stretch out in these monthly musings. In them is reflected the death of my mother, our only daughter's severe illness, the joy of grandchildren, remembrances of my parents, friends and acquaintances through the years, my Baptist roots, and the wonder of God's creation.

For whatever good there is in these pages, I give thanks. I am persuaded that whatever I write that has merit is a gift, a grace, and is not of me, but has come through me. Such are the gifts of God.

COM

October 1997

ACKNOWLEDGMENTS

There has been such supportive appreciation and encouragement from Trinity Parish as I muddled through these pages that I hardly know where to start my "thank you's." Ardell Shippy, church secretary and first typist of *Mullings and Musings*, put up with me for eleven years, all the while setting me straight on capitalization and other fine points. Then there were interim typists: Gerry Tatham and Hillary Ginas. Lastly, our new secretary, Mary Alice Burkhart, has changed our image on her wizard computer and has given the *Trumpet* a new-age outlook. For proofreading and editing, much time and effort were given to this project by Dorothy Ann Russo, Sylvia Dawson and Dr. Ed Irwin of Austin Peay State University. Bless them.

The true spark plug for this compilation has been Faye Hatfield, who on her own assembled every copy of *Trinity Trumpet*, put *Mullings and Musings* in her computer, grabbed me out of my lethargy, and demanded that we get it done. Without Faye, I would still be unorganized.

Thank you, all. I do love you.

                                                           COM

Mama and Daddy

MARCH 1995

Lo, children are the heritage of the Lord: and the fruit of the womb is his reward.

Psalm 127

My mother reasoned that the Lord was rewarding her too heavily since she gave birth in 1920, 1921, and 1923. In her last years, she shared her ordeal of diapers and became real about her feeling during those fecund years. "Three babies in three years! It was too much. When I was pregnant for the third time, I thought the world had come to an end. Little did I know that it was just beginning."

She and my father were married in 1915 and for four years all the neighbors' furtive glances at her waistline were in vain. Since most couples who married during this era usually showed the countryside something within the first year, Mama and Daddy decided they were going to be denied this heritage from the Lord. The Lord, no doubt, was giving my mother a four-year backlog, steeling her for the rewards of her womb.

Mama began her reproductive recitation thus: "Well, we got started and just couldn't stop. In the summer of 1919 I woke up in the night craving canned tomatoes, so I got up and ate a bowlful. Then about daylight, the bed started going round and round. I told Bracy I was going to be sick, and I threw up half-a-coal-scuttleful of tomatoes. How they multiplied that much, I don't know."

With the advent of morning sickness the curse of barrenness was lifted and my sister was a much-beloved firstborn in March, 1920. In 1921, my brother, the male heir in our long, distinguished line, was welcomed and admired by all for his infant beauty and intelligence. But alas and alack for 1923! In her utter dismay at this third pregnancy, my mother must have gone on an eating binge. She gained many pounds and I was labored into this world at over ten pounds, moon-faced, very red and red-haired, with an uncertain, floppy mouth that wouldn't close, as well as a flopped ear that is with me until this hour. Daddy reportedly said that the first two looked all right, but he didn't know about this one, as he attempted to close my mouth. Evidently, this was the mouth that closed down their fertility streak.

1

Mama & Daddy

With a wink, Daddy said that they finally found out what was causing all this, and as they grew older they told many stories of their raising "triplets." Somehow, Mama's stories were more graphic and had a sharper edge because she had the rewards of the womb in a time of few amenities—just washboards and diapers dried by the kitchen stove, two babies-worth at a time.

Mama gave this account of March 20, 1923, the day before I was born: "I was in the kitchen washing out tubs of diapers for the baby when a ring came at the front parlor door. 'Now, who could be ringing the front bell?' I dried my hands and with my babies hanging on my skirt, I answered the door. There stood the most dressed-up insurance salesman I'd ever seen, and just as I opened the door, the March wind flung the screen door back and pasted my wet apron against my huge pumpkin. With two toddlers peeping out at him and seeing my obvious embarrassment, not to mention his, the poor fellow turned to leave, only to stumble over our dog, Taffy, who was caught at the foot of the steps in a most compromising position with her latest beau. I knew the man thought that that was all that went on around this place."

Then there were my parents' stories of our illnesses, hanging between life and death; financial crises when Santa Claus almost didn't come and the taxes couldn't be paid; prizes at the fair and a fine Jack colt; war-time tears and separations; funny things that happened at my sister's wedding. The stories went on and on.

In their last years my parents declared if they had it to do over, they would have had more children. And I'm beginning to feel the same way. I sit with my husband and we look at our children and grandchildren and we wonder what we would be thinking about, planning for, and marvelling at if we had not had these three unique individuals. I glory in their diversity and talent, all the while remembering the pain of their growing up, their falling many times but getting up and trying life again, just as I did. Truly our life is a treasure from God and our parents, and I hand this life on in awe as I ponder this reward, this miracle of creation that was mine to bear.

Mama & Daddy

APRIL 1994

> *How beautiful upon the mountains are the feet of him that bringeth*
> *good tidings, that publisheth the gospel of peace.*
>
> *Isaiah 5:2*
> *Romans 10*

Grandma Wickham had taught my mother that you should never plant green beans until the maple leaves were "as big as a mouse's ear." At that time she said that the earth would be warm enough to resurrect the tiny bean embryos and the danger of frost would be past. Mama translated this same rule to our feet that had been encased too long in their winter tomb. They longed to be free again, to shed their wool and leather shrouds, to give us a heady lightness, to fly us through the spring grass like swift-footed Mercury. How beautiful were our feet in daffodils.

With the daffodils as our witness, my brother and I began our spring nagging campaign, "Can we do it today? See how warm it is and it's the end of March. The maples are blooming and we can see the leaves coming. Please, Mama, can we go to school barefooted today? Everybody says it's time and you can't play marbles with shoes on. Pleeeeease." Mamas can stand only so much nagging and they finally cave in. With shoes and stockings wildly abandoned and with Grandma Wickham's mouse-eared oracle ringing in our ears, we left, barefooted, for school.

Now Miss Mamie, our teacher, was an immovable object who resisted all forces. She ruled with a ruthless ruler. "Why are you two here barefooted this morning?" She gave us her contemptuous look saved only for white trash. With thin lips and matching nose, topped by cold, colorless eyes and a washboard marcel, she snapped, "I hope your feet freeze off before you get home. You both look like yaps." Her one comforting feature, which she never used, was her lap which extended halfway to her knees, accompanied by matching folds at each side that tormented her complaining chair. Daddy said he knew what her problem was, but we didn't understand problems.

"You know how the weather is in March—one moment sunny and the next cold. Your mother must have lost her mind."

"Yassum," we ruled to agree.

We had never before questioned the place of our mother's brains, but if God himself had forecast the weather, we would not have been more certain of its outcome after Miss Mamie's pronouncement. About noontime, as Abraham Lincoln and George Washington stared down on us, it began to snow. It was a calm, clinging snow with every twig, new leaf and stone caressed in belated splendor. I looked at my brother and we didn't care. With Mercury as our god, we knew we could wing it home even though our feet didn't yet have their stone-bruised soles.

And wing it we did. At 3:00 o'clock we light-footed it out, disregarding the rocks under the snow, tossed mushy snowballs down each other's collars and knew where we would place one for Miss Mamie. Mama met us anxiously at the door, went over the mouse-eared territory again, and propped our purple feet in front of the grate. How beautiful were our feet who had felt the good tidings of release.

Mary Magdalene knelt at Jesus' bare feet and found forgiveness as she bathed them with her perfumed tears and dried them with her hair. Then Christ, our master, taught us how to be great. At the last supper, the Lord of Glory took a basin and towel and bathed his disciples' feet, telling them that they must be servants to know greatness. And finally, our Savior was stripped and beaten and forced to bear the cross on bloody feet through the streets of Jerusalem. There at Golgotha he had nails driven through them that we might know the good tidings and the gospel of peace.

As the maples bud, grow into mouse's ears, and into full leaf, so may our release into joy come with this resurrection season.

APRIL 1992

> *Or who shall stand in his holy place? He that hath clean hands and*
> *a pure heart.*
> ### *Psalm 24*

On Sunday Mama saw to it that we three children had clean hands. As to our hearts, she worked on them too, but she concentrated more on *Lifebuoy* soap than the lives of our souls since cleanliness was more attainable in our kitchen than godliness. None could escape so mighty a cleansing on Saturday nights.

The story of our purification seems remote in our 1992 world with all its faucets of hot water on tap, great Jacuzzied tubs, and perfumed and bubbled unguents for "scurf" on your heels and elbows. We were purified in pre-rural electrification days by a mother who believed in seeking out each and every hidden crevice that might harbor "scurf," especially the "locks of your jaws" and the "bends of your knees," not to mention knuckles during marble season. Water was scarce and recycled and until this very hour I have never felt so clean and comforted as I did after our Saturday night's preparation to stand in his holy place.

We kept out a rain barrel for baths; this water was soft. But if it didn't rain it was to the well with a bucket and chain, filling the reservoir on the *Home Comfort* range, all the tea kettles, every available big pot, and finally a big zinc tub that was put up on the stove. After supper Mama stoked the stove until the surface glowed and the pots hissed and danced, sending vapors weeping down the window panes. Clean clothes, from the skin out, were stacked on the kitchen table, our last week's underwear made into the bath mat, the zinc tub was lowered to the floor, Mama got her scrubbing tools ready, and we were admonished not to "flinch or dodge." Our purification was at hand and we knew a purifying hand when we saw one.

There was a hierarchy for this ordeal by water. My sister, being the oldest and above frog-fondling and marble-swapping, got the virgin water. After her bath the water was left with a decent, milky tone with not too much soap scum accumulated against the sides of the tub; but for my brother and me it was repeated latherings. My brother was the second in line. Mama put two big pots of hot water into this decently clean water and put him in to soak. She soaped his head, held his ears forward and backward searching for "scurf", all the while giving him a soaped cloth to scrub the "locks-of-your-jaws." What these locks held in the way of impurities I do not know, but they received attention above all else on his budding anatomy. Then at last after his scalding and plucking, Mama would soap another great rag, "Now go over everything again."

Being at the bottom of this sibling stairstep, I was last. The water had to be thinned down. With two or three pails of lock-jawed water dipped out, fresh hot water went in with one bucket set aside to rinse my hair. I got the same treatment as my brother with a soak, two sudsings, and a rinse. By this time there was an evil gray fur clinging to the sides of the zinc tub, formed no doubt by some dire chemical reaction. It must have been *Lifebuoy* soap doing battle with elbow, knuckle, knee, heel, and jaw scurf; and it finally surrendered its lather to underwhelming amounts of hard well-water. Yet this water had its final uses. Mama added hot water, soaked her tired feet, and then mopped the kitchen linoleum with this triple-dip solution.

Mama & Daddy

Easter makes me remember these baths. Even though we Baptists were not a liturgical church, Mama put special emphasis on this day, retrimming one of her hats, and we girls had new dresses with Irish crochet lace on our collars and my brother a very starched and properly ironed white shirt. Shined shoes were also a pre-Easter chore with our patent leather shoes getting a good rub with a biscuit and my brother's shoes a coat of *Shinola*. Mama saw to it that we did our very best with what we had, and that is no small legacy. She said we had to have "Pride."

So we stood in the holy place on Easter Sunday with clean hands. I am persuaded that the example of this getting ready, the purification of our bodies, the anticipation of the holy, is a prerequisite that leads us into the mystery of true worship. The very death of our scurfed bodies in baptism by the kitchen stove to our resurrection from this mighty cleansing has lead us through the years on an unrelenting quest for our pure hearts. Never does Saturday night come that I do not anticipate the cleansing of my heart as well as my garments.

So to my mother who had pride, I say, "Bless you, for leading us to stand with clean hands in his holy place."

May the joy of Easter be with us all!

FEBRUARY 1990

A merry heart doeth good like a medicine; but a broken spirit drieth the bones.

Proverbs

For the past few Januarys and Februarys, during these short, bleak days, I have traditionally mulled and mused merrily, dredging into my remembrance of levity past to lighten our dried winter bones. Right now I need this. Having been away from you, my church family, for two months, I come back among you, broken and dried, but anchored in this Body of Christ that has sustained me with its prayers and consolation. My everlasting thanksgiving to you all.

With a merry heart I go back to my earliest memories whose shadows somehow become clearer as I approach the leeward side of life. Such is my recalling of my first singing of old Baptist hymns whose verses, all four of them, are still emblazoned in my memory and whose simple melodies began my life-long love for music. To you cradle

Mama & Daddy

Episcopalians, maybe you can hum along or perhaps you made enough Baptist and Methodist meetin's to sing along with me.

My daddy was the chief bass singer at Kirkwood Church. He had a true ear for harmony and didn't want any "dragging" singing. If the congregation got too slow, he would tap his foot a tempo and lead the congregation on to "Higher Ground." Long before I could read I stood by his side on the wooden bench and piped with much fervor the lines I knew by heart. Some of the words, however, were not in my innocent vocabulary, and the memory of these misinterpretations does lighten my January heart.

The King James version of the Bible, or the Holy Writ as my mama called it, seemed to sanctify or launder certain words whose connotations had changed from Shakespearean days to my infant days. From the Bible we could hear the account of Balaam's ass speaking without too much smirks and guilty looks at each other and read in Sunday school class of Sampson's slaying a thousand Philistines with the jawbone of an ass without choking on the word, not to mention our Lord's triumphant entry into Jerusalem on the foal of an ass. We got rather blase with this word. But it was the gentle ox and ass of the manger scene that confounded my earliest theology and confused the chorus of *I Am Thine, O Lord.*

"Draw me nearer, nearer, nearer Blessed Lord to the cross where thou hast died." My four-year-old ears had never heard the word *Hast,* and I figured if the ox and ass could be at the manger when Christ was born, the ass could show up to die at the crucifixion. I sang it loud and clear this way until one Sunday long after I could read I happened to glance at these long-ago memorized lines and saw this archaic form of the verb *Have* in the second person singular present indicative—"thou hast." Mortification was mine. But no one ever heard or seemed to notice. You ex-Baptists and Methodists sing this chorus and see if it doesn't sound this way!

But as I mull and muse about the poor ass's demise, this childish scene has real theological implication. Who among us does not need to give up his asinine self to die here at the cross?—our balking hearts, never truly taking our Master's bridle; our refusal to follow any path other than the ones we choose; our braying and bragging to shore up our gods of self and our possessions; and our petty nipping and kicking at each other's backsides. Our weaknesses die in the presence of the Lamb of God who *Hast* taken away our sins.

7

Over against my hymn of weakness was my hymn of power. "Would you be free from your burden of sin? There's power, power, wonder-working power in the blood of the lamb..." Having read *Popeye* and *Krazy Kat* in funny paper, I knew the word *Pow* well from Popeye's fists and Krazy Kat's brick bats. When we came to the chorus—"There is Pow, Pow, wonder-working Pow," I hit each Pow with firecracker crescendos to the sixth one which must have loosened a few wasps' nests in the tongue and groove ceiling, sending these threatened creatures down with dizzying anguish as we freed our burden of sin. My father's bass line resonates still in my lingering ear—"In the Blood"—"of the lamb" and then his answering *"Pow"* to my, "There is Pow." I knew from our singing there was some mystery, some unfathomable presence that made for all these Pows.

There is power in the blood. We know it anew each time we approach this sacrifice made for our weakness. We know its power to transform us into Sons of God. So with our old hymns and St. Paul let us say, "I am determined not to know anything among you, save Jesus Christ and him crucified." May his Pow give us peace in this new decade.

SEPTEMBER 1989

The people who walked in darkness have seen a great light.
Isaiah

We the people who walked in darkness were the graduates of Kirkwood Elementary School, I in 1936. There were no public school buses. The great light we saw was the dinner-plate sized headlights of a 1929 *Buick* limousine, one intended for a liveried chauffeur in some great city, not out by our smokehouse and chicken coops. If the coronation coach with queen aboard had suddenly appeared in our backyard, we, who had only known *Model A* puddle jumpers, could not have been any more pop-eyed or slack-jawed. What prophecy was fulfilled when my daddy drove this royalty into our backyard? Did she realize she had come to give her life as a ransom for many from ignorance? I as one who took my first feeble steps out of darkness into the light of Clarksville High School can attest that this lady, for the transportation of her people, was smitten and we esteemed her not. She was to be our school bus.

"Who hath believed our report?" There were silk window shades that went up and down on rollers just like in the living room, vases on

8

either side of the doors for flowers, plush seats that would ease the most delicate derriere, enough room between the front and back seat to completely stretch your legs without touching the back of the front seat, a grand metal footrest that flopped up and down, many tasseled straps for the ladies' decorous getting in-and-out, hand-painted ashtrays on all arm rests and the back of the front seat, and real wooden trim on the windows, doors, and dash. To me her length seemed a half football field, the straight 8 engine would do a *Mack* truck proud, and when we had to have tires, they were truck-sized tires. This queen was a dowager queen; but her enforced abdication and her sacrifice for our ignorance was imminent. Dwelling in darkness were Olivers, Marshalls, Moorefields, Masons, Doritys, Boyers, Harrises, Bournes, Harpers, Blantons, and others long forgotten.

"To whom is the arm of the Lord revealed?" My daddy in his travels selling fruit all around town knew a quite elderly Mr. Hurst, of Hurst-Boillin Wholesalers, who had this classic *Buick*, languishing, undriven, lo for many a year in his garage with about 800 miles on the odometer. Here was his answer! Being strictly of the swift school of Utilitarian Philosophy, my father made a quick deal with Mr. Hurst, left his jalopy and peach baskets behind to be picked up later, and dashed triumphantly homeward in a great cloud of dust and creative determination.

The first ostentation to go was the footrest in the back floorboard. Out came hammer and saw, 1 x 8 inch lumber was procured, her elegant innards measured and a wooden bench was built to fit behind the front seat. With this secured in place, there was in the breadth of Her Majesty room for twelve of us: four in front, four in the back, and four on the bench, these being chosen because of unsqueamish stomachs that could ride backwards. They also got a fifty-cents-a-month discount for their backwardness.

My brother, sixteen and swash-buckling, was the first driver of our school bus. He no doubt aspired to the *Indianapolis 500*; but in the meantime, for practice, determined to exalt every valley and lower every hill, make the crooked ways straight and the rough places plain. He gloried in the powerful engine and knew just how to switch off the engine, fill the carburetor with uncombusted gasoline, and then switch the motor back on to the most glorious backfire that rattled the countryside and sent the Rossview pedestrians into the ditches and over fences.

Mama & Daddy

One persistent neighbor who insisted on hailing us down for a ride into town on our already over-crowded bus was given the *Chariot-of-Fire* treatment. My brother set an all-time record from Kirkwood to Clarksville with 80 miles-per-hour in all straight-aways, every vehicle was left behind as though standing still, and when we went down the Red River Hill, all the fury of the gasoline gods was forced into the system at once, leaving such a trail of explosive fire as to render our freeloader dumb. We never saw him again.

With the muffler all gone and the parents in panic, my father unbuckled my brother's swash, but not before we brought down the window shades and silken tassels from hanging on. One of our passengers, Reuben Boyer, a most mature young gentleman and conservative driver, took over as charioteer. We and the chickens along the road gave thanks, and Mama didn't pray as much.

The grand old queen suffered every humiliation that a teeming carload of adolescent children could render over a period of years. She forgot what color the paint was underneath the mud baths; football sweat and chewing gum mocked her plush; the vases had long ago been missiles to toss out the windows; she had two plunges into ditches, one to turn completely on her side. The final insult was the result of our abandoned lunch sacks and half-eaten sandwiches crammed under the wooden bench. She had a bad case of mobile mice.

She was bruised for our transgressions, and I say, "Thank you and comfort ye wherever your old metal bones rest, my old *Buick* friend." You gave us our light and we count among us college professors, corporate executives, a priest and composer, teachers, successful farmers, and one who learned to scribble a few English language sentences with their syntax intact.

OCTOBER 1988

This is election year. How else do you account for the record hot air of '88? This, too, is the year of the *True Believer*. How else do you account for the zealots of righteousness, both Donkey and Elephant? Since Adam and Eve were given the knowledge of good and evil and the freedom to choose, the true believer has been with us. Hot-eyed and white-lipped, he grabs you by the lapels at the first suggestion you ride on the wrong party animal, berates you with his set of statistics, and heaps every cheap innuendo that has been ferreted out onto your candidate. Seething inside, you stand there, not giving credibility to a word

Mama & Daddy

he says, condescending to one so ignorant, waiting your turn to empty your wealth of righteousness on him. And so it goes.

My daddy was the first political true believer my infant memory can muster. The year was 1928 and the South was solid. But with a Tammany Hall, Catholic, wet Al Smith as the Democratic candidate, my father put his belief in the more dignified and humane Herbert Hoover and found himself proselytizing on his Democratic neighbors' front porches and at the general store at Hampton Station. There would be "a car in every garage and a chicken in every pot."

My father's true belief crashed with the crash of '29, and the derision of the countryside was on his head. He found hate letters in our mailbox and once a gnarled sweet potato, shaped somewhat like a combination donkey and elephant, with this inscription attached to the potato's trunk: "A jackass trying to be a GOP." But my father, from his bout with true belief, learned some lessons we all need to learn: You can be wrong; what's good and true in one time and place is not good and true in another time and place; you can change your mind, and should, from time to time; but above all, he learned the fallibility of all political personalities, their platforms and promises. He lived to be no longer totally dry and enjoyed a glass of wine and a good lace of bourbon in his Christmas boiled custard. Then, in 1960, back in the Democratic fold, he became a believer—but not too true—in the candidacy of Catholic John F. Kennedy.

Since I mull and muse in the name of Christ, I would that my commitment to party have a solid basis in some specific guidelines like *Tippecanoe and Tyler Too* or *Fifty-Four Forty Or Fight*. What Christ gives us, instead, is the all-encompassing, radical claims of the ages: "I am the way and the truth." Then he gave us one new commandment: "Love one another." On this should hang all our true belief.

With this way and this commandment we make our political commitment. His way is the way of acceptance of all men. In which party are all men and women fully granted their dignity as children of God? His way is the way of healing. In which party are the bodies of our neighbors cared for most fully? His way is the way of sharing. In which party is the great bounty of this nation enjoyed by the most persons? His way is the way of teaching. In which party is there the most opportunity to love God with the mind? His way is the way of the peacemaker. Blessed is the party that brings us nearer peace.

Our love is imperfect, our political judgment naive, and the correct choice is often obscure; however, I believe we are called to choose true

11

belief in the name of Christ. We are in our time the people of God, and we make our commitment anew in 1988 to the one who is the Lord of History and whose Kingdom shall come. We can say in faith with St. Paul, "I know whom I have believed, and am persuaded that he is able to keep that which I have committed unto him against that day."

JUNE 1988

June has Father's Day and so far Dear Old Dad has been ignored in the Trumpet. Mothers have had all the press, as though they were solely responsible for bringing forth the generations. As one old sailor said, "Fathers are necessary for the laying of the keel but can't do a thing at the launching"—but they can make all the difference after the launching. I had such a father.

He was Kirkwood's Renaissance Man in orchard and garden. We grew up surrounded by damson plums and nectarines, cherry trees, grape arbors, exotic varieties of peaches with names like *Georgia Belle* and *Stump-The-World*, apples that would be prized by the current collectors of the first settlers' scions, and trees with several varieties of apples and peaches grafted into the same trunk. From blossom time to picking time, my father communicated to his three stair-step children the miracle of growth and the wonder of our hand in this miracle.

However, the garden, not the orchard, was the training ground for his barefoot brood. This was the place of character-building and "sticking to your row," as well as the schoolroom into the way of beans. Beans, according to my father, had unique problems, especially butter beans. Now bunch beans just bunched up on the hill and made beans, unattended, but pole beans had to have lessons in astronomy. When the poles for the pole beans were put up in their four-stick tents and the bean tendrils started reaching out, we were required to instruct these young vines that they were in the northern latitudes and must be twined up around the poles, clockwise. This we did each morning after the new tendrils had the night with the Pole Star and had gotten themselves oriented. But the butter beans were another story. Bunch beans and pole beans were more or less round around the girth and had no problems with up and down when they were sprouting, but butter beans were wide and flat and could have their necks broken and their cotyledons buried backwards if the butter beans were not planted with their eyes down. Butter beans did not know about tropism.

Mama & Daddy

Thus our father began our education into the safe delivery of the embryonic butter beans. First he cut us a stick six inches long, the correct distance between the bean seeds. Then he laid out a straight furrow three inches deep down a long row where we placed the butter beans, measured true to the stick, edgewise, with their eyes down, to the end of our assigned row. Seldom was there a breech birth. Always there was the satisfaction, even at our tender years, that we had done our job well and that somehow we were assisting in the mystery of the seed that dies to give new life.

From my father's early instructions we children learned these profound lessons for the rest of our lives: Use a true measuring stick, keep your eyes in the right position, stick to your row, and remember that butter beans are flat.

FEBRUARY 1988

Honor the Lord with your substance and with the first fruits of all your produce; then your barns will be filled with plenty, and your vats will be bursting with wine.

Proverbs 3

My mother revered her grandmother Wickham. Grandma had been widowed and left with twelve children along with orphaned grandchildren, one of whom was my mother. I don't know my great-grandmother's religious persuasion, but her faith was bred into her bones from pioneer stock who crossed through the Cumberland Gap and came by the rivers to Montgomery County. It was a literal religion, austere and honest in its dealing with the Almighty: The first fruits were the Lord's and the tithe a small recompense for all his bounty.

If Grandma had ten fat hogs in her pig pen, the prize one was considered the Lord's; if she had wool for sale, the top ten percent was the Lord's as well as the tithe from all the crops from her land. Grandma said that the Lord did not eat at the second table. All this carried over into my good Baptist mother who absolutely labeled it sinful and insulting to the majesty and honor of our Lord to have any ice cream supper, bazaar, or—heavens forbid—a rummage sale for the furthering of his kingdom. The idea was repulsive! I found myself sneaking pies out the back door for the Salad Luncheon. In her last years, I kept my mother's bank account, and Grandma had trained her well—all the money from her farm and her small investments was tithed without question. That's just the way it was; there was no equivocation. My

13

eyes always bugged out when I saw her little country church's financial statement where the tithe was the norm.

So where are my priorities? We had a tithing sermon, rare in an Episcopal pulpit, that set me thinking. Where does the Lord of Creation eat at my table? How much of the table did I bring into the world and how much will I take when I leave this world? The answer to both I know—nothing. Naked I came; naked I go. I know all is grace, a gracious gift: my very life, my family, my food, my shelter, and, yes, the brains with which to puzzle my way through it all. This is indeed grace on grace.

St. Paul tells us that even the ability to know our need to give is a grace. Until we have had our eyes opened to see the totality of life as a precious gift, one we should respond to with overwhelming praise, we have not received the Holy Spirit which teaches us all things. This spirit envelopes us with the need to give our very selves away—to lose our lives to save them—and the tithe seems a small portion in return for what has been given us. So we need to ask first for this grace for giving. Then there will be no tithe to measure, no standard of law, but coffers filled by God's people, overflowing with gratitude for his bounteous mercy and grace.

APRIL 1987

> *For in this tent we groan, longing to be clothed with our heavenly dwelling—if indeed, when we have taken it off we will not be found naked. For while we are still in this tent, we groan under our burden, because we wish not to be unclothed but to be further clothed, so that what is mortal may be swallowed up by life.*
> *St. Paul*
> *II Cor 5:2-4*

We are still in Lent, but spring is here and Easter will soon be shouting resurrection. But for the past few days instead of lilies and dogwood and daffodils, I have been into crabgrass and bitterweed. Long deadly days and nights of hospital waiting with my ninety-five year old mother have put me into a morbid musing concerning my mortality and, alas, the mortality of us all. Does dying have to be so long? Where can you hide from tubes, tanks, and breathing machines and the impersonal probings of the naked self by many a professional eye—all of which, rather than prolonging life, prolongs death? Where do you find

14

dignity in dying in this technological age? Where do you wait in peace "for that which is mortal to be swallowed up by life?"

Across the years I still hear my father's pleadings to die. After some heroic surgery for prostatic cancer, he was left incontinent, humiliated, and at the last in a prolonged agony that made our Lord's time on the cross seem small. He pronounced this nation not Christian or there would be some means by which he could die. "My God, my God, why hast thou forsaken me," became our cry, and how my father longed to say "Into thy hands I commend my spirit"—but the prolonging of death had been done and there was no victory.

This time here called *Life* has become prideful and jealous of the victory of death. Man in his pursuit of knowledge, his dominion over creation, seems to have overstepped his bounds once again; and we are back to the original temptation where man is determined to be wise as the gods, even to the point of eating of the *Tree-of-Life*. His triumph of sustaining the heart, the lungs, the kidneys is a great victory if life is returned to joy and dignity, but a great defeat when man's allotted days are used up. These "pains of death" do not come from God but from his usurpers. This prolonging of death is idolatrous.

The sweet jargoning of the birds and the waft of daffodil perfume call me from such dark musings. Through the din of tubes and technology I hear St. Paul's affirmation, "What is mortal is swallowed up by *Life*." Resurrection is here with us each hour, each day, each moment. We know, though we die, yet shall we live. Our Brother has gone before us and we are not afraid. We only fear our misinterpretation of life.

When our time here has come to its end, may we say with Simeon, "Lord now lettest thou thy servant depart in peace, according to thy word: For mine eyes have seen thy salvation."

MAY 1986

My mother had the noble notion that she was going to make musicians out of the three of us. After saving her money for several seasons, she became the proud owner of a veteran upright piano with a jazzy twang that suggested it had seen better days in some dim-lit den-of-iniquity; but this inimitable instrument served well our budding talent which stayed, on my brother's and my part, in the bud, but came to full-flower in my sister.

Mama & Daddy

After the piano, the next hurdle was a teacher. Hampton Station's one claim to the world of art and music was Miss Molly Webb. She had studied in New York, was reported to have met Paderewski, and owned an original oil painting entitled *Cleopatra's Court* that covered one wall of her entrance hall. She played her square piano with a fury of feet and derriere and flailing arms to the utter amazement of my tender years. I was spellbound. She must have ridden to hounds in younger days because at seventy-five she rode a stallion, bareback, with a long, black riding skirt in fast pursuit. She was the original liberated woman. My sister, being the oldest, was judged by Miss Molly to have the promise of a prodigy and my brother "had the hands of a musician." With two down and my not being at the trainable stage, the judgment as to my ability was not made by Miss Molly. But well I remember my brother and sister's venture into the realm of culture.

This acculturation needed transportation. The year being roughly 1929, and our *Model T Ford* being regularly temperamental, my father decided what we needed was reliable transportation. The word became flesh in the form of a jennet. To you, gentle readers, who don't know what a jennet is—that is a lady jackass. Now the trek from our house to Miss Molly's was approximately two to two-and-a-half miles depending on whether you went by Hampton Station or down the Knott Lane; but either route was fraught with navigational hazards, dangerous to Jenny's delicate nature. There were trains and bulls and strange mechanical creatures in the fields. After each trip—some done in twenty-five minutes, others taking a whole morning—Jenny's idiosyncrasies were the talk of the roadside. Ears forward or back, tail up or down, nostrils flared with humped-backed braying—each nuance suggested some crisis on the road. It could be the *Pan American* approaching the crossing with whistle full-throttle. This called for dead *Stop* in the middle of the road which no coaching with bridle, two-by-four, or two full-grown men could budge. Only after her psyche had come to terms with whatever jenny psyches have to come to terms with, would she move. Every bush and tree, stray dog, or waving piece of paper along the route called for "shying," which meant a buck and a fast side-step that could send you off in the dust. Her final act of desperation was the full-fall-forward, sending her double load over her head. When she was headed home, she would twitch her tail in a most hopeful manner and pick up speed in excess of two miles per hour. One hung on at this dizzy pace. After my brother and sister rebelled and took to walking did we find that Jenny was in a family way, at which point she was relieved

16

of cultural pursuits, put out to pasture, and ultimately redeemed herself with a fine jack colt.

My sister learned well from Miss Molly and played the piano for church with much volume and flourishing runs up and down the key board. We were all proud. My brother decided he didn't have the hands of a musician and, being tone deaf, settled for plows and football instead. My poor mother, frustrated with too many duties, along with Miss Molly's departure to glory, put me out to grass along with Jenny. But enough culture filtered down that I learned F A C E and Every Good Boy Does Fine, which has allowed me through the years to hum along in many a choir. So whatever "joyful noise" I have made has been an indirect legacy left me by Miss Molly, my sister who learned her scales, a tinny piano, a mother bent on making something out of us, and the stubborn brays of a lady jackass.

AUGUST 1984

My father was an inventor. Sometimes his grandiose contraptions went awry but they were always innovative and ingenious. The electrification of the churn was one of his most spectacular projects.

If you don't know a *Daisy Churn*, which was a notch ahead of the dash-up-and-down kind, here are more or less the specifications of this gem: It consisted of a square, five-gallon metal bucket topped with two wooden lids which kept the buttermilk from splashing out. Down into this churn through a small hole in the lid came a wooden paddle wheel that was powered by a flywheel which you had to turn. Having seen the many monotonous hours that were droned away at this cranking job, my father decided with the advent of electricity that he must liberate the household from this chore.

His intentions were 100 per cent for our release from a tedious job, but his information about motors and their ability was zero. Someone had donated a one-horse-power motor to his inventive genius, and this to him was the very one to power the churn. After some days of building a rolling platform for the churn and motor and fitting the right belt between the drive shaft and the flywheel, he was ready and the countdown day arrived. What a day it was!

When the Tennessee Valley Authority was turned on, old Daisy took off in a mighty dance across the kitchen tossing her lids and flinging buttermilk to the ceiling with noble abandon, all the while losing the soldering from her old seams and streaming buttermilk down her sides. She was caught in a mighty force until we, through our buttermilk-splashed amazement, could get this mad scene in focus and unplug the motor. Daisy was retired to the attic never again to be gently cranked or wildly ravished. She couldn't hold her buttermilk anymore.

I mull and muse for the moral of this domestic intranquility: When I consider my father's ignorance of power and Daisy's unpreparedness for it, I see us—the human family—who so dimly grasp the glory and wonder and might of the only source of our lives. We resist the source with inordinate pride or with sniveling weakness. We wind up with the grand schemes for ourselves out-of-hand or relegate ourselves to Life's attic.

Give us wisdom, Lord, to know you through whom and by whom all things were made. Amen.

JUNE 1983

In the early 1900s when the rural South was deeply impoverished, my father, in his late teens, decided the thing for him to do was to seek his fortune in the North. So with his straw hat in his suitcase, he was off to Pittsburgh. As long as he lived, he recounted the stories of his venture into city life with a vivid freshness as though they had happened last week. Probably his most lasting and life-changing experience was the one into Lutheranism.

With no Southern Baptist Church at hand and with newfound German immigrant friends, he attended their services with regularity. The one service, above all, that remained in his memory, and one he could not tell about without becoming quite emotional, was their service of reconciliation before the Communion. If there was anyone in the congregation with bad feelings and unforgiveness toward his brother or sister, he was forbidden by the strict Lutheran teaching to take Communion until he made peace within the brotherhood.

There were specific prayers and names named. "While you (name) were yet a sinner Christ died for you and forgave you. Father forgive them (name) because they know not what they do." And being grounded Lutherans, they emphasized God's grace and reminded each other that of themselves they could not forgive but must open themselves, as St. Paul said, "because God's love has been poured into our hearts through the Holy Spirit which has been given to us." If they resisted this gracious gift of the Holy Spirit—the ability to forgive—then God would not forgive them their sins and they would be left in their miserable state of a bitter and unforgiving heart.

The denouement of my father's account was the reconciliation of actual brothers, two powerful German men who worked in the steel mills and had not spoken in several years. Both continued to attend church and had, as their church so ordained, been excluded from the Communion service. There was a stony, impregnable anger between them even after years of prayers and admonitions for their mutual forgiveness. But at one Sunday night service—and here is where my father's eyes filled and his lips quivered—one of them had the experience of "God's love poured into his heart" and he leaped over a pew, grabbed his brother in an overpowering embrace, and they washed away their anger in repentant tears while the beauty of their forgiveness flooded the whole congregation. They at last took the bread and wine together.

For more than fifty years one country boy never forgot this Communion service, and he reminded us that we should harbor no unforgiveness even though we had not been asked to forgive. "For while we were yet sinners, Christ died for us."

JUNE 1996

Far-away mice have long tails.

A family epigram

Daddy's double first cousin, Jim Warner, left Rossview for California in the early 1900s, seeking a golden life away from farming, which was about the only opportunity for rural boys at that time in Montgomery County's history. My father stayed rooted to the land, except for his two-year venture to Pittsburgh, and managed a meager living for his family, never dreaming of a gold rush; but with reports from Jim, Daddy's small farm must have looked like payless dirt compared to Jim's picture of his touring car with His Highness, Jim, at the wheel, his Knob Hill home in the background.

Daddy spoke Jim's name with reverence. With his being so far away in California and reports of a wealthy marriage, inventions with patents, and accolades from the world of golf, we knew we, indeed, had a celebrity in our family, one who would soon grace Kirkwood with his world of flashy automobiles and golf knickers. We couldn't wait for this hero's return. We waited and we waited and we waited and the tales of fame and fortune grew weightier until, alas, we despaired. We became resigned to the bare fact that Jim could not condescend to such a mundane world as ours.

Time passed, World War II ended, farming got better, and Daddy had a few loose nickels in his pocket. With his new-found wealth, he convinced another cousin to accompany him to El Dorado. At last, he would behold Jim and bask in his world of wealth and pleasure.

The far-away tales were the tail-end of a mirage. Poor, disillusioned Daddy! The truth did out: Jim had married into a wealthy family who were Dutch immigrants and most parsimonious. They allowed Jim to use their car and house for a prop for pictures back home. In fact, his in-laws disapproved of their fifteen-year-old daughter's marriage to this Tennessee upstart. The inventions and patents and royalties were wishful thinking, and the only proof we ever had of any creativity was a crossbow that he made and, in his old age, gave to one of our sons. He had no job. His wife was given a small allowance from her family, and Jim spent his days on the golf courses around San Francisco picking up lost golf balls and selling them.

All this information came from neighbors. Daddy had been in Jim's home two days when he knew the families on both sides. Jim knew no one; spoke to no one. All up and down the street, Daddy charmed the children and dogs, and after he got home he carried on a lengthy correspondence with one of his new friends.. There was such a careful allotment and general paucity of food in Jim's household that Daddy and his other cousin would gather up the neighborhood children after supper for a visit to the Dairy Dip to assuage their hunger. Daddy said he had never seen a scrambled egg divided between two people. When he got back to Tennessee, Mama's bountiful table was at last appreciated.

In his old age, Jim came home to his native sod. He was a widower, in his eighties, dirty, completely alone, and uncherished. He had no children. During his visit to California, the neighbors told Daddy that there had been a pregnancy but no child?? On his family reunion visit, Jim said to Daddy that he had made a mistake about not having children. Daddy had no patience whatsoever with his fallen idol. When Jim started some puffy tale, Daddy hid behind his newspaper. One day, in desperation, he looked over both his glasses and the paper, impaled Jim with a cold stare, and blurted out, "I'm tired of that B—S—." And remember, Mama allowed no strong language in the house. To add to his fallen image, Jim presented me with the engagement ring he had given his wife. The setting was dangerously worn; whereupon, I took the ring to Mr. Sites for a new mounting, worthy of the "sapphire" and diamond ring. Yes, the small diamond was real. The sapphires—glass.

So it goes for far-away tales. There are the Christmas letters where all the children are straight A's and the four-car garage is finished, not to mention the family genealogist who has traced her blue blood back to Charlemagne and finally to a Roman centurion, cheek-by-jowl with Julius Caesar. With some family members in mind, the line could probably be traced back to the She Wolf.

Looking at our long history of far-away tales, I know they go back to Adam and Eve. We are made of the earth, and we try to rid ourselves of our dust. Eve could have told in her Christmas letter how nicely Cain and Abel were getting along, that Adam had a fine family enterprise going with "no sweat", and that they had a ten room tent East of Eden. The Lord God, however, told her that she could not live by tales and unreality. Labor and sweat and nakedness would be for her and Adam and for all of us, their children, throughout the generations. Therefore, let us pick up handsful of dirt-reality and fling it in the face of pretense.

> *For all our days are passed away in Thy wrath:*
> *we spend our days as a tale that is told.*
> *The days of our years are threescore and ten;*
> *and if by reason of strength they be four score years,*
> *yet is their strength labor and sorrow;*
> *for it is soon cut off and we fly away...*
> *So teach us to number our days,*
> *that we may apply our hearts to wisdom.*
> ***Psalm 90***

JUNE 1997

> *For ye suffer fools gladly, seeing ye yourselves are wise.*
> ***II Corinthians***

Ah, it's April Fools' Day and how gladly I would suffer again some of the foolishness that has delighted us through the years. How good it is to be light-hearted, to dwell in the enchanted land of pure tom-foolery, and to be liberated within to laugh at ourselves and with each other. Wise foolishness is a rare wisdom.

21

Mama & Daddy

My father was the master schemer of April l, a trait he inherited from his mother who has endowed her posterity with the elfin passion and patient waiting to bring off the perfect trick. During his childhood, each April Fools' Day my father was on red-alert for he-knew-not-what: One year it was shoe buttons sewn in the knees of his pants. When he knelt down to shoot marbles, he had pebbles in his pants. Another year it was a promise after school to him and his schoolmates to see, captured in a box, a "red wingless bat." Grandmother had a piece of brick nestled in straw for the breathless children to see. Another trick my father remembered ruefully was his favorite fried apple pies, beautifully browned and stuffed with cotton.

My father and his mother were such buddies, such lovers of laughing, savoring any interjection of fun they found in the ordinary tenure of their days. This grandmother's gene for April l has bred true: to my father; to me; to my brother; and in these last years amassing itself in a great-grandson, that great-grandson being our youngest son. How wisely he plays the fool-especially to fool his mother.

While I was visiting this son in Columbus, GA, he took me to his favorite flea market where I found a *Rainbow* vacuum cleaner for $35.00. Impossible! It was practically new with nary a flaw, pronounced absolutely perfect by this engineer son. Little did I know that he was writing down the vital statistics of this cleaner for his devious foolishness. Now I have a brother in Atlanta of rare foolish-gene infestation, who was waiting for my visit like a spider in its web. About as soon as I got to his house, I started the garrulous account of this prize cleaner and what a bargain I had found. With this, my brother began his Oscar-winning act. Inhaling on a long pause, he told me that this was quite a coincidence, recounting how he had just bought his wife a new Rainbow because she was totally dissatisfied with her old one and how while he was parked at the grocery someone had broken into his truck and had stolen the cleaner and how he was trying to collect on his insurance policy and on and on. My vacuous brain should have known.

After we went over all these "coincidences" again and again and lamented my brother's loss, he went to his desk, got out the *papers* on his machine, and said, "Let me see your vacuum. I have the serial number of mine right here. Your vacuum might be stolen." We went out to my car and you know the rest. The numbers matched exactly. Our son had called the night before and set up this act.

To add to all this foolishness, my brother started bargaining with me about how to straighten out the finances of this purloined cleaner and

Mama & Daddy

even suggested a share-the-vacuum deal. He was insistent that I let our son know about this hot merchandise; whereupon, gullible old me called our son who responded with much feigned indignation, "Mama, I'll have the police close that place before night." Finally, after too many twinkles in my brother's eyes and wink from my sister-in-law, I knew I had been flim-flammed by masters of the art.

This story will live long after me, and I set it down for our collective funny bones and as an example of the liberating wisdom of mischief and fun. Too much we go around mirthless and miserable, when all about us there is a world of joy and light-heartedness.

This is not whistling in the dark. "A merry heart doeth good like a medicine," and a wholeness of spirit can plumb the depths of death and sorrow; but counter-weighted, can rise to renewed life with its joy and imaginative humor. We will not get out of this world alive—we know that—so let us not take our years too seriously, but put a smile on our faces and as much bounce as we can get in our steps, and walk wisely on the sunny side of the street. As St. Paul tells us, "God has chosen the foolish things of the world to confound the wise; and God has chosen the weak things of the world to confound the things that are mighty." In light of God's tolerance of foolishness, let us love one another and follow our merry hearts until we come to that place where we shall understand all things wise and wonderful—and foolish.

Kirkwood

DECEMBER 1994

> *In Him was life and the life was the light of men. And the light*
> *shineth in darkness; and the darkness comprehended it not.*
> ***John 1***

Ignorance is darkness; illiteracy is darkness. However, I have seen a tropism, an insistent movement toward the light that has refused to be denied. "We who dwelt in darkness have seen a great light."

My early school years were cast in an era of both darkness and light, with privilege for some and poverty for many. There were no buses, no attendance officers, no requirements for the beginning and ending of one's school years. All these decisions were the parents'. Caught in this rural, tenant-farmer, tobacco-based economy, were a group of young boys/men who came to school only when they didn't have to work. The tobacco had to be planted in the spring, housed and fired in the fall, and stripped for the winter market. Maybe they had learned to read or maybe they hadn't, but there was a powerful pull to school. Already showing full beards and chewing tobacco, they came and made chills run up and down the older girls' twittery nervous systems.

The "Christmas Tree" brought out all these young saplings. This light of expectation was the height of their dark-fired year. Whether by permission of their parents or by raw rebellion for a glimpse of another light, they came like shepherds to Bethlehem.

All activities seemed to center around these young men. The big project was to go after the Christmas tree, and here was muscle, newly arrived, to cut it. With axes and saws, and rising expectations, they managed to cut a tree that would serve well on the White House lawn. Dragging such a cedar was a feat for a bulldozer, and it had ever so many shortenings and prunings before they got it through the door into the room where we were to have the Christmas pageant, then herald the arrival of Santa Claus.

Our infrequent scholars were tall enough to be Joseph, and their voices had lowered so they could howl like the winter wind in the Christmas play. They kept all fires stoked because of a need to be outside to spit and smoke, and they moved our desks and chairs to make room for this celebration. One made us most joyous at "what-you-want-from-Santa-time" when he said he wanted "one of them type-rit-ters" so he could write his girl. He was hopelessly illiterate.

We knew down deep that this was their Christmas. The play, with its drama and make-believe, away from the tenant-farmer homes, the Christmas story read and enacted; the noisy arrival of Santa (my father) with his banter and teasing; and, finally, the Christmas presents—all this climaxed a year of anticipation.

The teacher gave the big boys combs and handkerchiefs, and the younger students got three pencils in a slim box with their names on each pencil. There were candy bags and wonderful raisins on stems and fruit for all. What a magic night, full of light!

Three generations have passed since this Christmas recounting. What light did these young men take back to their fields and barns? Enough and to spare! Out of these families have come lights of rare intelligence and beauty and goodness. And I have beheld their light. There are university professors, an astronomer of international fame, a museum curator, a seminary graduate and some of our neighborhood's best farmers.

We praise him who has called us "out of darkness into his mar-velous light," and we know that this light of men shall never be put out.

Peace and love and joy to all.

NOVEMBER 1995

> All the king's horses and all the king's men / Couldn't put Humpty-Dumpty together again.

No one has a chicken house anymore. I was privileged to learn the lessons of the chicken house. We children had chores after school, mine being the careful gathering of eggs from the hen's daily duties and the rightful discerning of eggs, which had to be done before dark. "Now be careful with the eggs, and don't bring in the nest eggs."

The nest egg, which became slick-polished with use, was the one left to encourage the hens to lay in certain nests. You wouldn't dare gather this ripe one. If by chance or carelessness, you forgot your chore, you had to light the lantern, get your basket and face the dark chicken house with all its eerie shufflings, cluckings and chortlings as you squinted in the dim light lest you bring in the nest egg.

Kirkwood

One goblin-filled night after Halloween and after my daddy had told a ghost story of headless, sheet-shrouded bodies appearing in the hay loft, I forgot my eggs. Out in the cold breathing night I went with my lantern and basket. There was no star over the chicken house. Carefully I opened the complaining door, held the lantern to discriminate against nest eggs when suddenly an old white hen was taken with some powerful paroxysm of squawking, flew down at my egg-gathering expedition and flogged my head with her ghostly feathers. That's when I learned to scramble eggs. Abandoning the lantern and assaulting the back screen door, I brought in the eggs. A few were whole, many cracked, and some oozing out of the split basket. Humpty-Dumpty was mine.

After this night's discipline, I never forgot the eggs again. Mama was forgiving and declared the broken eggs just the ones she needed to make the Thanksgiving boiled custard and pies. The saying, "You can't unscramble eggs," has become more real for me each year as I creep with a dim light into the dark chicken houses along my way. But "Thanks be to God" you can take scrambled eggs and Humpty-Dumpty can become whole again. He may be an elegant souffle, or a chess pie, eggnog or our traditional boiled custard. His form is changed, but he is made new.

Some years my prayers have been mostly supplications and confessions; but in 1995, they have been thanksgiving. Scrambled eggs have been made by God's hand into beautiful gifts. There has been a long illness healed, a quiet restoration of bitter relationships, and an in-gathering of forgiveness all around. Tragedy is made triumph.

As the People of God at Trinity, we have corporate thanksgiving that wells up with praise for the triumphs over tragedy. Each week we have choir practice and welcome new voices. I see Tom Cowan's face and know his presence. His scholarship fund has brought us a taste of the heavenly choir.

Then I gave thanks for such triumph as the whole congregation, diverse though we be, coming together for the celebration of Dorothy Ann's birthday. Joy and inspiration were ours from a life so dedicated to the life of this parish. But best of all, we give thanks for the gospel, the good news about our scrambled eggs:

> Humpty-Dumpty was gathered in a pot; You won't believe what God has wrought!

27

Kirkwood

JUNE 1995

Charm is a delusion, and beauty fleeting. Extol her (a good wife)
for the fruit of her toil and let her labors bring her honor.
Proverbs 31

The matriarchs of Kirkwood were many. Among the many was one stellar example, Maggie McCraw, mother to Turner, Judith, Lynn, Joe, Emma Lou, Sarah, and Bill. Maggie had complications and frustrations by the throat and strangled them with horse sense, laughter, and kindness.

Logan McCraw liked to move, about once every two or three years. He never owned a farm but was farm manager for big acreages and was noted for his organization of labor and discipline of boys and mules. Maggie was his perfect complement. The first time she came into my childhood focus, her family had that day moved from Barren Plains in Robertson County to the Morgan Farm next to my family's. In the late afternoon of the moving day, my mother took us for a call to see what help was needed and if we could lend a hand the next day. Maggie was sitting in front of the fire crocheting! Her necessary household appointments were in place, she had cooked supper for the family, and she welcomed us from her rocking chair, "Come in, come in, sit down," as she drew a circle of chairs around her hearth.

She was a squat, square woman with the merriest eyes that ever squinted out at you. Her breasts, overlapping her lap when she sat, were eternally swathed in a great utilitarian apron wherein she gathered vegetables, carried kindling wood and jars of fruit from the cellar. Her legs, in parentheses, listed her body back and forth in a see-saw that would have left one of a lesser heart in great complaint. There was never a word. In her voice there was a hearty tremor, a vibrating good humor that made you forget the warts with their hirsute adornment that she, no doubt, never favored with a glance in the mirror. Her hair was abandoned to widow locks that felt her collar and refused to be confined to a hat. Comfort was her fashion goddess. Maggie had no consciousness of self, only good cheer for everyone, combined with much laughter at oft-repeated tales of her family's history.

One of her favorite stories was an account of her son Joe's birthday. All her sons were giants among men, ones you would never tackle in a fray. When they got together, the foundations of the house shook. They had a tradition that on each one's birthday, the honoree would be put under a bed. When it came Joe's turn, this called for a mighty struggle since he was perhaps the strongest of the four. Maggie found no problem with this situation. She had her three other sons hold Joe in place and she promptly rolled the bed over him. She doted on each of her children, quoted them, and never found a flaw in any of their doings.

Maggie McCraw cooked for more wheat thrashers, strained more milk, washed more clothes, canned more vegetables, gathered more garden produce in the heat of the afternoon, made more pickles, sewed more seams, and moved her belongings more times than anyone before or since at Kirkwood. She was, however, oblivious to the fruit of her toil and its honor.

I remember in particular her compassion for one tenant farmer family who moved on their farm. They were without food and clothes; they owned nothing. There were many children. In one afternoon, Maggie made dresses for all the little girls—cut them butterfly and bound them with bias tape—and the next day made pull-on pants for the boys. The mother had a new baby, sick with colitis, and Maggie was there with milk and bread and other food for their supper and continued to support and encourage this impoverished family. She was food stamps, Aid to Dependent Children, and Medicaid, all rolled into one.

Maggie's simple and uncomplicated world and our fast and frenetic world seem eons apart. Who could move and crochet on the same day? Who would be content with the barest of necessities in our households of magic appliances? Who would be joyous over two bushels of black-eyed peas to shell? Who among us would nurture an outcast family, full of sores and reeking with poverty? Maggie wasn't considered terribly "religious" by the community, but her testimony was in her law of kindness, her earthy wisdom, and her recognition of "least brethren."

All her children and all we children who remember Maggie "arise up and call her blessed." The fruit of her toil left a legacy of honor far exceeding any fleeting charm or beauty.

OCTOBER 1995

The world goes round and round; Some folks up and some folks down..

A saying in my family

From my travels from Kirkwood to Kenwood, I've seen some down folks—way, way, way down—depression and tenant-farmer down. Mary Ann, my friend and protege, turned her tenant-farming world upside down with muscle and horse sense. She had no patience with laziness and people staying down. "You've got hands and feet to work with, ain't you?" and she used the one gift that she recognized.

She was of the tenant-farmer family that I mentioned in *Mullings and Musings* when I wrote about Maggie McCraw. Mary Ann was next-to-youngest of ten children. Of an Irish-Cherokee mix, she was red-haired, raw-boned, big-footed, high-tempered and could fight or work herself out of any situation. She had to be tough. Her father was a hard worker, but alcoholic. When he got drunk, the natives of Kirkwood took cover. They locked their doors, and his children spent the night in the barn or under the house, as he threatened with guns and knives. His abuse of his wife and children was more or less ignored. The Law was called a few times, and he was jailed once for public drunkenness.

Tobacco was the tenant-farmer's mainstay. Mary Ann and her siblings were matted with tobacco gum from the time they were about six until they departed their serfdom. School was sketchy and only attended during slack time in the fields and barns, leaving Mary Ann to rely on her native intelligence, which she applied with an iron-clad ethic and immovable opinions.

"Can't no man outwork me. I'd like to see him try. I can hang tobacco faster than anyone, black or white." In our west field, I saw her do just that one hot August afternoon with seasoned field-hands all around. She led the rows, barefooted and bareheaded. When the laborers stood in the shade for a drink, Mary Ann never stopped, and she led the crew until the sun went down. My father-in-law told of this feat as long as he lived. Too bad she couldn't have challenged The Citadel.

With my husband away at sea and with three small children, I had Mary Ann's sister, just older than she, living with us. We were helping her go to high school but, being overcome by romance, she left to be married. With this event, Mary Ann appeared, without notice, to replace her sister. Our household would never be the same again.

To recount the Mary Ann stories would take a book. She was all ideas and energy and muscle with no aspirations for school—just work. In her sixteen years she had never had access to a sewing machine, but when machine and Mary Ann met, that was it! She knew from the first stitches how to design, fit, alter, and co-ordinate. She had a "gift." She was on her way up.

Kirkwood

Now to shorten this account of Mary Ann's going around in the world, I realized she couldn't be with me forever; therefore, I launched her into the world of "public works"—*Frosty Morn Packing* and later the *Dairy Queen* on Riverside. As kind providence would have it, a most honorable and "born again" Fort Campbell soldier came by Dairy Queen, saw Mary Ann's Dolly Parton-styled red hair, claimed her for his own and took her home to Indiana.

There Mary Ann has had her own business, making draperies, slip covers, bedroom trimmings and wedding attire. Woody, her husband, has worked for the same company since their marriage and is supervisor in his division. The world has gone round and round and they are up. To add to the upness, they have three children, all of whom are up.

I was feeling a bit down last week when the telephone rang. It was Mary Ann. "Where's Cap'n Bull?" (That's what she called my husband because she says all he thinks about is bulls.) "Now don't say a word and don't sass me because I'm 'flying' you and Cap'n Bull to Indianapolis. I've been going through old letters and you promised to come. We'll meet you any day."

Since this call, I have marveled at this child of the tenant farmer's fields, overcoming her down world. And the preposterous idea of this child having resources to buy airline tickets to "fly" me—I, who felt so up. From all these ups and downs, the message is clear: Kindness is the only way. It will return to you, multiplied, beyond your wildest imaginings. So as our world goes round and round, let us love one another, up or down.

AUGUST 1986

If we must become like little children to inherit the Kingdom of God, sometimes I pity the Kingdom of God. I find myself mulling and musing at length back to my childhood. Maybe this is good—a bringing forward of those experiences, still painful and unexamined, into the light of the wisdom and charity one has gained. As children we had no charity. A lifetime of penance would not make restitution—only the grace of God.

With anguish I recall one pale boy, myopic and adenoidal, who arrived one September at our country school. With all their worldly goods on a wagon, he and his family had moved into a two-room shanty that was little more than a shelter from the rain. There were five children, my subject being the second, with a sister just older and two sisters and a brother younger.

There were two rooms to our school and most of us had known everyone from the first grade, which meant that any new pupil had to have his measure taken and placed into the hierarchy of the baseball team. The older sister had a mean swing, long legs, and a true arm. Right away she was chosen for a side just after the best boy players. But not her brother. He sat under a dogwood tree at the edge of the schoolyard, breathing through his mouth in dry gulps and squinting to see the world of fun at recess. He was left in his blurred solitude, and as far as we were concerned he did not exist. However, when the teacher rang the bell at the end of recess, we found out that he did exist.

With a book in front of his nose, he was lost in another world. He knew all the multiplication tables long before anyone else, won all the spell-downs, and stayed ahead of the class in his lessons. We were sour grapes at such scholarship.

As October progressed into November we were shod in our winter shoes, having been barefoot all the fall if that were our preference. For about two weeks we noticed the head-of-the-class was absent. After some more days the word got around that he didn't have any shoes; and we knew, judging from his brother's and sisters' handed-down clothing, that there wouldn't be any. Whether it was the deprivation of his books or the threat of his parents that brought him back, I don't know, but he finally appeared one morning. He wore his older sister's tattered shoes. He sat, desolate, his feet hidden as best he could under his desk. There were snickers and pointing while he made some feeble attempt to read and not care.

In time they bumped away on their wagon, back on the grim road of the tenant farmer of the 30's. I could fantasize some glorious ending to this recounting with a benefactor appearing with shoes and scholarships and glasses, but the reality of the times when we last heard from this pale young boy was World War II and work in a defense plant. Since then, no other word.

So many years have passed, any rectitude on our part is impossible. My penance for our childish cruelty can only take the form of a prayer: Wherever this unaccepted friend went and whatever happened to him, may the grace that accepts us all keep him. If he is no longer here on earth, may he look kindly on us in forgiveness as we acknowledge our manifold sins and wickedness and lament the unfilled potential of this child of sorrow, acquainted with grief.

Kirkwood

NOVEMBER 1994

There are they which came out of great tribulation and have washed their robes in the blood of the Lamb.

Revelations 7

In the early 1930s, a frail black woman, wizened beyond her years with fatigue and perhaps malnutrition, set her face each Monday to go to the white folks' house and do their weekly wash. Being a widow with two small children and with no food-stamps and no aid-for-dependent-children, she had no other choice. She was paid fifty cents a day. There were side benefits: left-over food, discarded clothing, and a noon meal for her and her children who tagged along. All day long this dignified black woman toiled: first, the water drawn from the well; the fires kindled around the wash pots; the series of tubs assembled with hot suds and washboard; then the rinse tubs and the blueing water, all clothing and linen being hand-scrubbed and hand-wrung; and finally, the wash put on the clothes line. Thus she filled her day.

In the summertime under a plum tree, this drudgery of lye soap and washboard was set in motion by seven o'clock. The mistress of the house organized the children, both black and white, to assist with the wash and, in fruit season, to peel bushels of apples and peaches for a mighty canning operation inside the kitchen.

A white girl of the house and a small black boy of his mother's cabin were the main peelers. With cicada and dry fly rhythms playing through the breathless air, they sat through seemingly interminable hours, peeling, forever peeling, for the maws of the mistress's insatiable jars. A turn at the washboard was a release.

But time marched on. In 1937, TVA released the South from the washboard. The black mother moved away. World War II came and dispersed the children of both races, and the white girl and the small black boy lost each other in the century of swift and sure upheavals.

At hand was one of the great tribulations of our time: the Black nations' demands of their rights and their dignity, set over and against the entrenched order that often heightened their struggles with murder and intimidation. Just as the Hebrews were taken into slavery, refined in Pharaoh's brickyards, and then liberated to be a light unto the nations; so there is a parallel with the tribulations of the slaves of this land. They had a dream and the dream is turning the world upside down. It is slow and unsure, buffeted and belittled; but surely and inexorably the outcome of the tribulation is in the hands of the Lamb, the one who makes the robes white for those who wash in his blood—even the white girl's and the small black boy's.

A few weeks ago, an older white woman and a few-years younger black man were standing at the desk in the office of the Parish House when the man said to the woman, "Don't I remember you from somewhere? Didn't my mother help your folks wash? All I learned about work, I learned at your house."

He went on to recount his life after the wash days. He had a steady job at *Frosty Morn Packing House* for many years; he had reared four children, some being college graduates; he owned his own home and was a respected member of the community, speaking out on many issues; and he was trustee of his church, St. John's Baptist.

Yes, they knew each other! They fell into an embrace of recognition that breached the barriers of the years, and they stood in an equality that is for all who have washed in his blood.

The white girl is I. The small black boy is our sexton, Alonzo Smith.

SEPTEMBER 1996

> *Those who come to see me do me honor; and those who stay away do me a favor.*
>
> **Samuel Johnson**

Honored or favored, we, instilled in a long Southern tradition, entertained summer visitors. These visits were no weekend affair; this meant at least two weeks. Mama said that the higher the sun in its zenith and the fuller the butter beans in their pods, the more she exposed her derriere sunward to feed the butter bean-starved hoards. Among the regulars, two ladies linger in my log book of summer memories.

The first, Miss Beulah Lee Beaufort, came each July for the two weeks protracted meeting at Kirkwood Church, which, morning and night, began on the second Sunday of the month. When we children knew she was on the way, we moved all activities away from the front porch into the backyard shade, and the dog slunk under the house behind the chimney's foundation. She arrived with a son-in-law who wordlessly beat a hasty retreat, leaving her grip leaning against a col-

Kirkwood

umn on the front porch. She had no husband. From what Mama knew and what Miss Kate across the road had heard, he had gone "out West for his health."

With one eye in a perpetual jaundiced squint, she surveyed her lodging and began a rigorous and spiteful superintendence of us children and our domestic progress. She no doubt had liver problems because this biliousness had yellowed her hair into a wash board wave that had never seen a blueing rinse and had tinged her false teeth into old piano keys. Or perhaps this yellowing could have come from the sulfureous fumes absorbed from too much hell-fire and damnation revivalism. One snap of the teeth, however, and we children were at attention.

With her palm leaf fan in one hand and her voile dress on for the morning meeting, she began her inspection: Did the *Kentucky Wonder Beans* have all the strings off? Was there one silk left on the "rossen-ears"(fresh fried corn)? Did the front porch get swept and the chicken dabs washed off? Is the water bucket filled and the kindling wood straight in the box? And on and on. We, too, wanted to go West. Mama was more charitable and felt sad that she was so embittered and had no place where she was welcomed and loved.

When the two weeks were up and Miss Beulah further yellowed and homeward bound, the dog once again lay across the front door, we played marbles in the front yard, and we probably squished through some missed chicken dabs.

In contrast to Miss Beulah's visits, we got Julia Lockert Dunn. The dog jumped with pleasure, we children couldn't wait for her fun and laughter, and Mama considered Miss Julia's visit her vacation. There were long, leisurely afternoons on the front porch with our pumping back and forth in the swing and with Julia's unique melody of laughter filling the languid air as we shelled butter beans and left strings on the Kentucky Wonders. There was no yellow with Julia—only black curly hair and the kindest and bluest and truest eyes you would ever behold. No longer playing marbles in the yard, we children were a nuisance, sitting around so we wouldn't miss a word. Occasionally, the sleeping dog thumped his tail, and we all basked in Julia's gift of joy.

Unlike Miss Beulah, who resurrected every illegitimacy, illicit affair, and scandalous indiscretion, Julia was a woman of vision for a new world of Kirkwood and Montgomery County. When you read the history of our county, Mrs. C. C. Dunn was the first woman to be on the School Board. Education was of the highest value in her family.

Kirkwood

The old Lockert School and the Lockert Community were named for her forebears, one of whom was a respected teacher in this Rossview Road Community. The contrast of a constructive and joyful life versus a critically closed one could not be more aptly shown than through Miss Beulah and Miss Julia.

They were both women who lived with loss. Julia lost four of her children—Beulah a child, a husband, and a home. St. Paul writes of the gifts given to us, and a merry heart which must be *Hope* was certainly Julia's; I personally knew her love, not only for me but for the children who through the years have come through the Montgomery County School System. During the most economically depressed era of the 20th century, she was tireless in her efforts to improve the rural schools, and I remember well the music teacher who, through Julia's influence, came to us once a week.

So let us give our days, not to narrow criticism and picky trivia, but to Julia's way. Let us enjoy the strings on the beans and the silks on the corn. Let us open wide our hearts to whatever we can give ourselves to that will be constructive and enabling for the future generations of God's children. This is our "reasonable service."

SEPTEMBER 1997

The love of money and the love of learning rarely meet.
George Herbert

"Why, when we were in the first grade at Kirkwood School, a million dollars would have educated the State of Tennessee. What is all this about buses, consolidation, sports programs, special education and multi-level tracks, art and music, and in-service for teachers? ...A bunch of tom-foolery! A couple of rooms, a chalk board, a teacher with a good head and a tough hide, and some knothead pupils—that's all you need."

This knothead lived in sight of Kirkwood school's two rooms. Later on when the enrollment went up, a third room was added with a portable partition and behind this was built a stage, a board worthy of our Thespian efforts at Halloween and Christmas. It was beside this stage on the other side of the partition that I had special education with a special educator. For me, love of learning began, and there was no money involved.

Kirkwood

The school's rooms were furnished with single and double desks, and if you were of certain deportment—didn't poke ribs, talk too much, chew tobacco in class, or pass dirty notes—you could share a double desk on the other side of the partition. Being threatened by my mother with violence for misbehavior, I was one of the favored ones. Lucky for me, one Keith Powers, the third son of Miss Gloria Powers of the "True Eye", took me as his protegee; there, I had a private tutor as we shared a double desk away from the other four classes in our crowded room.

Long division was a mystery to my non-mathematical mind. With the utmost patience, this gangling fourteen-year-old boy, wise and wonderful in my eyes, took me step-by-step through division problems as only a master teacher could do. From Miss Gloria's example, Keith gloried in reading. After our math lesson was finished, he would choose a book for each of us from the library-on-wheels where we lost ourselves in the worlds of King Arthur, the Swamp Fox, and Tom Sawyer. Often the teacher forgot to call us when our class's turn came to go up front to recite. To Keith, across the years, I give the highest acclaim to one who taught me how to study and how to travel into new realms.

During these Depression years, there was no money to love. But love of school and the love of creating our extracurricular activities kept us charmed. As near as I was to the schoolhouse, I refused to go home at noon for lunch but wolfed down sausage biscuits and fried-egg sandwiches lest I miss the first inning of the baseball game. We played with homewound, string balls and soap paddle bats. The PTA sacrificed its entire treasury for a basketball, which brought on a flurry of activity: scraping the school grounds for a court, building the backboards, and salvaging hoops from the community's junkpiles. We lived in Tarzan's jungle, swinging down long saplings in the bordering woods while practicing whatever ape-related yells and melodies we felt in our bones. With long poles, we high-vaulted wet weather branches for "Cross the Atlantic" and sent the law after Bonnie and Clyde until Bonnie took refuge in the privy and fell through the floor. Graciously, the WPA furnished us with two sanitary "government" toilets.

There were no buses; we walked to school. There was no remedial reading. If you couldn't learn to read, you went home to farm or to "help Mama." We read the Bible every day, said the Lord's prayer, and saluted the flag. There were no protests or lawsuits. The Health Officer came once a year for shots and that was our health care. Our innocent age had no inkling of the unimaginable upheavals awaiting it at the close of this century. Our *OK Tablets* and chalk boards are lost in the revolution of the computer age.

Kirkwood

In this new age, there is money, and to be honest, we love it. Luxuries unheard of are ours. The love of learning has been in many instances endowed by this money so that the twain seem to have met. A dear friend of mine upon his death so endowed Austin Peay State University because he loved his home community and the people who made his inheritance possible. The constructive use of our money, as in the parable of the talents, is our duty as the People of God. Rather than a narrow hoarding and worshiping of wealth, we are called on to love its use for our families' welfare, for the education of our communities, for the larger purposes of our nation. For sure, we will not take one thin dime when we die.

Therefore, those whose destructive use of money compels them to hoard it and worship at its feet shall lose it; but those who love it for Christ's sake and give it away, shall have it returned, heaped-up with joy, to keep for eternity.

Being Saved

FEBRUARY 1989

Mama preferred Kentucky preachers. She said they were more filled with the spirit, more grounded in the Scriptures—chapter and verse. Daddy said they were more filled with chicken and beans and used more volume than brains. However, there was no sermon topic too obscure nor verse too hidden that these Kentuckians, so grounded in chapter and verse, couldn't ferret out the exact text for any situation. The sins of pride and gluttony were put to this test in my time.

My earliest recollection into the chapter and verse dispensation was one Brother Jordan, strutted to a girth of some sixty inches, who came to us via the train to Hampton Station, down each Saturday night from Russellville. Mama put a high premium on this Kentucky preacher. She said he just had more "fire" than Tennessee preachers; but Daddy said it was hot pepper sauce, and reluctantly hitched old Topsy to the buggy, if it were wintertime, to haul the corpulent chapter-and-verse man-of-fire for Saturday night and Sunday.

Mama always got ready for the preachers on Saturday. She lopped off chicken heads on a chopping block in the chicken yard while we children shelled butter beans and shucked corn on the back porch. This was summer fare. Apple pies were lined up to cool, the prize pickles and preserves uncapped, and if there were ice in the icebox, ice cream was readied for Sunday.

Now some preachers, like Brother Turner, were long and lean, with bad color and bad appetite, but not Brother Jordan! (Philippians 3:19). We peeped through the keyhole into the dining room when there were other guests, waiting our turn. Long after everyone had finished, Brother Jordan, complimenting each dish afresh, had the second and third helping. There would be a few necks and wings left, no gravy, and only the biscuits made from the final gathering of the dough into the corners of the biscuit pan. Mama did hide an extra pie in the safe. I understood at last why we called it a Safe.

In the summertime, after Brother Jordan had given Mama a Proverbs 31:10, he took to the front porch swing for his rest. One hot July afternoon after his regular gormandizing, he stress-tested the chains on the swing, all the while settling his bulk into as near a prone

39

position as an overwhelmed wooden swing would allow. The porch was L-shaped, and we children were given our Sabbath seats around the corner to be quiet while the preacher napped, Daddy read the paper, and Mama fanned. She was secure in the knowledge that she had been a blessing to the Lord's anointed.

Suddenly the Sabbath calm was shattered. A great alimentary symphony in the swing began, the bass line augmented by what Daddy called "Fatty Heart" problems. The rumbling began somewhere under his no-neck, which he raised for a breath; then there was a resounding expulsion of butter beans and buttermilk fermentation in a mighty belch that allowed his neck to return to its non-existent position. This was the overture. Across his gravied front, his watch fob undulated, as flute-like "tweets" came from some pie-muffled organ behind his left gallus. Then after about thirty minutes of digestive jockeying, the butter beans and corn came in for their solos, counterpoints, and variations on themes, building to such great crescendos in the ascending and descending passages that they bristled up the dog.

We children finally were allowed to escape behind the house to collapse with laughter; Daddy had enough of this day of rest, and we heard him mutter down the front hall and slam the screen door; and Mama, being a lady, disappeared to meditate on 1 Timothy 2:12.

Now Brother Jordan considered himself a pulpiteer par excellence, one whose dignity must not be compromised. He had gotten wind that we had enjoyed his "symphony," and, red-faced, took to the settee out in the yard to search the Word, knowing the Lord would reveal to him the chapter and verse that would make his gastronomic upheavals into the Lord's own revelation.

For that Sunday-night's preaching, he announced his text with trembling jowls and heaving paunch: Isaiah 55:2, "Eat ye that which is good and let your soul delight itself in fatness." And Isaiah 63:15, "Where is thy zeal and thy strength, the sounding of thy bowels and thy mercies toward me? Are they restrained?"

Mama declared the sermon the highlight of the summer season and became a disciple of unrestrained mercies and souls delighted in fatness. Eventually, she outweighed Daddy by forty pounds.

When Brother Jordan was caught chewing tobacco by his flock, we got Job 7:19, "How long wilt thou not depart from me, nor let me alone till I swallow down my spittle?"—and Daddy said that if he didn't have

Being Saved

any more sense than to swallow "ambeer," he ought not to be preaching; and the best I remember, he didn't too long. The Lord called him home because of his Fatty Heart.

JULY 1987

July was the month for the "meetin" at my childhood church. This month was no doubt chosen for its heat which reminded us of where we were going if we didn't get saved; and if *Tarpley's Funeral Home* hadn't furnished us with fans on thin, wooden handles with Jesus blessing the little children, we would have surely entered into the fiery state right there in the pew.

How the preacher could concentrate on his hellfire and damnation amid this frantic fanning was a wonder of concentration. Minus his coat and eventually his tie, he exhorted us with frog-croaked virtuosity through the fiery furnace with Shadrach, Meshack, and Abednego; and for the clincher gave us Lazarus and Dives separated by the burning lake where the worms never die. To add to the heat were temperamental gasoline lamps that were pumped up with bicycle pumps, and these lamps housed the most delicate mantles in the *Coleman* collection. One flutter of an errant moth would shatter the mantles, making a sizzle and hissing above the fans and the battle with sin. Then the devil himself would send in his panzer division—giant flying black beetles that zapped the mantles with one dizzying attack, then whizzed away, scorched, against the wall and ricocheted down the front of some saved lady who hesitated to dance and undress in church.

Along with the black beetles came some little green stingers who seemed to be particularly attracted to heat and sweat at the collar line. Just as you turned your head around to see what passion might be flaming on the back pews among the fast crowd, where you weren't allowed to sit, there was a sharp stiletto that turned you around. You squashed him and the blister was bigger, and then he fell down into your unmentionables to blister your weaker members. Too, these creatures that wafted lightly were easily inhaled on a volume of air for singing praises. I remember the lead praise-singer, whose Adam's Apple rose and fell in his long neck with the ease of a Radisson Plaza elevator, who had it—his Adam's Apple—stuck in mid-rise by the inhalation of a green stinger. He clutched his neck, pointed down his bellows, and could utter nary a note. He was taken out behind the church and turned over a stump. We heard he was devising a strainer for his solos, but all

41

we ever saw was a waving white handkerchief and a quick survey of the air waves before he sucked in for full throttle.

To end the meeting and the heating, there was the baptizing in Spring Creek. Bathing suits were the Devil's own device, and it seemed the Lord wanted us fully clothed, shoes and all, to go down into Jordan. He knew good clothes and shoes were scarce, but he did provide. Old tennis shoes were greatly in demand; and there were mismatched shoes and shoes without tongues or laces. The ladies who feared too much cling against their wet bodies, lest they caused their brothers to be tempted, boiled out feed bags and fertilizer bags for extra underclothing; but you could still read *Purina's Pride* through their wet white dresses. They waded out, cool at last in Spring Creek's eternally frozen waters and were baptized in the name of the Trinity. No dove descended, but there was a dinner-on-the-ground that the angels from glory would have gladly shared: three kinds of barbecue and real caramel pie.

At that end of the two weeks, there always seemed to be a great storm, a purging of the elements tormented by our sin. The heat was broken, the powers that had held us in the hands of our angry God gave us respite in rain, and we knew we would not be faced so heatedly with our sins again until next July.

FEBRUARY 1982

I was raised a Baptist, the kind that was baptized in the creek by a shirt-sleeve preacher. Every summer during the hottest spell in July, we had a protracted meeting and souls were saved far and near because of the analogy between the weather and the hereafter. Then after I married and moved across the county, I was a Presbyterian for a while and found they used much less heat and water and the preacher wore a long black robe and knew how to use "whom." Now I am attending the Episcopal Church and the only mention of the heated hereafter is "He descended into...". The preacher's robes are grand enough for glory and not only can he use "whom" but "vouchsafe."

In my wanderings through denominationalism, I have found in them all the same faithful Christians, those great souls who are the Holy Catholic Church. I've seen them in the Baptist Church, when the congregation was divided by some hair-splitting doctrine propounded by an untutored minister, stand to declare they followed neither Paul nor Apollos but Jesus Christ. When the sad division came, they quietly put their light on the lamp stand and were Christ's continued presence where they had been called.

I've seen them in the Presbyterian Church during the dark days of integration when some in the congregation threatened to withhold funds because the minister dared preach that God was no respecter of persons. They stood and declared that they would love their neighbor and would finance the good news of freedom and respect for all men.

I see them standing now at Trinity. They know that the only permanence in this world is change, and with their faith in an unchanging love, they accept the vagaries of man-made institutions. Their hope lies in no earthly personality, no printed page, no legalistic ritual. They may have a preference for prayer books, but they know true worship is "in spirit and in truth," and that, in spite of man, God's word will prevail. Like our Baptist brothers, they know to whom they belong, and I see in them the Church Triumphant as they follow neither priest nor prayer book nor fallible ritual but the infallible word made flesh.

SEPTEMBER 1993

Dear Brothers and Sisters in Christ at St. Paul's Episcopal Church, Kansas City, Missouri:

As editor of the paper for Trinity Episcopal Church, Clarksville, Tennessee, I repeat for you the September 1983 *Mullings and Musings,* which is the title of my monthly effort for the *Trinity Trumpet.*

> All of life is a series of beginnings and endings, meetings and partings. We have a beginning at Trinity with one Robert E. Wood. From the search committee's outline of Robert's accomplishments, qualifications, and attributes, I spotted one that said he had a sense of humor. Good news! If we can laugh together and love each other with our mortal mess-ups and misunderstandings, we shall be off to a good start. Welcome to Trinity, Robert E. Wood.

> Some of us are probably already disapproving of calling you Robert, and I assure you that you will get called, among other things, Bob, Father Bob, Robert, Father Wood, Woodie, Mr. Wood, The Reverend Mr. Wood, and "Hey, you." Now this is to point out to you the diversity of the flock you have chosen to shepherd, each

of the lambs knowing he has a corner on what is the proper salutation for a man-of-the-cloth, not to mention right theology and correct liturgy.

My prayer for you and all of us at Trinity is that we love and accept each other as Christ has loved and accepted us. May all we do from this beginning abide in him who is the Beginning and the End, the Alpha and the Omega.

After ten years I have learned some new names for Bob. Yes, that's what I call him. I suppose the first one for me, personally, would be "Emancipator" because of a bondage I knew. Having been reared in a fundamentalist tradition, I for years had yearned to do good and to be good, to earn my points, to deny myself daily and struggle with crosses; but Bob at length communicated to my do-it-yourself soul the Amazing Grace of God. I know now "denying myself" is giving up my self-righteousness and resting in this all encompassing, all-forgiving, unfathomable love. What liberty and how sweet the sound! Thank you, Bob, for helping me know freedom, away from hellfire and damnation.

Then I would call him "Counselor." Prone to shoulder burdens as "good girls" do, I blamed myself for too much. Bob's sorting out, his hard hitting observations—no *Pablum* here—made me come to see things I could change and things I could not. From him there was no judgment or windy wise words, just listening and sharing with me his humanity, his nights-of-the-soul. No holier-than-thou preacher here. I know now there are no pat answers and that life was not promised to be easy. I only know I am loved, no strings attached.

On a less personal note, I would call Bob, "Builder." I saw him lead a fractious and divided congregation—and what congregation is not fractious and divided?—through the total restoration of historic Trinity Church, built just after the Civil War. It was in shambles. Knowing the buck stopped with him, he set his face to the task to be done. The product of his resolute effort is a restoration that has been lauded, near and far. All who come to see stand in wonder. Your new priest is not a back slapper—not of the good-old-boy tradition, but rather a thinker and at times almost an absent-minded professor in his preoccupations with matters that matter.

Then at last I would call Bob, "Friend." Christ in John's Gospel told his disciples that from henceforth he would no longer call them servants, but friends, because all the things he had heard from the Father he had made known to them. For ten years, all the things Bob has heard he has made every effort to make known to me, and he has given me a new vision of my Self. I have heard the good news of the Gospel. What greater gift than this, other than laying down one's life?

I borrow Paul's words as he sent Phoebe to the Church at Rome: "I commend to you Robert, a fellow Christian who holds office in this congregation. Give him, in the fellowship of the Lord, a welcome worthy of God's people, and stand by him in any business in which he may need your help, for he has himself been a good friend to many, including myself."

NOVEMBER 1992

Let the high praises of God be in their mouth, and a two-edged sword in their hand.
Psalm 149

When I was teaching at New Providence Junior High, I had one dear student who truly cared for me, especially for my immortal soul. She knew me doomed, teetering, unsaved on the brink of the fiery pit. In her loving, quiet way she would slip onto my desk tracts with great flames of hellfire leaping up across the pages with barbecuing faces screaming in their agony for me to be saved from their torment. My student belonged to the *Only True Holy Ghost Pentecostal Church Of God In Jesus Christ.*

My real problem was her many, many invitations to one of their services. How could I refuse one who truly loved me? After the fall was growing into winter and I had spurned "so great salvation," she stopped at my desk, without much hope, and invited me to a Friday night musical celebration, a praising of the Lord for Thanksgiving. That sounded like a service that wouldn't hanker after my lost soul. I could relax, sit back, and enjoy whatever high praises to God that my Pentecostal friends could raise up with "psaltry and harp, stringed instruments and organs, and loud crashing cymbals," not to mention full sets of drums, guitars, electrified piano and organ, accordion, and "sound of trumpet."

Not being familiar with the exact location of the church, I got there early; but not before my student and her family. How graciously they received me. My student, flushed with zeal, took me inside their concrete block church and proudly seated me with her family. Needless to say, I was not prepared for my "flight" nor was my soul awake for its challenge on what I thought was a "safe" night.

Being Saved

Up from Nashville came the visiting musicians. If the Heavy Metal Rockers had been setting up for Madison Square Garden, they couldn't have had more electronic entanglements or amplifiers. These black giants squatted in every corner of this modest enclosure; and when the musicians turned all the stereo sounds loose on super-loud, every instrument and voice with its own microphone, the concrete walls pounded, pulsed, and reverberated, the mortar joints seeming to bend on beat. The first tune: "I'll Fly Away."

Literally we flew away. The sound so enveloped me that there was no other communication; I was transported on sound. My family, with eyes closed and hands high above their heads, immediately began to praise into this cacophony. Ecstasy, wonder, and visions of delight seemed to be theirs. One good sister, who filled almost a whole bench, began a strange keening on high C-sharp that somehow pierced above this maelstrom. She never stood or moved. For the whole night she did not cease her other-worldly wailing—and no one seemed to notice. Maybe that was Pentecostal Primal Scream.

After we flew away a few numbers and the Devil was awakened so we could do battle with him, the preacher got in his hand his two-edged sword, a hand-held microphone. He began to roar up and down the aisle challenging all to be saved, to flee the wrath to come, to confess, to be healed, to speak to God. I was frozen in my seat. But my family went to the floor or to their knees beating their benches and falling into various paroxysms of anguish. At length, the invitation was for all to come forward so the spirit could descend. At this point my family deserted me, leaving me alone with Satan, knee to knee, on our bench. The spirit slew them, they dropped out cold, awoke, spoke in tongues, and the spirit slew them anew. Even the piano player was prone on the floor.

The preacher never ceased his amplified invitation and soon there was just a handful of us hard sinners left. He roared by me with baleful and accusing eye, warning me that Satan was telling me not to come forward. I evil-eyed him right back. He never looked at me again. The good sister wailed on and I, deserted in my pew, didn't know what to do. The program started at 7:00 and it was getting on toward 10:00. I had to go home. So bidding Satan good night I quietly stood up to leave and with my standing the whole family came out of their "slaying," walked me to the back of the church, said all the proper words of appreciation for my coming, and showed absolutely no signs of having dwelt in the spirit world. I recall this night with a mixture of anger, amazement, and wonder; and I wonder too, what time did they ever go home?

46

Being Saved

My parents and grandparents called these people "Holy-Rollers." And roll they did.

After being in Washington at the National Cathedral on September 13, as I wrote in the last *Trumpet*, I find the contrast between high Episcopalianism and Holy-Rollerism practically incontrastable, if there be such a word. It's all order vs. all disorder; all keptin vs. all hungout; symbolism vs. literalism; intellectualism vs. emotionalism; and, lastly, privilege vs. deprivation.

When my Pentecostal family greeted me with, "We've been a-settin' here, a-waitin' for you," I knew from whence they came. Probably their forebears landed in Virginia as indentured servants, made their way from the Tidewater across the Smoky Mountains, where some were left to handle snakes. Many came through the Cumberland Gap and down the rivers of Tennessee, away from school and church, and languished there for several generations. On the frontiers, the great awakenings and revivals and brush arbors were the sole outlets for many families and certainly the emotional outlet for their cruel lives, away from all gentrifying influences.

These Pentecostals are God's beloved people. I know their personal lives of honesty and hard work, living apart from the vanity of the world; and I believe God accepts true worship, whatever its form, wherever it occurs. Had I been trapped in lower Palmyra, where my mother was born, and never had any opportunity for education, I probably would be the head "Holy Roller" in some remote hollow.

Along with Peter, who felt in his Jewishness he had all the right answers, we must say, "I now see how true it is that God has no favorites, but that in every nation the man who is God fearing and does what is right is acceptable to him." Therefore, let us with St. Peter be a respecter of all persons.

At Thanksgiving, we count our blessing of privilege.

Being Saved

OCTOBER 1991

> *But Abraham said, "Son, remember that you in your lifetime received your good things, and Lazarus in like manner evil things; but now he is comforted here, and you are in anguish. And besides all this, between us and you a great chasm has been fixed..."*
>
> **Luke 16**

Great chasms are also fixed on this side of Abraham's bosom. I know this brutal fact from a chasm that divided a black mother from my comfortable place as a privileged white mother. This division was a watershed in my life, and its grace opened my "seeing" from that time until this moment.

When we moved to our farm on Pollard Road forty years ago, the post Civil-War system of tenant farming was still the *Modus Operandi.* This meant that the landowner furnished the tenant farmer his most basic needs through the year and when the crops were sold, the owner took what was owed him, and the tenant got his share afterwards. Many times, through dishonesty or crop failure, there was nothing left; and often, if the tenant farmer stayed, there was debt carried over into the new year; however, many tenants moved from one landowner to another in January and February after the tobacco was sold. So these anguished people, both black and white, eked out a subsistence, and their shacks across the countryside, fallen-in and overgrown, bear witness yet to the "evil things" and the chasms that separated us— landowner and tenant.

Thus I bring to memory Cal and Minnie who moved on our farm in March, away from somewhere, with their six children and another protruding prominently through Minnie's ragged apron. After the family had been here about a week in a cabin down across the railroad, Cal came to the back door to see if I could call the "doctor," which meant Minnie's time had come. The doctor was a mid-wife that the black community knew to call at those times, and she was not long in coming.

Now I had my first child about six months before Minnie's imminent delivery, and I, of course, had every hospital and doctor amenity, every receiving blanket that could be blanket-stitched, every gown and petticoat, hand-embroidered, stacks of Curity diapers, every bottle and brush needed and all powder and pins that must be assembled for this event. No royal child could have had more. My baby and I had all the good things, received here in our lifetime.

48

Being Saved

Across the railroad, the chasm divided Minnie and me. No child born could have had less. After we had gotten the message to the nurse-midwife, I naively decided, since I was a good "Christian," that I should go check on Minnie in her travail. During this encounter of mother-to-mother, all that was inequitable and divisive overwhelmed my smug station, and the world of the broken and dispossessed came alive, crucified, in these impoverished and pitiful circumstances. Six pairs of eyes, glazed with unsuppressed terror and perhaps hunger, pierced me outside the door of their mother's agony. Inside the room there was worse to come. On the bed where Minnie was lying, still in the ragged apron, there were no sheets, only a filthy mattress and some sack pillows. There was absolutely not one thread of clothing for the baby, no clothes or towels for delivery, not one diaper or blanket to welcome this wailing stranger into the world. There was *Nothing*! Not even a manger bed.

I managed, amid my shock, to get back up to the big house, gather together some things out of my over-abundance and get them down to the nurse who seemed to shield her resigned eyes from the recognition of my bounty. She took it without comment. She knew the gulf. She knew this manchild's hope and inheritance in his world. Her vision of justice certainly was not of this time and place—it could only be in Abraham's bosom.

So what shall my response be to Father Abraham when I see Minnie and her child comforted, across the great gulf that will separate us? What will my anguish be? Surely Christ told us this story of Lazarus and the rich man so we can be working on our great chasms on this side and face our anguish here. My guilt is so overwhelming in the light of my sister's pitiful want that my prayer can only be, "Lord, have mercy. Christ, have mercy. Lord, have mercy." But in this confession, by God's grace I am given the gift of compassion: to be broken with and enter more deeply into the Cross of Christ and his sacrifice for the world of the outcast and dispossessed.

In Abraham's bosom may Minnie and I both be comforted—she from her poverty, and I from my poverty of wealth.

49

Being Saved

JANUARY 1991

A "tender and scrupulous conscience" is a good thing. In the winter of 1939 I was a thief. We were children skating on a big pond at Kirkwood when we slipped into a poor man's backyard and stole all his firewood to warm ourselves. How many times through the years this scene has flashed upon my inward eye! I must not truly believe God forgives or I could let this go; but it has made me mindful of the suffering that poverty has as its lot. God has then blessed me with the memory of this long-ago thievery.

Remembering more, I lied to my grandfather about money he had given me for the movies when I detoured by way of the soda fountain with the change. Still repeated, this scene has weighed on my conscience, serving to keep me honest. God has blessed me with the memory of false witness.

So sin is useful. Sin, well-confessed, enlarges the soul and dwindles the ego. Sin, well-remembered, guards the steps and clears the pathway of entanglements. All our sins, so well-atoned for, give us new life in glorious and unexpected places and keep us safe wherever our place may be. Our prayer for the New Year is to remember such glorious grace, never forgetting its source.

Dear God, if we drag our guilts along with us into 1991, may we know that we are the ones who remember them—not you. If we refuse to let go of our sins, may we never forget you have already borne them. If we lose hope in the next year, reassure us that you are the God of this place, this year, the years past, and the years to come. Amen.

JULY 1990

But when sin abounded, grace did much more abound: That as sin has reigned unto death, even so might grace reign through righteousness unto eternal life by Jesus Christ our Lord.
St. Paul

Ah, the second Sunday in July! As this Sunday approaches and the heat builds to its mid-summer apogee, my inner child returns to its innocent place at our annual revival meeting that began on this preordained Sunday. Heat, hellfire, and liver problems all converged for me into one sharp focus, pointing to man's "utter depravity," with my consigning myself at so tender an age to the front seat reserved for the depraved. There was no "grace abounding"—just sin.

This summer spectacular consisted of two weeks of services that threatened, night and morning, all three categories of mortal flesh: Sinners, Saved, and Mourners, the latter being sinners "wrestling with the spirit and under conviction." The morning service was for the Saved who needed to give their testimonies and rededicate themselves. The night service was for the Hard Sinners and the Mourners, which called for the deacons to be on their knees around these ones enslaved to Satan. The visiting preacher proclaimed our Ancient Foe's domain so vividly that none should have been able to resist being saved from so great damnation. I feared to go to sleep lest I wake, unsaved, in the lake of fire. I never felt sure I was safe.

These meetings were our spiritual and cultural outlet for the summer, and the deacons combed Kentucky for a man filled with the spirit. This spirit often boiled down to flamboyancy and showmanship because his act would have survived well on the stage. He knew all the techniques of crowd-pleasing: He thundered and threatened, rocked the pulpit while holding the Book high, had his tear ducts at full flush, and was a master impersonator. How well I remember the hypocrite, the Pharisee, and the Prodigal Son in the pigpen. What a flood of tears when the father saw the Prodigal coming home!

Play-on-words was another attention getter. With tongue-in-cheek, Brother Jordan, during my eighth summer, gave us a morning service on the different kinds of Livers: Among them were *Abundant Livers*, *Right Livers*, *Loose Livers*, and *Livers Forever*. It was the Loose Livers that got my attention. After a reading from St. Paul, this condition seemed to doom one to be either a whoremonger or a fornicator.

Now livers I knew, but fornicators and whoremongers were mysteries to my digestive knowledge. Aunt Lucy, whose bad disposition was ever before us, was plagued by liver problems, and she was forever taking "powders" to touch this stubborn organ. I figured she had touched it so much she had loosened it, and I sure didn't want to loosen mine and wind up a fornicator with a bilious temperament. Afraid of deranging my insides, I quit jumping off the high limb of the apple tree and studied my food intake for disturbances. Horehound candy I wondered about. Tomatoes and potatoes were suspect for creating fornicators if there were any power in rhyming vegetables. After a summer of butter beans, fried corn, and squash with onions, my whole family was probably guilty of fornication. The Loose Liver Syndrome had me in its grip.

Along the way from 1931 to 1990, I have done my play-on-words and joyfully trust I have now joined the ranks of the Loose Livers. Too long I was a *Tight Liver.* Perhaps it was my finally understanding "man's utter depravity" that set my liver free. There is no way I can make myself good and righteous. In other words, I am a mess and so are all the rest of us, and there is no reason for us to have tight livers and try to pretend we are good. Anytime we point a finger at each other, we are only insuring our tightness and revealing our own bilious judgments that we hide behind. Those who relax solely into the Grace of God for their worthiness are the Loose Livers. What a loose freedom in knowing your worth is not weighed against your "goodness" or dependent upon your manufacturing righteousness. All our righteousness is an amazing grace.

Let us rejoice in the unrestrained flow of blessings from a loose liver.

JULY 1985

Therefore confess your sins to one another, and pray for one another, that you may be healed.
James 5

I have a friend, a very dear friend, who often blurts out his prejudices and angers to me to see what my response is; and my response is that I see myself, a comrade-in-arms, one who probably experiences anger more than he but is not so honest about it. His expression of hatred, confessed head-on, is far nobler than any of my pious pussy-footing that does not let me look squarely at my inner conflicts, leaving me open to self-righteousness, resentment, and self-pity. Nice girls do get angry, and if I, like my friend, could confess to someone who cares about me then I could be healed from anger's iron grip. But if I hide my anger behind pretense, smile and act holy, then confusion reigns in the very place where the peace of God and the Kingdom-of-Heaven are to have their dwelling place. My friend, I am persuaded, is nearer the kingdom than I because of his honest confession, this purifying of the heart when he faces his unvarnished self.

While I mull and muse about my friend and our mutual struggle to enter this longed-for Kingdom-of-Heaven, it becomes clearer and clearer that honesty must be the key to unlock the door. When Jesus talked about his kingdom he certainly made no impression on the professional religious people of his time—the Scribes and Pharisees—who wanted an earthly king. His own disciples were worried about their standing in the kingdom and who would get what seat on the right or on the left; and the faithful women, even his own mother, seemed to have little idea what he was all about. It was an honest criminal who was the first in the gospels to recognize the kingdom on Jesus' own terms. He confessed he was a sinner and worthy to die. He faced himself head-on. Then he turned to the ultimate innocence hanging there beside him, the one who that very moment could claim him: "Lord, remember me when you come into your kingdom." At that same moment, with total acceptance of a thief without any preparation except his honest confession and his abandonment of himself, Christ welcomed him into his kingdom, "Today thou shalt be with me in Paradise."

Now Paradise my friend and I have not found. Like the thief we've got to "cross over Jordan" for that perfect peace. In the meantime we are left with our struggles here. But we do have intimations of this paradise when we choose what we know is right and true. When I see my friend wrestling with old angers and prejudices, he reveals through his anguish a great heart, one so finely tuned to what is good and just, that when it comes right down to the wire, he faithfully chooses dignity and respect over his inbred prejudices. Behind his stiff exterior, a loving warmth radiates in spite of his best efforts to hide it, and I know I have a trusted comrade who helps show me the way through our confusion here and points me down the road to Paradise.

FEBRUARY 1985

Be careful—watch out for attacks from Satan, your great enemy. He prowls around like a hungry, roaring lion, seeking someone to devour.

1 Peter 5

The Old Devil was one of my first literary acquaintances. As children we stretched out on the floor, stomachs down and feet up, and poured over a great tome of a book entitled *Character Sketches*. On many a besmudged page we pondered at length this lascivious fellow with his evil leer who called us down the easy road to perdition. His horns, his cloven feet, his arrow-barbed tail, and his ever-present pitchfork would eventually send us turning for comfort to the few pages devoted to the old gentleman with the long beard who was handing Moses the Ten Commandments. But his evil fascination would call us back to the most worn page of all: "The Devil Fishing." Here on the edge of a great lake with poor mankind as his fish, the devil baited his hooks with the sins of the flesh: whiskey bottles, cards, cheap novels, dice, dollars, hearts (we couldn't figure out why the devil had valentines on those lines), and cigarettes. Other more formidable sins got their own chapters. Here we found our ancient foe plunging his pitchfork into his victims infecting them with anger, malice, jealousy, lust, envy, pride, slander, judgment, and the whole gamut of sins that he has planned for us.

I mull and muse at length, wondering if I have abandoned this anthropomorphized devil of *Character Sketches*. He has not abandoned me. In the middle of the night, I wake with his demonic pitchfork at my throat. In my innermost self, where even I fear to tread, he releases his poison of repressed anger, a foolish mistake made long ago, a morbid jealousy, some unforgiven stab-in-the-back, a bitter disappointment, an all-absorbing fear. He has the exact barb in his repertoire to fit my specification. I can identify it by my loss of objectivity and the all-consuming hours it eats on my innards. The devil has gotten his pitchfork of anger into me. When it finally erupted I was frightened at the intensity, the irrationality, the total absorption of its passion. Here was a demon, a force beyond me, that possessed me. I mull and muse further, wondering if he does not probe deeper into those struggling to overcome his power than into those whom he has already devoured.

Christ gave the devil the prominence of including him in his prayer. "Don't bring us into temptation, but deliver us from the Evil One." Other translations read, "Do not bring us to hard testing, but keep us safe from the Evil One." Each month as I attempt to write this first page for the *Trumpet*, I am amazed that whatever approach or detour my thoughts may take they ultimately converge at the same place: the all encompassing and all conquering love of God as revealed to us in Christ Jesus. Rather than surrendering to Satan's snares and barbs, we must surrender ourselves to the forgiving and restoring love that makes all things new. This love is our only hope.

> *Stand firm when he attacks. Trust the Lord. And remember that other Christians all around the world are going through these sufferings too. After you have suffered a little while, our God, who is full of kindness, will give you his eternal glory. He personally will come and pick you up, and set you firmly in place, and make you stronger than ever. To him be all power over all things, forever and ever. Amen.*

> *1 Peter 5*

Being Saved

MARCH 1985

This morning on my way to church I tuned-in our black Pentecostal brother who was admonishing his congregation, amid many "Amens" and "Praise the Lords," to control the most sinful member of the body. Having come in during a long and fervent exhortation against the evils of this unknown-to-me member, I envisioned the roving eye which should be plucked out or the cheating hand that should be cut off, or other members best left unidentified. But I should have known. When he thundered: "You sets on yo' front porch and talks about yo' neighbor when you should be talkin' 'bout Jesus," I knew. The culprit, of course, was the tongue. During a long decrescendo he challenged his congregation to "rise to the holy way" and anytime, anywhere when criticism and unkind words rose to their lips to stop them right there. In their place: "Say somethin' Jesus would say! Amen. Somebody say Amen!" I said, "Amen."

This fragment of sermon set me mulling and musing about the wisdom and world-changing consequences of such a discipline. "Say something Jesus would say." Then my mind did take off on a fantasy and I envisioned a great world council where war and peace, boundaries and treaties, armaments and disarmaments were parried back-and-forth by presidents and other potentates. When these world leaders rose to speak, some inexplicable force, at the moment of deception or maligning, would stop the words on their lips and a counteracting compulsion would "say something Jesus would say."

One, arrogant with power, would rise to denounce his adversary nation and from his lips would come, "Blessed are the peacemakers, for they shall be called the children of God." Another would say, "As for our country we shall love our neighbor nations as ourselves." Another, "I am meek and lowly and I will take up my cross and follow in a place of servanthood." And yet another, "Those who live by the sword will die by the sword."

Fantasy, yes. But the fact may be that the way pointed by our black brother is the way. "Say something Jesus would say."

Doesn't the answer, which man, being what he is, will not hear nor use, lie in these simple words? A Thoreau, a Ghandi, a Martin King have dared say what Jesus would say. Through them we have seen a burning light to the way. Humble men seem to see more clearly the path than those in high places.

"Somebody say Amen! Gonna lay down my sword and shield down by the riverside. Ain't gonna study war no mo'." I say, "Amen and Amen. Glory!"

Saints Marching In

Thou hast been faithful over a few things: I will make thee ruler over many things:..

Matthew 25

Saints. Who are they? The first one who comes to my mind is our long-ago hired hand. He was of one of the tall African tribes, stately and austere, and in retrospect our "Uncle Thomas" sounds patronizing, but that is what we children called him. When I first remember him in the late 1920s, he was in his 60s, no doubt born in slavery or just after Emancipation. Recounting his life's history, he always told of his childhood spent in the fields with his mother who must have instilled in this little boy the mystery and majesty of God and his creation.

Thomas Moody was a poet. He may have been illiterate—I don't know—but a literacy of spirit had been breathed into his being that no tutoring could impart. The black church was about a half mile as the crow flies behind our house. My father, even though a born Southerner, never knew anything about segregation, and we would go to Foston's Springs to hear the preaching and the singing. Invariably, the preacher called on Tom Moody to pray. From thence we were transported on a voice, resounding and prophetic, as he extolled the glories of the heavens, the vastness of the teeming seas, the mystery of God's stooping to salvage sinful man, the assurance of our place in the "house with many mansions," and the goodness of life and the joy of being a lamb washed in the blood.

This lamb had meager pasture, indeed, and how easily his prayers could have been selfish petitions rather than soaring praise. When as a child I first remember Uncle Thomas and Aunt Quance, they lived in a one-room cabin with a lean-to where she spent her days alone in bed. She had been an invalid for years. Each morning before coming for his day's work, he tended her needs with utmost care and patience, meticulously arranging her bed and food so she could care for herself during the day. Then upon his homecoming from the fields, there was her bath, the laundry in the washtubs at night, and the preparation of food again for the next day. Always there were starched pillowcases and newspaper "lace" on the mantelpiece. This he did for many years, alone, since they had no children. He never wavered once in his faithfulness; he had taken his vows for better or worse.

After Quance left for the house with many mansions and Thomas had retired, he would call on my father. Stately in his best clothes and watch fob, he commanded respect; and even before the days of civil rights and our awareness of the indignities we had done to black people, we granted him an equality—and perhaps a superiority—because we knew a presence was with us, one who had seen the glory.

JULY 1992

> *Great grief is a divine and terrible radiance which transfigures the wretched.*
>
> **Victor Hugo**
> **Les Miserables**

On the 4th of July my thoughts should turn to flag waving, barbecues, and firecrackers; but, at an age where the years bundle closer and closer, I delve, as I understand older persons are wont to do, into my past for memories, some lovely and lyrical, some almost too wretched to bring forward into the light of a new understanding. However, years seems to press these memories against our retelling lest we fail to pass them on and their meaning be lost in this space we call Time. The time was about my twelfth summer.

If you stretched a straight string, Miss Naomi Doak and her brother, Doug, lived about a mile across the field from our home at Kirkwood. Their two-room, board-and-strip home leaned forward to a tiny front porch, held together by a one-plank shelf and water bucket, and sat well off the road, dwarfed among giant oaks that must have been left from the continent's original forest. It was a doll's house in this setting. Miss Naomi's rocking chair took up most of the space on the porch as she rocked the long summers after her great grief.

She and her brother, Doug, were of lean, angular stock who kept rather to themselves and made their home together after they had failed—or perhaps never tried—on the marriage market. Mr. Doug with his missing teeth, tobacco-stained mustache, and humped-back from too-early plowing could never have been the neighborhood's beau-at-large; nor could Miss Naomi whose eyes didn't quite adjust to the same focus be the belle of anything, at large or small. Their lives as they lived them were right for these two. "They kept the noiseless tenor of their way."

But their young half-sister, Alice, was different. She was small and squeezable and caught herself a husband who was reported to work on the railroad for "big money." From these long-ago reports filtered through my childish ears, I remember the husband vanished and poor Alice died from causes I cannot dredge to the surface; but out of this tragedy was delivered into Miss Naomi and Mr. Doug's hands their tiny niece who was the absolute treasure of their world. No two could have ever lost themselves so completely into loving this unexpected gift, one so treasured as to be labeled "spoiled rotten" and "too hovered-over" by the neighbors.

Jean Alice grew up in our church and I, being several years younger, remember her as a teenager, just beginning to be allowed out of sight by Miss Naomi and Mr. Doug. After much begging by Jean Alice, they finally agreed to let her go with the "young people" to Horseshoe Bend, the neighborhood's favorite swimming hole in Red River. The terrible and awful hour's report reverberates yet where my fears live: "Jean Alice Burton has drowned!"

They were long in finding her body. Mama went to Miss Naomi and came home with one anguished phrase I could not understand—"vale of tears"—in which I pictured Miss Naomi in a hat weeping so many tears that they literally made a veil for her face. I do not know of Miss Naomi's and Mr. Doug's immediate grief; but I do remember well Miss Naomi's great and interminable grief. In the course of her remaining years all the "whys," the guilts and angers must have been crushed under the rockers of her chair because the community at length began to see in her a radiance, a dimension that became to be known as a holy acceptance, a sort of Baptist sainthood. She had moved to a plane of transfiguration beyond her wretched rocking chair, and we sensed that the state of her mourning had been comforted. Mr. Doug hoed in summer and spit in the fire in winter. Little was spoken of his grief.

To my childish senses, Jean Alice's cold, lost, underwater death was the most horrible one I could imagine. Death came alive for me on this 4th of July.

How did Miss Naomi and Mr. Doug ever reconcile themselves to such an ending for their treasure? Only they know; or, perhaps, only the Infinite Love, whose keeping is not of our knowing, knows.

Saints Marching In

Each of us has his great grief. Often it is death; often it is not. Grief has its peculiar form for each of us: We grieve for our loss of love, our shattered relationships, our might-have-beens, our broken bodies, our broken minds, our children's tragedies; and to add to all this personal grief, the hunger, the wars, and the hatreds of the world. These agonies can transfigure us by acceptance, as it did Miss Naomi; or they can trample us into bitterness and morbidity. Only by Grace can we lean our weariness into a strength not ours.

From across the unknown chasm, I hear through my fatigue and grief a comforting call that beckons me. I believe in the Communion of Saints, those on the other side of grief who are at peace and wish this peace for me. The call is to a new body, to rest, to joy, to completeness, to a freedom beyond our boldest earthly imagining. The Book of Wisdom says it best:

> The souls of the righteous are in the hands of God, and there shall
> no torment touch them; in the sight of the universe they seem to die,
> but they are at peace.

APRIL 1986

Each year the little country church where I was raised had a drive devoted to *Home Missions*. One special field for attention was Louisiana where "those Catholics were getting a real toe-hold" according to the Amen corner. Through my childish eyes peering through the narrow cracks of my world, "those Catholics" were some diabolic breed sent by Satan to practice witchcraft, burn candles and incense, and worship statues. They prayed with beads and rather than worshiping the true God, they had a Pope who decided who went to Hell and who earned his wings. Such was my understanding of Catholicism.

During my journey through Christendom, I have seen the beginnings of a reconciliation between Protestants and Catholics. Perhaps it was Pope John XXIII who loosened our unloving hearts and gave us a glimpse of our oneness through the candles and incense and around the Amen corner. Praise be to God! The real clincher for me, however, has been a view of the world through Trinity's Soup Kitchen. Here in the flesh are my Catholic brothers. These servants of Christ, come to us via Fort Campbell, via Immaculate Conception, are on fire with love for mops and recipes and schedules and mousetraps and above all, love for the hungry brothers among us. Each of them has brought a special dimension to the smooth running of this all-volunteer project.

Saints Marching In

First is our dynamo, Tom McGilloway. We will follow Tom right through Purgatory because we know he has heard Christ's clear call: "If you love me, feed my sheep." What he says, we do because we know he is the good shepherd; and some days when his body almost refuses to go, we know that he is literally laying down his life for the sheep. No greater love has any man than that. Each morning after Mass, he comes early to get the pots boiling, to see if there is plenty of food, and to list the supplies for the next day. His creative and peppery culinary combinations are filled with surprises (and wieners), and you do believe in the feeding of the five thousand after some stealthy addition that keeps the pot forever full. His coordination of many a willful Presbyterian, Methodist, Baptist, Church of Christer, and an occasional sinner is soup kitchen diplomacy at its best: We surrender to Tom because we know he knows. You even learn which side of the bread to butter. His love for us who work with him, for the people who come to the kitchen—especially the children—and for his Church and the Church Universal shines through this good and true man. The Soup Kitchen owes much of its life to Tom McGilloway.

Then there is John Clark. Immaculate Conception knew we needed a quiet and deliberate attendant to the main keeper-of-the-fold, so they sent John. With a bemused smile, he watches all the vagaries of human nature around him and rises above it, all the while doing his duties as if by slight-of-hand. Amid all the prattle, John keeps his counsel, but if the Soup Kitchen ever needs a word-of-wisdom, John will be our man.

The latest shepherd from "those Catholics" is a firebrand, Rick LaValley. He is Mr. Clean and Lee Iacocca all rolled into one. He must be a shepherd intended for goats because he can see all the wrong traffic patterns, the wrong placement of equipment, the inefficient working areas, and the mouse playgrounds. He even knows how mice think. The ones he hasn't caught, he has starved. Poor church mice. Added to this is a passion for *Clean*—I mean in the corners behind the stove, under the drawers, and beyond the cracks. There is a glow, a shine that is beginning to transform the faces of all cabinets and appliances; the old refrigerator is gone and the new one turned around; and the next move is a new floor. Rick says, "Give me four good men and a few hours and it will be fixed." The Virgin Mary or the Pope couldn't have blessed us with a more sorely needed leader for organization and Get-It-Done. Like Tom, we do what Rick tells us because he can separate the sheep from the goats when it comes to cleaning out a kitchen. Bless all these good Catholic men!

Saints Marching In

Such humble service as making big pots of soup together and giving them in Christ's name is an answer to Christ's high priestly prayer. He prayed that his followers might be one so that the world might believe that God had sent him. Our oneness at the Soup Kitchen has made him real to all who come to this fold—the hungry sheep as well as the servant shepherds.

JUNE 1984

> *And one of the Elders answered, "What are these that are arrayed in white robes? And whence came they...?" And he said to me "These are they which came out of great tribulation and have washed their robes, and made them white in blood of the Lamb.*
> **The Revelation of John KJV**

"These are they which came out of great tribulation." These haunting words from the Apocalypse are beyond my grasp of symbolism, but they always bring to mind one of my childhood saints—Miss Kate.

She lived across the road from us at Kirkwood right next to the church, and even though we had been admonished by my mother time and again not to be a burden to Miss Kate, I would slip off with great regularity just to bask in the feeling of being somebody who mattered in her world. There were usually tea cakes, but always there were biscuits in a speckled, enameled pot that, with a bit of butter, were the food of the gods. So with biscuits in hand and my dusty bare feet pushing the swing back and forth, Miss Kate and I sat on the front porch and engaged in conversation. She could not have been more attentive to President Hoover.

Not only were we children drawn to her but adults as well. When my mother needed a shoulder to cry on or the release of a good laugh, she, too, slipped off to Miss Kate's. Hearing the fun across the road, there we children would go to invade my poor mother's need for some communication with a joyous spirit and a chance to let her burdens go.

So I mull and muse "Whence came this spirit"? Miss Kate had to be one of the *Theys* who came out of the great tribulation. She had an only son, Robert Lee. This son was the most grotesque aberration of the human species ever seen in our parts, and I almost fear to write this account less I wax too emotional or lessen the impact of her life's statement with sentimentality. There is no way, however, to exaggerate.

Saints Marching In

When this son first focused into my childhood memory, he was about twenty years old, and he frightened me because he picked and pulled at me with gnarled hands, plaited with a cold multitude of fingers. But as I grew older, he was part of Miss Kate's house and we children paid Robert Lee no attention. He was able to walk on stalk legs and each foot had two massive toes that began at the heel and splayed out like ostrich feet. He spent his days eternally pacing, beating his head on the wall, beating himself in his vacuous face with a rolled-up newspaper, uttering the same interminable idiotic phrase, and tearing apart whatever he could find to destroy. He was restricted to his pacing areas, back and forth, so there could be some respite; and there was release also when he slept. He was always in diapers, always to be fed, always to be watched for putting things in his mouth. Once he swallowed a door key!—a big brass one. This tribulation was the forty years, and this was before electricity and running water and bathrooms—just a well behind the house and a wash board.

Miss Kate devoted her life to caring for her son without complaint or bitterness. She had grasped a strength beyond herself that buoyed her and all around her in a joyous acceptance of her life, one given to loving the unlovely. She knew how God himself loves.

When she was old, she contracted tuberculosis, and Dr. Jack Ross, who at this time had his office in Guthrie, told her she must rest, or better, go away to a sanatorium or she would soon die. But there was no one to care for her son! When she told my mother of her circumstances, that was the only time I ever saw her weep. In a few weeks she could no longer get out of bed, and the county health authorities came and took Robert Lee to the county farm, or the "poorhouse" as we called it then. She died the night he was taken away. Like some animal away from its familiar surroundings, he died a few days later. The two, so united in life, were released together in death.

They shall hunger no more, neither thirst anymore... for the Lamb which is in the midst of the throne shall feed them and shall lead them into living fountains of water: and God shall wipe away all tears from their eyes.

The Revelation

63

Saints Marching In

Be ye kind one to another, tenderhearted, forgiving one another,
even as God for Christ's sake has forgiven you.

Ephesians 4

I met, quite by the accident of a lemon car, a Good Samaritan whose mother's influence has kept a watch on my life. From time to time, we need some sentimentality to soften our cynical responses and tears to loosen our tight faces. So here's my Mother's Day remembrance:

Two teacher-friends and I had been to a concert in Nashville and were on our way home by 41A, our only highway at that time, when suddenly the electrical system of the car failed, the lights went out, and we klunked to the easement of the road. It was almost midnight, moonless and starless. Visions of rapists and murderers were all one of us could see, but all I could see was a night on the roadway without even a flasher to wink our distress. Within minutes of our stop, a car appeared along this now-deserted road, somehow saw our predicament in the dark, and wheeled right in behind us. The rapist for sure! Out popped the most helpful and gracious man that heaven itself could have sent us. First he declared our car beyond his help. Then he loaded us into his car and brought us home, delivering each of us to his front door, all the while refusing one penny, nor would he accept gas from the gas tank here at our home. Now there was a Good Samaritan!

On the way out in the country where I live, I had a chance to ask him about himself. He lived in Dover, had a job in Nashville that required his traveling quite a bit, and was on his way home for the weekend so he could minister to his flock at some unknown-to-me Pentecostal Church. By this time, I was convinced that this congregation had the ultimate in good shepherds. I had to ask him what had compelled him to stop for us, and wasn't he afraid to stop. And he answered, "No, I am on the mission of my life, and I am not afraid."

He had been thirteen when his mother died, and the last week of her life she called him to her where he wept with fear for life without her. My benefactor then brought tears to my eyes. "She took my face in her hands and declared, 'Son, if you learn to be kind, you will be a success.'"

How many times since then have this mother's words turned me around. My hard heart with its nasty little responses cannot escape such simplicity.

Saints Marching In

Two weeks ago, I was on my way home from Atlanta on I-75 when the traffic got caught in a two-and-a-half hour hubcap-scraper. Finally, I inched off the Interstate onto the old Highway 41 Exit just before Chattanooga. There, at a filling station, I found two precious little Oriental girls—probably Korean—who had been stranded in their car, insulted by a rude truck driver, and were weeping great tears of total desperation. They were on their way to a track meet, couldn't find Daddy back in Marietta, and had only $47 for a $60 wrecker. My Samaritan's mother's words sounded in my ear; whereupon, I produced $20. At first, they refused; but giving them my name and address, I told them they could return the money. Surely, I knew I had been helped by a stranger who asked nothing in return but the joy of being kind. How could I do less?

Promptly, I heard from my high-school friends on a special "Thank you" card they had bought. The $20 was enclosed. The call to kindness had been passed on, and I am persuaded that they, too, shall never forget.

There is so much anguish and tragedy and hurt in all our lives that it seems so reasonable to be kind to one another. The whole measure of the second commandment is held in the profound wisdom of a mother from Dover, "Son, if you learn to be kind, you will be a success." I am learning.

MARCH 1992

Enlarge the place of your tent and let the curtains of your habitation be stretched out; spare not, lengthen your cords and strengthen your stakes.

Isaiah 54:2

What better lines for a modern-day Prince of Israel—for one who has dedicated himself to the preservation of the tents—than these written to encourage the exiled people of Israel. Dan Ross of Grace Chapel, Rossview, Montgomery County, is the preserver of his heritage. His lineage goes back to patriarchs like Reuben Ross and Edward Barker Ross whose devotion to loving God first and neighbor second has bred true in this son.

Dan is a scion of their best yearning. There is no smallness in his bones, no dishonesty, no self-aggrandizement. He is ethical to a fault, fearing he might not be fair, or not do what is best for his neighbors or community. He has lengthened the cords of this mission church, established in 1866, in large part by his grandfather, Edward Barker Ross, to reach out to the total community and to welcome several new families. Since his retirement in 1974 from Southwestern University as Professor of English, Dan, by his dedication and determination to restore Grace Chapel, has mightily strengthened its stakes. He has come home to the family farm to be a patriarch in his time. Part of his understanding of himself is that he must continue to be creative, to serve his neighbor, to shine with use.

I still have things I am trying to do. My father, a physician, said that he had observed that people die often after they retire, or, even when they don't, they live as though they were dead... The idea is to keep from being caught up in myself... There's nothing in this world that can make you happy... You make your own happiness. Then, miraculously, there's something in the world to make others happy...

Born Danforth Raynolds Ross, January 12, 1911, in Panama, where his father was one of the young doctors working on the eradication of Yellow Fever, Dan lived there until he was two. His family at that time consisted of his parents and an older brother, Dr. Jack Ross of Trinity Parish, Clarksville. Later there was a younger sister, the Diocese's own Dorothy Ann Russo. Always an intellectual and a creative and humorous journalist, he was studying for his Ph.D. at the University of Minnesota where he met Dorothy Gertrude Sunnenfeld, who has been his most able assistant in tent-enlarging and stake-strengthening, not to mention organ-playing. These two have been the leadership that enlarged the vision of a handful of members, brought about the total renovation of Grace Chapel, and proclaimed a fresh pronouncement of the gospel.

The first repair of the mission church began in 1988 when the roof was in a state of collapse. Then when the roof was uncovered, it was discovered that the walls were buckling outward and the foundation was not too secure. Dan said that they built from the roof down. One repair opened up another area of disrepair until finally a general contract was let for a new roof, a lovely new, all-wood ceiling, the cinching of the walls back into their proper girth, and the installation of electric heat. But the greatest of the enlarging of the tent was the installation of a new privy. Dan, with his wry humor, got many laughs from his writings about this structure:

> Shortly after the installation, Bishop George L. Reynolds paid his annual visit to Grace Chapel... The Bishop saw to the proper hanging of the Episcopal shield above the door, examined the facilities to his sat-

isfaction, and pronounced Grace Chapel to be the most backward-looking mission in the Diocese, as for that matter, in Tennessee.

In the meantime, one of the mission's members has run a water line and there is a hydrant on the outside of the chapel—as yet, no inside plumbing.

Dan and Dorothy's dedication to Grace Chapel has sparked a fierce loyalty among its members, and this devotion will leave a bequest that will honor the patriarchs before them. Devotion does seem to be the standard for all the service there: the planting of the yard in spring, the keeping of the grounds year-round, the maintenance of the building, and the constancy in attendance. Love of place is there. Dan remembers the service when the yard was full of horses and buggies and he was running and hiding with his friends after church. The children do the same today, and Dan delights in this continuity.

But the delight of all delights is the laid-back proclamation of the gospel by the one and only lay-reader, Dr. Dan Ross. He lets the curtains of the habitation be stretched out. Whether it is a reading from *Moby Dick*, *The Emperor's New Clothes*, or a short story of his choosing, always he brings into focus some ethical point, impaled on his exquisitely sensitive love of what is good and right—or he calls our attention to the follies of us all.

Dan approaches the addressing of God the Father, God the Son, God the Holy Spirit as though God were a farmer neighbor who is more than willing to hear what we mortals have to say. There is a comfort of closeness here, that God really cares, and that he has a funny bone.

Dan, as well as Dorothy, somehow seems eternally young. Nineteen hundred and eleven! Dan is eighty-one! However, his spirit exudes triumph over fleshly ills. Even though he is not so straight as he once was, there's an inner twinkle that makes him vibrant and alive, and he seems to follow knowledge and the world of the spirit by a special star appointed just for him. Yet there is an earthy simplicity that belies his depth. He delights in saying *Ain't* and tending his cow herd with fatherly affection. His chosen order for the foundation of his life is his aliveness! "In my private prayers that I make at the beginning of the church services, I ask Christ to help me follow his two commandments: to love the Lord my God and to love my neighbors as myself."

On those two, the Prince of Rossview has hung his life, and his prayers have been well answered.

Saints Marching In

MARCH 1993

Blessed are ye when men shall revile you and shall say all manner of evil against you falsely for my sake...

Matthew 5

One whom I love is blessed among us. He chose deliberately for Christ's sake to be reviled and have all manner of evil said against him. I saw him wrestling with himself to be Christ-in-the-World as he understood his calling. This embodiment of Beatitude is George Garrow of Trinity's congregation.

We, George and I, are enrolled in the *DOCC* program that has met for twenty weeks or so each Monday night here at the church. The essence of these lessons has been an attempt to fathom the unconditional love of God as revealed to us in Christ; and the challenge to us is an attempt to live out his unconditional, no-strings-attached love. Can we accept each other, without judgment, but with understanding, no matter how different or however much we might disagree with this other one? This is hard stuff.

George has taken these lessons deep within himself. In an effort to be a voice for ones he felt persecuted, he chose to write a letter-to-the-editor defending homosexuals and has opened himself to much vilification in the local press. He has chosen to humble himself; but, in my eyes, he is exalted. He is Christ in the World. This is what we in the Church are called to be.

Giving up a practice as a cancer specialist at Vanderbilt, George has taken a year off to experience the hurt of God's people. Each Monday for some weeks you would find him in the role of servant as he ladled up soup at *Loaves And Fishes*. He brought his small daughter with him to experience this ministry. I saw the glow on his face as he patiently heard some prodigal's story. He was never too busy to listen. As I watched him, "Saint" was the word that came to me.

As Christ loved the unlovely, included the excluded, touched the untouchables, and forgave the sins of all even before they asked, George aspires to love this way. For him, homosexuals are God's beloved children and are not to be discriminated against. They are to be accepted and cherished, loved and forgiven.

The sad history of unconditional love is crucifixion. Our hidden guilts and angers are too great in its light. But to those who are capable of such selfless love: "Rejoice and be exceeding glad for great is your reward in heaven, for so persecuted they the prophets which were before you."

JUNE 1991

Hence I remind you to rekindle the gift of God that is within you through the laying on of my hands; for God did not give us a spirit of fear but a spirit of power and love and self-control.
2 Timothy

There is a laying-on-of-hands every Sunday at Trinity. If you watch closely as the congregation comes up for communion after the choir has received the bread and wine, you will see a most distinguished gentleman lay his hands on two kneeling choir members. This blessing rekindles in one, who long remembers, a great gratitude for this good man. He was my obstetrician, our pediatrician, our general surgeon, oncologist, eye-ear-nose-and-throat specialist, orthopedic surgeon, urologist, dermatologist, and all the time our good-sense psychiatrist and personal friend. This one who found in the Hippocratic Oath his servant role and, thereby, his greatness is Dr. Jack Ross, Trinity's own for all these years.

Gina Ross, of soprano fame, receives her blessing and I, if I am lucky and look imploringly, get mine. We cherish this laying-on-of-hands. If only Dr. Jack could be just a little bit holy, these hands would be worthy of one of St. Paul's *holy kisses*, for surely, they were ordained for every good work and have done such good works for more than fifty years.

Born John Walton Ross, Jr. in 1909, the first son of the beloved Dr. John Ross and the incomparable Helen Danforth Ross, he claimed the exciting genes of both and came into the world athletic, witty, dapper, handsome—just an all-round charmer. Even after the best part of a century, these "endearing young charms" are still there, only toned down a bit, their patina softened. But there is another Jack, other than this charmer. As his patient and friend, I have seen more. Beyond the smooth charmer there is a man of great sensitivity and sorrow. His enigmatic smile; his far-away, yet twinkling eyes; his elegant head bent toward you in greeting; his quiet, professional listening—all state here is a man of true empathy, one who knows "a time to weep and a time to laugh, a time to keep and a time to cast away."

Saints Marching In

After graduating from the University of Virginia Medical School, Dr. Jack came home and brought along Mildred who remains, even until this hour, his bride. He began his medical practice in Guthrie, Kentucky, where their happiness seemed secure upon the birth of their first son, Jackie Boy, in 1938. Before his second birthday, Jackie Boy died, and there was no miracle to save him. Almost unable to cope with their child's death, they lived numbly, wholly bereft and disconsolate, until weeping was no more. With their son's absence always present, they chose to leave Guthrie. Called from his grief, Dr. Jack knew other children waited his expertise, so he joined his father's practice in Clarksville. At this point in his life, Dr. Jack became the Wounded Healer.

I write subjectively of Dr. Jack's graces. He delivered my three children. His laying-on-of-hands began in me the overcoming of the spirit of fear, fear for our premature daughter's life and my fear of fear itself. Knowing all the hazards of premature birth, he laid the cold facts before me, yet gave me the utmost reason for hope. His power of presence and reassurances held me during those seven long weeks that our daughter struggled for her place in the world, as I also struggled for mine. From this time, I date my long journey out of fear into the power of love and self-control. Incomplete though my journey is, Dr. Jack was one who helped point the way.

Caring and concern can be translated into mundane matters such as money. Assuredly, Dr. Jack did not serve Mammon. When I asked him about the bill for tending our daughter in the nursery, he answered—"Nothing, the nurses did all the work." Mildred said he never turned anyone away, didn't charge enough for shots to cover their cost, and when he retired there were bills on the books to make a small fortune. Thank you, Dr. Jack, for serving the true God.

All the preceding may make Dr. Jack sound like a plaster saint—which he *Ain't*. If you've seen the imp in his eyes, you know. How he loves a good story—risque or otherwise—a practical joke, a good point to tease about, a good stiff drink with friends, a festive meal with the family, and his favorite of all pastimes—golf. And what a great golfer he is! His peers declare he is the sharpest player who ever hit Clarksville, outside the pros. He scored a hole-in-one to crown his four score and two years.

For Jack and Mildred, much was taken; much has been given. So after Jackie Boy's death, Olivia Ann sparkled her way into the family;

then there was another Ross charmer, Charlie Dan; and now there are three tall grandsons. Since his retirement, Dr. Jack lives quietly with some golf, much family, and the accolades of the Clarksville medical community. One emergency-room nurse expressed her devotion to him in my presence: "If all doctors were like Dr. Ross, this place would be heaven."

The love and care Dr. Jack has given to others in his lifetime are an intimation of greater service, of his going from "strength to strength." This "heaven," this place of perfect love—the where, the what, the way of this place—we cannot know. But it has been said, "Little children shall lead them." The way, Jackie Boy knows. In the natural course of the years, you, too, Dr. Jack, shall know the way; therefore, when you pass Gina and me by, please continue to lay your hands on us. We must be rekindled to finish our time here and then we also shall join this heavenly kingdom where we shall know as we are known. "For it is written, eye has not seen, nor ear heard, neither have entered into the heart of man, the things which God has prepared for them who love him."

Beyond Knowing

MARCH 1996

> *For he looks to the ends of the earth*
> *and sees under the whole heaven,*
> *to make the weight of the wind...*
> **Job 28**

The weight of the wind can be a long wait. It must be right—not too strong, not too balmy, but steady on, prevailing high from the northwest, with scudding clouds tickling the underblue of heaven and the cold sun suddenly more bright than new copper. This is the March day to fly a kite. Winter waiting days, dull and barren, are to be given up in this resurrection of wind; and we children are to know the exhilaration of the Wright Brothers as they moved heavenward at Kitty Hawk. The vast vacancy of the sky was to be invaded.

As February moved toward March, we started getting ready. My daddy wasn't the engineer of any little flimsy, sissy kite, but a giant fellow that on the right day would get you light-footed as you got it airborne; and its tail was a study in ragbag artistry to dazzle any student of aerodynamics.

Early on, we graduated from paper-bag paper to a cloth-reinforced paper, called "building paper," which was used to chink cracks in the plastering. With this sturdy material came the need for strong, but light laths; then from our local merchants at Christmas, we hoarded a cache of yardsticks for cross pieces. Daddy no longer engineered the regular kite shape but moved on to a six-sided one which stood almost to his shoulders and took half a gallon of flour paste to hold it to its strings. If you have ever flown a kite, you know what a delicate balance it can be to get the correct amount of tail attached. What tragic crashes I have seen with a too-light one! Then for string we had to have strength. This brought out a round, grassy ball of binder twine, the variety used in wheat harvest, and a metal rod for hand grips was placed into its core. With the paste thoroughly dried, the tail prayerfully attached, the controlling strings strung into place, and the master string attached, we were ready. Now the wait for the wind.

Beyond Knowing

The day came, cold and clear, with the wind increasing as the morning grew older. In a broad meadow north of the house, free from any entanglements, we stood with held breath as Daddy tested his engineering. The tail had to have more ragbag; it was dipping dangerously. At length, it was deemed in perfect harmony with the wind and sky, and a crescendo of string, paper, and paste was let go. It pulled with a wondrous whirl against the rod that held the twine; and in my eyes, my father could have been the master of a three-mast schooner with all sails unfurled.

When the twine was all reeled out, the kite was so high, so far away that it was no bigger than a postage stamp; and I felt a pull beyond my childish self where there was mystery beyond knowing in this pasted paper that had claimed the sky. There was another dimension; and I was left, earthbound.

In my grandchildren's eyes I see the same wonder of kites even though they are plastic imitations. There is a communication along the string as though one is seeking another sphere of being, of venturing, of knowing, and finally of letting all the string out. The final weight of wind and string can snap the petty hold of earth and over the fields and far away, the kite can fly, uncharted and unfettered. Its final resting place is in the unknown. The snapped string and the fragile paste will hold fast to some place where "he sees under the whole heaven and to the end of the earth," and the weight of the wind is no more.

So when you are told, "Go fly a kite," do it with joyful awe. "There are more things in heaven and earth than are dreamt of in your philosophy."

MAY 1995

Whoever has lived long enough to find what life is, knows how deep a debt of gratitude we owe to Adam, the first benefactor of our race. He brought death into the world.

Mark Twain

Christ has risen indeed! During the Easter season this joyous affirmation has been so muted by the steady passing of my generation that I have mulled and mused morosely and felt the cold breath on my collar as I look from this side of the Great Adventure. Death, we know your sting. My faith tells me this final fear has been vanquished, those whom I have loved have been loosed from earthly pain and passion, and Christ himself tells me to let not my heart be troubled. Being thoroughly Adam's child, however, I am sad, sad I suppose from unknown dimensions of separation that cannot be breached until I, too, travel on, my time here spent.

When we are sad, we need comfort. I need comfort not only for me, but I need the assurance that those who have been here and endured much grief and pain have gone to a perfect place of rest. The first account of such comfort beyond death is Christ's story of Lazarus in Abraham's bosom. Now whether Abraham, by literal interpretation, took on hermaphroditic characteristics, and snuggled Lazarus into an ample bosom, or whether some metaphor crept into the King James' translation is for further exegesis. But Christ's own words tell us that Lazarus, full of sores and weak with hunger, was carried by attending angels to Abraham's bosom.

As a child, I remember being held against soft bosoms that comforted me for a stubbed toe, a fight with my brother, or a booger-bear in the night. Surely, the children of God are given equal comfort on the eternal bosom as warped and diseased bodies are abandoned, tangled brains are untangled, lustful passions and addictions are loosed, and fears and guilts are forgiven. Only death can reveal the totality of Grace "reconciling all things whether they be things on earth, or things in heaven."

After comfort, the promise dearest to worn-out, weary ones is the assurance of perfect peace. Christ, after his resurrection, declared, "My peace I give to you." As my father died I saw this peace come over him and heavenly calm filled his room. In a dream I saw my mother after her death with a softened and loving countenance as if she were saying, "I am at peace; I love you; I understand all now." As the poet, Keats, wrote: "I have been half in love with easeful death"—but not head over heels.

Christ, our older brother, has gone to prepare a place for us. It sounds splendid. The place has many mansions and some versions say "rooms." I will settle for one small room. The gates of pearl and the streets of gold have no great charm for me, but I would like to sing in the heavenly chorus. After whinnying in many a choir all these years, I will ask to be rewarded (for faithfulness) with the ability to sight read and sing like Tom King. There's no male or female there, if I understand correctly, so I can sing in any section. With the new body Paul talks about, it won't need to be fed, cleaned, clothed, mated or sated, which will take a lot of bother out of eternal life. No tears, no sorrows, no night, "For the Lord God giveth them light: and they shall reign for ever and ever."

JUNE 1990

My daddy told this story about cleaning off the cemetery where he attended church as a young man: One crotchety old fellow with a long history of chronic complaints came around with a shovel and scythe, determined to make trouble. Someone made the mistake of uprooting some bushes too near his family plot and tossed some of the rubble on the graves. Irate, he bristled up to the digger, "Get that damned dirt off Grandma's grave," and with that he threw his shovel down, stormed out of the graveyard, and, yes, left the little country church. So in our family when someone got too near our "sacred places" or special opinions, we responded, "Get that damned dirt off Grandma's grave."

So there is dirt on Grandma's grave, and we need to sort out just how sacred a place her grave is and whether, from eternity, Grandma cares. Our Senior Warden communicated to me the importance, yet unimportance, of cherishing place. His point was that there is no physical building and its content worth a division in this Body of Christ. Clearly, I got into my mind from his wisdom the difference in Temple (or graveyard) worship and True worship.

I mulled and mused at Jesus' responses to temples and sacred mountains and "right" worship. His most heated language and his long list of woes to "Snakes" and "Sons of Vipers" were pronounced in Herod's Temple. To distract him from his anger, his disciples wanted to take him on a tour of this beautiful place. "There shall not be one stone left on another," he prophesied. The temple was totally destroyed in 70 A.D. He knew the blindness of all of us who would follow through the generations. He knew we would often choose wailing walls and forget love and faith, justice and mercy, and choose the transitory over the eternal.

We are like the Samaritan woman also. When we are offered "living water," we change the subject and return to Grandma's grave. "Our fathers worshiped in this mountain and you (Jesus) say Jerusalem is the right place to worship."

He pointed out to her the impermanence of all places. "The hour comes when you shall neither worship in this mountain nor yet in

Jerusalem." Then it was back to his point of true worship: "But the hour comes, and is, when the true worshipper shall worship in spirit and in truth: for the Father seeks such to worship him." So let us not refuse living water and true worship in our determination to worship in the "right" place.

Does Grandma care about place? A thousand years from now, how firm will be the foundations of Trinity? Will the floors be higher or lower, the lamps brighter and the seats softer, the organ piped or unpiped, the altar forward or backward? Now, only Grandma knows.

From our finite understanding of eternity, let us make every subjection of ourselves to plumb the heights and depths of true worship—"in spirit and in truth." In spirit, let us have faith that this People of God shall use their best judgment to restore this transitory temple, and whatever their best judgment is, we shall accept. We shall refuse to wail at wailing walls of old temples and empty graves. We shall only wail at our hardness of heart and lack of acceptance and love for one another.

> But, beloved, be not ignorant of this one thing, that one day in the sight of the Lord is as a thousand years, and a thousand years as one day... Seeing that all these things shall be dissolved, what manner of persons ought you to be in all holy conversations and godliness?
>
> **2 Peter**

FEBRUARY 1996

> The old order changeth, yielding place to new,
> And God fulfills himself in many ways,
> Lest one good custom should corrupt the world.
>
> **Tennyson**

Sitting here staring at a blank piece of paper and clenching tightly a stub pencil, I, a remnant of the blackboard and *OK Tablet* age, protest the change of the old order of communication. My rubber eraser has been insulted by a smart alec computer that corrects mistakes with nary a smudge and then has the gall to scan the pages for my errant spelling. Would you believe it offers choices of spelling? No fool, this contraption! Number 2 lead is obsolete—and maybe the dictionary, not to mention the one who peruses its pages searching for meanings for new-order words.

Beyond Knowing

Time was when a mouse was a mouse, a wee creature who instilled panic in Southern ladies, causing them to grab their skirts tightly around their thighs, mount chairs and scream out "EEKS!" Online meant just that. On Monday morning you got the wash on line just as soon as you could so the clothes would be dried and offline before the solar clothes dryer set. Software was put online also. There were teddies, Grandma's flannel gown, Sunday petticoats, and the good linen napkins. Concerning hardware, it was kept in a shed by the smokehouse. It was an internet of chicken wire, garden hoes, abandoned burlap bags, and pitchforks and spades for uploading and downloading. An occasional mouse surfed this tangled web. As for the mainframe, that was the one on the four poster bed with the 2x8 slats. When Brother Jordan, our fire-and-brimstone preacher came down from Russellville to spend Saturday night, his main mass put the mainframe on overload. Our disc couldn't be floppy because it had to disk the barn's unload into the garden plot. With this lexicon of golden oldies, here endeth my extended megabyte of computer ignorance.

Had I lived in the 1400s, I probably would have protested Gutenberg and his upstart printing press. But ignorance is brushed aside by powers beyond our knowing. When man's creativity and God's foreordination for his creation converge, a dazzling confluence is recorded in the pages of history. The beginning of this merger is often quiet, quite unnoticed; but, oh, the difference one spark of creativity can make. The printed page has been the herald of freedom, the great liberator, the great educator for all the world; and the liberty we know in this country can be traced to a printer in Germany who gave the power of the written word to a new age.

Lest one good custom should corrupt the world, the old order of communication is obsolete. The new order for eye, ear, and hand is here. It is so sudden, so overpowering, so all pervasive, that I tremble at one small microchip—amorphous, uncharted, and forever on the frontier. In the blink of an eye the world is in my kitchen. I do not know what God is about. Children of the new age seem to have a mutated gene that instantly makes them knowledgeable of technology so swiftly moving. God is somehow preparing a new work.

Could it be that he is bringing the horror of war into our living room so we see the gore, rather than hear-say glory? Is he letting us see the plight of the unempowered who live by guns and drugs? Is he letting us feed on every sort of perversion so that we understand our "total depravity" and gag on our own rottenness? Is he revealing the poverty of most of the world so we sicken on our affluence? Is this world-wide communication a warning of the apocalypse? Will he use this new work to make his name known to all nations?

When God reveals himself, there are always surprises. So far the greatest surprise was a baby born in a stable. Is there a new son of freedom to be born? Here is one fossil ready for "yielding place to new," and for the coming of a new age...and I won't set any mousetraps.

> *For since the beginning of the world*
> *Men have not heard, nor perceived by ear,*
> *Neither hath eye seen, O God,*
> *Beside thee, what Thou hast prepared*
> *For him who waiteth for Him.*
> **Isaiah 64**

JUNE 1994

> *Practice random kindness and senseless acts of beauty.*
> *- on Scott Lee's Door*

Several winters ago, I was standing at the counter at the Farmers' Co-op, ordering a hundred pounds of sunflower seed, when a tall figure appeared at my elbow. It was my friend, Bill Biggar, with his wife Mabel in tow. They always seemed to shop together and enjoyed neighborly greetings and funny stories all along their route. To know this pair was to appreciate their natural goodness.

Bill had heard my order. He inquired in his usual whimsical manner, "What in the 'wurld' are you going to do with so many sunflower seeds?" and I gave him the obvious answer: "Why, Bill, feed the birds; it's cold and they're hungry." With that he laid two crisp twenty dollar bills on the counter, smiled down at Mabel, and paid my bill. "I want to do a little something for the little 'burds'," he explained.

This random kindness was cast on the water of caring and was to be returned in a way beyond my imagining.

But I knew yesterday. I was at Bill's funeral. His family asked for a grave-side service at Grace Chapel. Family and friends from many points gathered to honor Bill on a flawless day, all blue, all redolent with honeysuckle, alive with wild roses and bees. And the birds!

Singing a cappella, a glorious baritone of near operatic quality began to fill the morning with music. He sang three hymns, the last one being "Amazing Grace." With his first note senseless beauty—if senseless can mean beyond understanding—broke out all across the cemetery. The birds joined in! It was a miracle, a grace, a symphonic background that emanated from the mystery of being.

The communication seemed to come with the first note: "We must join in this praise. This is our brother who loved us when we were cold and hungry. His random kindness was kept by our Father who knows when any of his creation falls. Our brother Bill has fallen and we rejoice at his being lifted up. We too shall fall, and our Father will know. 'When we've been here ten thousand years, bright shining as the sun; we've no less days to sing God's praise than when we first begun'."

Let us rejoice in the promise of that perfect place of random kindness and senseless acts of beauty.

MARCH 1994

> *The ice was here, the ice was there*
> *The ice was all around;*
> *It cracked and growled and roared and howled*
> *Like noises in a swound!*
> **The Rime of the Ancient Mariner**

Last night, February 10th, we were in a "swound" of fear. With cracking howls, the maple trees in our yard gave up their limbs, one after another, as we huddled with held breath inside the house. Truly, the ice was all around. A benevolent hand guided our last summer's shade to a safe landing that didn't harm the house, but left us encased in a shining array, like a crystal bird cage. Next morning, standing in the cold, we were awed by the marvel of ice, however destructive; and in its shambles we surrendered to the knowledge that we have no control over the vagaries of wind and water, ice and snow, for "who can stand before his cold?" The trees, the power lines, and our car didn't stand.

The push-button world stopped at 6:20 Friday morning, the 11th. The kerosene lamps came off a high shelf in a closet, candles were sorted out for use down to the stub, wood came in from an abandoned stack in the fence row, down comforters from my mother-in-law's household were fluffed out, the *Coleman* camp stove was untangled from the attic's disaster, the refrigerator's contents were relegated to the back porch, and we began our back-to-basic life. We continue in this state. On our dead-end line, Clarksville's Department of Electricity is teaching us patience and humility as well as thankfulness for the luxuries of our time.

But we have had blessings "unaware." With no television to rivet our eyes and little light to read at night, we, like the Ancient Mariner, have had time to feel the beauty of creation in this icy silence. If you remember your high school English class, the old seaman lost the alba-tross around his neck only after he became aware of the beauty and majesty of nature and could love all of God's creation, even the water snakes ... "A spring of love gushed from my heart and I blessed them unaware."

Amid the shattered trees, we bless the ice storm. The trees are topped, new maples will fling their winged leaves in the March winds, woodpeckers can perform their tree surgery deeper in hollow limbs, grass will spring up in too shady places, and our vaunted selves will learn better what to pray for, what to love and bless—even though "unaware."

> *He prayeth best, who loveth best*
> *All things both great and small*
> *For the dear God who loveth us*
> *He made and loveth all.*
> **Samuel Taylor Coleridge**

MAY 1993

> *And all the trees of the field shall know that I have brought down the high tree.*
> **Ezekiel 17**

Last week the sighing of the wind among our walnut trees, the paw-paws, the Paulownias, and the maples let me know their sadness. The Lord had brought down the high tree in our yard.

When we moved onto Pollard Road forty-one years ago, a great maple, already gnarled and splitting at its fork, shaded the whole of the eastern side of our house with its sheltering arms holding the roof and the yard against the summer's sun. Gladly in winter it tossed aside its golden umbrella to let in the radiance, cheering our morning kitchen. For these many years, even though crippled in its old age, this high tree had been a refuge and a strength; but we gave little thanks for its gifts. The massive stump with its year-after-year-after-year of concentric rings is monument to its faithfulness.

Beyond Knowing

The trees know the plan of the Lord who raises them up and brings them down: his winds, his rains, his woodpeckers, his termites, his tree-borers, his lichens, his whole entwined plan for his creation. "To everything there is a season and a time to every purpose under the heavens: A time to plant, and a time to pluck up that which is planted." So the Lord, with the help of the tree cutters brought down this high tree.

Our birds have lost a true haven. One of the first high limbs to go was the one on which a pair of robins had built their ragged nest each year. How they arranged their scant assortment of twigs to withstand the wild rides in the wind was an engineering feat comparable to the Golden Gate Bridge. They seemed to know the fork to which they belonged, and their tree held them fast. Forty generations of woodpeckers claimed the trunk, decaying and laden with choice grubby morsels; and they inspected every inch of bark to protect their home as best they could. Parading up and down with their heads always coming down first, the nuthatches joined in this inspection and discussed the menu for the day. Spring romance came from the tall tree's top-most branch. The brown thrasher, day after day, sang his flute song until some lady thrasher joined him and they flew away to nest in a safer place. Even our suet feeder for the birds must find a new home.

The high tree was a "very present help in trouble" for our children. When there were problems to solve, I would see them swinging in heart stopping, monkey-gymnastics among its top branches. Our daughter decided when she was about ten to have her long, beautiful hair bobbed. After seeing herself in a mirror, she spent a whole day in consolation among its branches. And I, myself, with too many "musts, oughts, and have to's" would gather my soul and body together at this friend's feet. This summer its stump, fully exposed to the sun, shall surely hold many memorial plants.

Already—in all the cracks in the walk, in the flower beds around the house, and scattered widely in all the fields—are tiny, two-leaved maple seedlings. These winged seeds from the tall tree are still attached by their baby roots to an expectant shoot. How many thousands of potential great maples are there? Creation is extravagant beyond imagination, and we sit on the edge of its wonders, stolid and unimpressed.

As the height of God's creation, we fail to see the fecundity of his mercy when our tall trees are brought down. We limit ourselves to tiny seedlings in a rich forest of joy and creativity. Oh, the fullness of creation! "Let our soul delight itself in its fatness—and the trees of the field shall clap their hands." (Isaiah 55)

Beyond Knowing

One March morning when we hadn't been on Pollard Road too many years, a knock came at my front door. An old man stood there, dressed in clean overalls and a many-wintered hat, who wanted permission to go to the back of the farm to visit the hillside where his two-year-old brother had been buried. He said he had been eight years old at the time, and after all these years the pain of his loss still swam in his eyes. His father had been a tenant farmer on this farm in the early part of the century. Several abandoned cisterns, a few scattered foundation stones, and stray daffodils in gallant cheerfulness mark the sites where these poor families lived out their twentieth-century serfdom.

"Before I die," he said with averted eye and shifted hat, "I want to see that hillside again, if it ain't no trouble." I knew the spot well. In a grove of elm trees—high overlooking the creek—was the burial ground chosen by whatever small hope arises in people of such little hope. There were three graves—two long ones and a small one—all marked by flat limestone rocks, buried upright. These anonymous stones were mute testimony to the goings of their generations—unnumbered, unsung, often unmourned and long forgotten. The sting of death was there.

A few days ago, mulling over the meaning of Easter beyond our rote rehearsal of "Hallalujah, He is Risen," I sat on this hillside. Our cattle have trodden the headstones flat, vines have overgrown the graves until their outlines are barely discernible, and a busy groundhog, in an ambitious engineering project, has thrown dirt over the whole scene. But in my musings' imagination, I went back to this hillside with an eight-year-old boy who stood with his mother as they placed his baby brother in the finality of earth. I could see no coffin—only a small figure wrapped in a blanket, placed in a crude box. I could hear no clergy—only a father or perhaps an uncle who knew a few verses. I could sense none of the insulation that pretends death is not present. This bereft eight-year-old followed his family home, carried his grief through the years, and as an old man brought it back to my doorstep.

I have no pretty consolations for my sad old man. I am certain he has joined his brother on another hillside somewhere, and he leaves his sorrow and his questions to me: Will God's poor from all generations be claimed? Are they to be resurrected? Why did they have to suffer such indignities? Where lies their hope? With Job, my questions can only be answered by the questions of God:

Beyond Knowing

"Where were you when I laid the foundation of this hillside and set it on feet of stone above the flood? What did you understand of re-creation in the realm of the fungi and decay, the nourishers of creation? Can you plumb the mystery of birth and death, and my infinite care on either side of these mysteries? 'Do you know I can do all things?'"

My only certainty and my long-gone friend's certainty is hope in the face of uncertainty. With Job, I know nothing. We have far-off intimations that we "have heard by the hearing of the ear." Grief and Death are our resurrections and the door to our certainty. Then, and only then, can we say, "But now mine eye seeth thee." Job's Easter affirmation shouts through all our doubts: "For I know that my redeemer liveth and that he shall stand at the latter day upon the earth." Hallelujah!

JUNE 1987

We know that the whole creation has been groaning in travail until now; and not only the creation but we ourselves...
                              Romans 8

The groaning of the whole creation—this inaudible sound in the past weeks—has been the filter through which all my feelings have passed, and indeed the groanings: My brother reported the duck's nest of last months' *Mullings and Musings* destroyed one sad night with only a barren crumple of shells left behind; my mother was released from her groanings on April 30th, and the wisdom to understand her suffering after her long life eludes me; our dear friend of Soup Kitchen fame, Tom McGilloway, bears without ceasing his constant pain; my husband took the hay rake out of the barn and nestled against one of the wheels was a wren's nest, replete with three minuscule eggs; just this morning our dog, Tess, killed a kitty whose screams still resound in my ears; and the news blares forth with thirty-eight young sailors dead for no rhyme or reason. With Job, I find the mystery of suffering beyond my ken; and with his wife I find the temptations to "curse God and die."

"Who is this that denies providence with words void of knowledge?"... and I am the guilty one.

In all my searching for the understanding of the mystery of suffering, the writings of the French philosopher and theologian, Teilhard de Chardin, along with St. Paul, speak to me with a clarity of hope:

Beyond Knowing

In a bunch of flowers it would be surprising to find imperfect or sickly blooms, because they have been picked one by one and assembled with art. On a tree, by contrast, which has had to fight the internal hazards of rough weather, the broken branches, the bruised blossoms and the shrivelled, sickly or faded flowers are in their rightful place; they reflect the amount of difficulty which the trunk that bears them has undergone before attaining its growth... The world is an immense groping, an immense search... It can only progress at the cost of many failures and many casualties. The sufferers, whatever the nature of their suffering, are the reflection of this austere but noble condition. They are not useless and diminished elements. They are merely those who pay the price of universal progress and triumph... it is exactly those who bear in their enfeebled bodies the weight of the moving world who find themselves, by the just dispensation of providence, the most active factors in that very progress which seems to sacrifice and to shatter them.

Give us grace to understand that "the sufferings of the present time are not worth comparing with the glory that is to be revealed in us" and to all of creation. May each egg, each twig, each kitty, each sparrow, each hair on every head await its redemption, resting in the sure knowledge that it is known and cherished and that its redeemer liveth.

OCTOBER 1984

> *Remember to show hospitality. There are some who, by so doing, have entertained angels without knowing it. Remember those in prison as if you were there with them; and those who are being maltreated, for you like them are still in the world.*
>
> ### *Hebrews 13*

When we who work in the soup kitchen at Trinity get going on our assigned morning, we are jarred awake by the fact that we are indeed still in the world. I am amazed at the diverse ways of cooking squash. Anyone who has been in the world two weeks would know you don't cook squash that way! Then there are the dishwater critics—too cold, too hot, too polluted—and those cooks who use cup towels for pot holders, and the germ generals suspicious of strange packages in the refrigerator and unidentified flying odors. All the while we are jockey-

85

ing around each other delving into the realm of group dynamics to see who the leader will be. By the grace of God and his grace only do we come together, forgive each other our dirty dishwater and desecrated squash, and become Christ in the world.

When we have said our prayers, the task at hand is to look over the serving counter at the hungry who begin to gather as early as 9:30. Our Christ-eyes suddenly grow dim; prayers forgotten, our judgmental glasses go on...." Now if she can sit there and smoke a half package of cigarettes and drop the ashes in her baby's eyes she could afford some milk for that child; you can tell he has been drunk for years by that shuffle; look at all those children she has, and you know the more you feed them the more they breed; that black girl has such hate in her eyes and is so impudent I could slap her face; they just use us and laugh at us bleeding hearts; we know they have a job and come here for a free lunch day after day..." Being in the world as we are, we recognize about as many angels on one side of the counter as we do the other.

By the power of the Holy Spirit, however, we can see with the eyes of Christ. When he fed the five thousand he asked no questions of color, beliefs, worthiness, cigarettes consumed or sleeping arrangements. He simply fed them. He said to us who are his body that what we do to the least, most unworthy, drunken, and outcast that we do it to him. I mull and muse how to keep my Christ eyes in focus and my heart open to his spirit; and being, sometimes I feel hopelessly, in the world, I have to begin anew each morning, ask Christ for his compassion, and lay aside my judgmental glasses. Then my mind plays over the hungry ones whom I have served. I ponder who among them were those angels I did not recognize and how well did I become Christ to them as we ladled the hash over the counter.

Was I arrogant and condescending as I served them or did I suffer with their humiliation and brokenness? Did I hear the Song of Mary as the dirty dishes accompanied in the sink? "...He hath scattered the proud in the imaginations of their hearts. He hath put down the mighty from their seats, and exalted them of low degree. He hath filled the hungry with good things; and the rich he has sent empty away."

Beyond Knowing

JANUARY 1984

"Do not lay up for yourself treasures on earth—." For the past two years I have been digging and delving through here-on-earth-treasures, some going back four generations. After the experience of dismantling my mother-in-law's home and now my mother's, our families must admit, mortals that we be, that we have treasures here on earth. They somehow plant our roots to a place and knit our hearts around old dining room tables stretched to their last leaf and Christmas tree baubles that long ago lost their outward glitter.

At my mother-in-law's division of treasures, the most tears and nostalgia came over the bread board. This wooden board, carved all the way around with *Be Ye Thankful*, had come over from Ireland with the grandmother and had been used to slice the bread as long as any of the children could remember. This was real bread, no plastic-wrapped sissy stuff. When I left the scene, the best I could understand of the destination of this almost Eucharistic piece was that it would rotate from household to household. Then there was Granny Fry's picture, the old checker games and the balls and bats, the butter dish, the family albums, the "dress-up" clothes, and the books, oh, the books. Moth, rust, and silverfish had gotten to them, but still they were treasures on earth.

At my home the past two months, we have repeated this scenario. The pepper mill in the attic where we ground the hot pepper for hog-killing was lovingly taken from its rusty screws to its new home in Atlanta; the pseudo-Tiffany lamp shade that hung over our dining room table made a journey to Chicago where it is considered a treasure indeed; and from Kirkwood to Pollard Road came the favorite pot roast pan that was bestowed on me because I, as a child, had sat on the fast talking salesman's hat and crushed it beyond recognition... On and on, the sorting, the joys recalled, the sorrows not spoken, the mute memories handled and once again dusted, another layer of a generation assigned.

"For where your treasure is there shall your heart be also." Knowing that all things here on earth are ours briefly, on temporary loan, and that we are bankrupt except for the bounty of grace, may we at this New Year be given a clear eye to sort treasures from possessions. May our hearts be knit around a stretched table in an upper room where we are offered treasures beyond price: The Bread of Heaven and The Cup of Salvation.

Beyond Knowing

MAY 1996

Whither shall I go from thy spirit? Or whither shall I flee
from thy presence?
If I ascend up into heaven, thou art there;
If I make my bed in hell, thou art there.

Psalm 139

I seem to have made my bed in hell, suffering from post-flu mortem; and I am frozen with negative thoughts and dire reports of illness and misfortune. I am in bad need of resurrection, of coming up out of the gray fog, and for "wings of the morning" when I rise up.

Too long the spring has been belated, held in a winter of blighted dogwood and daffodils. But there is an Easter insistence that no blight or morbid feeling can discourage. Each marvel of creation—be it animal or plant—comes up out of the killing cold and flings its life on a disappointed world. Frozen blossoms and barren nests are suddenly forgotten as the countryside is filled with verdure and song. At last, with the coming of spring, my spirit has risen on the wings of songbirds and indefatigable dandelions, and I know resurrection.

Along with me, the wings of the morning have claimed the songbirds in our yard. The sassy mockingbird has been hanging around for some weeks, popping in and out of the holly tree by the kitchen, but this morning he ascended. Up on the television aerial on the roof-top and then to the top of a power pole, he has announced life anew that would lift any spirit from the doldrums. A woodpecker picked up in the percussion section and drummed out a head-rattling rhythm on the chimney-flue announcing to the lady woodpeckers he is ready and willing. On the top limb of the tallest maple, a brown thrasher has sung his three-note song for two mornings; and when he is gone, I know he has found his beloved and is ready to descend from the treetop and tend a new generation.

There is respite and promise for the trees. The pear trees in our yard had a 7 degree blossom time; therefore, no pears. But on their tired old limbs, probably a century old, the new leaves are half-grown and are ascending with only slight damage from the many freezes. The trees needed a rest from too many pears last year, and loss of fruit will be found in lush foliage. Dogwood blossoms show small promise. With three freezes on tender blossoms, they will have difficulty making a spectacular show and, along with the redbud, will wait for a gentler spring. Creation cares for its own in inexplicable ways. "Wonderful are thy works."

Psalm 139 is my favorite psalm. It is to be read at my going-out party. The totality of God's love and care, within the womb and beyond the grave, is expressed for all depths and heights. I have known these depths and heights. Who among us has not? In 1972, I was diagnosed with the Great Depth—Cancer. A chill fear was my constant companion on my "downsitting and uprising" and the spirit seemed far away and uncaring. Where could I go for solace? Where were the wings of the morning after a sleepless night? Where could I go from Job's Comforters who declared my disease a consequence of poor thought patterns or my sins? "Surely the darkness will cover me."

Out of the depths, my cry was heard: I asked to live to see our younger son through high school. And here I still am—twenty-four years later. My body was restored as well as my spirit and from the depths the whole creation for me has been made new. I see with eyes filled with a grace from a spirit beyond my blindness. With a new dimension of caring, I can see the spring with eyes of wonderment and my fellow sufferers as persons called out for special lessons.

The worst consequence of any terrible disease is death. This must be faced. Only do I live when I accept my mortality. Only beyond the barrier of inevitable death, do I find life. And again with David, I say, "When I awake, I am still with thee."

Beyond Knowing

NOVEMBER 1996

While he was still speaking, a man from the ruler's house came and said, "Your daughter is dead; do not trouble the Teacher anymore." But Jesus on hearing this answered him, "Do not fear; only believe and she shall be well." ...All were weeping and bewailing her; but he said, "Do not weep; for she is not dead but sleeping." And they laughed at him, knowing that she was dead.

But taking her by the hand he called saying, "Child, arise." And her spirit returned and she got up at once, and he directed that something should be given her to eat.

Luke 8

The miracle of Jarius' daughter coming back from death is recorded in three of the Gospels. I record such a miracle in a new gospel, one whose lines I write in wondrous awe and boundless thanksgiving. Our grandson was dead; yet he lives.

Three weeks ago our daughter who lives in France found her nine year old son, unconscious, not breathing, blue from lack of oxygen, choked in the night on his own vomit.

Lamentations arose from all quarters—from neighbors, from strangers off the street who came to the distress call, and from patrons of a near-by restaurant. "He is dead; he is dead."

But our daughter heard another voice, "Do not fear; only believe and he shall be well." Belief, coupled with divine prompting, took her back to mouth-to-mouth techniques long ago lost to memory, but suddenly flooding back in every detail.

"Don't do that! Don't do that!" the cry went up from the mystified on-lookers, not familiar with this form of resuscitaion. Our daughter heard none of them but breathed breath after breath into her son's powerless lungs and useless diaphragm, all the while communicating to him, "Charles, don't you die; don't you die. Hear me. Live, Charles, live!"

Oblivious to the tumult around her, she heard another voice and did not stop the mouth-to-mouth until the emergency squad got to her apartment. In the ambulance on the way to hospital, our grandson's spirit returned. He could not speak nor focus his eyes, but he knew his mother. By morning, it was directed that he be given something to eat, and suddenly he was well. From the doctors' reports and extensive tests, there is absolutely no trace of damage to any part of his brain or body. We have lived a miracle. In stunned thankfulness, I am over-awed by this divine intervention; and my perception of things known and my grasp of things unknown are new before me, radicalized into a dimension of faith beyond my understanding.

Two things I know. I know now what life is worth, and that for which I would die. Before I knew our grandson was completely restored, I lived David's agony. "Oh my son, Absalom, my son, would God I had died for thee." My life is a cheap exchange for my grand-son's. I would gladly die for him. Then the pricelessness and the fragili-ty of life, bound together as an ephemeral gift, came into such sharp focus as to make me weep anew. Why have I been so dull, so unaware, so taking-for-granted the treasures given me? Never again will any of life be taken cavalierly. I shall hold my grandson and all other treasures ever so closely, all the while knowing that the day or hour for letting them go may be upon me. Where can I find the strength to hold my treasures in an open hand? "For all flesh is as grass, and all the glory of man as the flowers of grass."

That leaves the unknown before me. This miracle of my grandson's restored life must have its divine purpose as Isaac's spared life had its purpose. Perhaps its purpose is to bring the gospel, the good news, up to the present moment so that our flagging faith can come alive. Or is it to underscore once more the sovereignty of God—that he is in con-trol of his creation even to the sparrow that falls, the number of hairs on our head, and the breaths that we take?

"The grass withers and the flowers fall, but the word of the Lord abides forever." Whether we live or whether we die, his word is forev-er and the gospel is ours—the good news that we are safe. Do not fear; only believe and we shall be well.

Unorthodoxy and Questionable Theology

NOVEMBER 1991

Giving thanks always for all things unto God...
Ephesians 5

Always for all things give thanks. St. Paul, do you literally mean to give thanks for all things? As I sit here in the hallelujah of the trees, awaiting Thanksgiving, I shall give thanks for all things—small though some of them be—just to let you know I am listening to your exhortations after these hundreds of years.

There is Tess, our dog, basking prone in the leaves, soaking up the failing rays of the summer sun. Our cat, Marble, comes across the yard with a dead bird—whether fallen by its length of days or snatched up by Marble, I do not know. A woolly-worm wends its way across an uncharted path in the walnut tree's twigs, frantically searching for some mystery in the woolly-worm world, and I am nursing a sore finger that I cut in a frenzy of slicing. For these, I give thanks, St. Paul.

Tess has shown me how it is to be laid-back. I need this lesson. When her old bones need a rest, the sun is just right, and the fallen leaves nestle just so against her rheumatism, she spends hours tending her needs. No stray cat that ambles by tempts her to her favorite chase. There is a time to run and a time to rest. I give thanks for her example. Basking time is mending time.

Then there is Marble. How do I give thanks for her and her dead bird? All things follow the order of creation—something must die to give life—and the cycle is unending. Marble eats the bird, the birds eat the insects, the insects eat the leaves, and the leaves are nourished by the earth, air, and rain. In certain parts of the world, Marble herself would be fair game for the human species. I give thanks for the economy of creation, knowing full well that nothing created is ever lost; it only changes its form. And even when we die, we make space so the next generations might live and our elements are added to the fecundity of creation.

And the woolly-worm and its frantic searching? I am persuaded that some hand beyond my knowing guides its humping determination to some safe winter haven and to a secure nest for its progeny. It has sustained itself for millions of years, and the wisdom of worms is bound

93

into its certainty of the guiding of its creator, and it follows no other path. Oh, for a worm-like faith that charts our path when winter comes. Thank you, fellow-travelers, for your example.

Then by my sore finger I give thanks for the one body I am and its innate care of my members. The ministration of white cells comes and nurses this throbbing finger back to health and makes it well again—a miracle in itself. This is a small foreshadowing of the final healing of this worn-out body when its time is gone and a new time will take it. There will be no more cut fingers, broken valves, motor malfunctions, or plumbing problems. "Behold, I make all things new."

So for this Thanksgiving, give thanks for all things, even a burned turkey. This sacrifice is made that you might live.

APRIL 1990

But that which beareth thorns and briars is rejected, and is nigh unto cursing; whose end is to be burned.

Hebrews 6

Saw briars have had me nigh unto cursing. A long one, well-hidden in undergrowth, can entwine around your ankle like some barbed serpent and relieve you of several inches of skin. They stand as sentinels along all our fence rows, guard the entrance to the lushest blackberry bushes, and patrol the edges of the bluff where the wild flowers flourish. They seem to say, "Stay out!" The vines spring up from nowhere, trailing their tendrils for yards in an entanglement that defies tough old heifers—both bovine and otherwise—who dare venture into their prickly domain. Some builders and grain farmers wish these thorn-bearers cursed, rejected, and burned—but not Brer Rabbit, a symphony of songbirds, and all small, vulnerable creatures on our farm. They welcome them. "They were born and bred in the briarpatch." Here is safety.

At this moment as I write these lines, a dove is calling from the protected boundary at the west side of our house. Her mournful call, so close yet so far away, would not be heard, this melody in a minor key, if some great bulldozer "improved" our fence row. From the uppermost branch of a wild cherry tree our mockingbird is singing a trill that would lessen the bold notes of Israfel. Underneath the briars, if you walked quietly, you would hear a stealthly towhee and her mate whispering their secrets for a safe nest. Like Christmas tree ornaments, a pair of cardinals, considering co-habitation, flirt on a low-hanging sassafras limb; and a sparrow argument with many debaters has gone on all afternoon. Such is the delight of a briarpatch fence row. This is the gift of thorns.

Briars and thorns are necessary. Ask the birds and the rabbits, and, yes, ask St. Paul and me. Even though St. Paul resisted his thorns vigorously and suggested they be cursed and burned, he held one thorn-in-the-flesh dear to his heart and found rest in it just as Brer Rabbit did in his briarpatch. It was his stabilizer, his safe-haven from himself, his anti-pride prickler. When I consider my life and its thorns and entangling briarpatches, what would be my priorities and what would I be worth without the discipline of the thorns? Certainly I would be some egomaniac who would have no heart for my briar-torn brothers. But as it is, with my being wounded in my briarpatch, I do not judge and condemn as you struggle in yours.

If I do get into judging and condemnation, it tells me that I am not dealing with my thorns and their lessons, that I am trying to place my prickles onto someone else so I can forget my thorns. The lesson I must learn is compassion—to suffer along with you. Here is the place I know the sufficiency of Grace for the whole creation. Here is the beginning of peace and joy. This is the blessing of the briarpatch:

> *For ye shall go out with joy, and be led forth with peace: The mountains and the hills shall break forth before you in singing, and all the trees of the field shall clap their hands. Instead of the thorn shall come up the fir tree, and instead of the briar shall come up the myrtle tree: and it shall be to the Lord for a name, for an everlasting sign that shall not be cut off.*
>
> **Isaiah 55**

NOVEMBER 1985

We have a cow lot with a shallow, muddy pond much prized by our cattle for a summer cooling place. It is full of their droppings and covered by an unsavory green. Wee creatures—tadpoles and minnows—surface and bubble for air in this polluted milieu which only has fresh water when it rains. On the clay bank a profusion of barnyard thistles prickles the passing parade of hooves and threatens man or beast who dare invade their province. Overhead several elm trees, long dead from the elm disease that has decimated this species, dangle their broken arms into the pond while a woodpecker beats out his staccato as he makes a nest hole in their barren limbs. To Tess and me, in our quest

95

for action and beauty, this seems a lifeless place, and we pass on the other side of the fence.

We envision the perfect place: a garden with flower-catalogue blossoms, everything pruned and weeded, all bugs bombarded. But that's not the way it is, nor will it ever be. The cow lot is the honest place. It is the hopeful place. Those cow droppings with all their nutrients make the algae grow and oxygenate the teeming life beneath the "slime." The tenacious thistles hold the bank against trampling and erosion. And, alas, the woodpecker is not only making a home for himself, but in his quest for grubs, he makes multiple holes, ones used by the bluebirds who have come back in profusion to our farm.

I must cross over the fence. I must inhale those lusty smells so full of struggle and life. If I listen with my inward ear for the triumphs of hope as the mud sucks beneath the cattle's hooves and as the woodpecker hammers away at his home, I shall hear the promise of all time and eternity: "Behold I make all things new."

OCTOBER 1992

And what does the Lord require of thee, but to do justly, love mercy, and to walk humbly with thy God?

Micah 8

Who said I was not raised in a liturgical church? These uninformed ones are only exposing their ignorance of liturgy: "the prescribed form of ritual for public worship in any of various Christian churches." You of the hierarchical persuasion, that chain of command of the Princes of the Church, even to the Pope of Rome, should quake before my infant instruction into the all-encompassing infallibility and power, once revealed for all time unto all generations: *The Book.* Our pope was the Bible. Each person had his straight line up to the throne, no priest to soft pedal his confession, and he stood eyeball to eyeball with the Almighty. The liturgy of the word, read and expounded upon, was the cornerstone of all our worship.

If any preacher worth his share of the collection plate could not find between the lids of the Bible a text for any sermon on sins—committed, omitted, or cogitated upon—and couldn't flip the pages in an expeditious manner from one book, chapter, and verse to another without hesitation and hem-haw reading, he "just didn't know his Bible." Brother Jordan, to whom I have extended superlatives before for gluttony and garrulousness, was the first on the list for Bible dexterity, coming forth with instantaneous and extemporaneous exegeses on obscure texts.

He held the book higher than any chalice, waved it above our heads with its black morocco binding and its golden-edged leaves flapping like some great vulture of the apocalypse waiting to devour our mortal flesh. Mama allowed no book stacked on or above the Bible. The word indeed dwelt among us.

Then there was the Liturgy of Baptism. Always and always was read at the creek's edge Acts 8:38 ——"and they went down both into the water, both Philip and the eunuch; and he baptized him." At one baptism, Verlean Thomas, who must have had hydrophobia, resisted her immersion with such splashing and back stroking that the top of her head didn't get wet. Yes, you guessed it. She was a double-dip Baptist, which was certainly better than the Methodists just across the field. Brother Jordan said they had just been "dry-cleaned."

So what of this liturgy, this prescribed form of public worship? Sunday before last, September 13th, The Most Reverend and Right Honorable George Carey, the Archbishop of Canterbury, was the preacher at the National Cathedral in Washington. I was there. Archbishop Carey didn't have to be nimble with the Book. The readers saw to that. This good and wise man was just that, a good and wise man who proclaimed the meaning of grace. Every liturgical correctness was aspired to in this service; every note of music carefully selected and practiced; every detail of the procession and recession ordered to traditional protocol; every symbol was in its proper place, raised and lowered and praised in its due time. "What we aspired to be and were not" in this setting comforted me. There in the cathedral all was well-ordered, except for our common humanity.

I found myself gawking rather than worshipping; judging my brothers' and sisters' attire rather than longing to love them; listening for the wrong inflections and pronunciations to make myself feel in-the-know rather than facing my own imperfections; and worrying when I knelt for communion about the *Guinn's* sale price tag on the bottom of my new shoes rather than marveling at the gracious gift of any salvation. I am persuaded that God must love us so much that he is amused by our foolishness.

At length, I knew amid all this pomp and pageantry that we do not worship the liturgy or a book or a tradition, but a living God who is going before us, surprising us in our narrow concentrations, and puncturing our pretense so that we might bloom in a new place.

Our true liturgy and liberty are found only in the grace given us. We accept because we are accepted; we forgive because we are forgiven. By this grace we are Christ's own, his redeemed sinners. Among us are The Most Reverend and Right Honorable George Carey, the Archbishop of Canterbury; Brother Jordan; the "dry-cleaned" Methodists; and, yes, even you and me.

SEPTEMBER 1991

> *And when ye hear of wars and rumors of wars, be ye not troubled,*
> *for such things must needs be...*
>
> **Mark 13**

When I had seen the PBS Series on the Civil War, these words of Christ "for such things must needs be" began to haunt my mulling and musings. These things must needs be! As a student of history, I long avoided the pages devoted to the Civil War. These accounts were too close, too personal, too irrational, too gory, and certainly too painful, because as a child and even into the 30s and 40s I was aware of the hot-eyed angers on both sides of my family. "Yankee" was still a dirty word. "Damn Yankee" was a Yankee who came South and stayed. If Abraham Lincoln had had horns and tail, he could not have been more vilified.

My grandmother Winn chilled our bones with the account of her father being taken in the middle of the night to show the Union Forces the fording places in Red River at Port Royal; and she recounted still with fear in her voice how the soldiers cursed and threatened, leaving the family huddled in the dark until daybreak. Out in North Carolina in the path of General Sherman's march, Aunt Hattie told us in many anguished details of her home's destruction. Every piece of furniture was piled and burned, all china was broken (enough to make a path to the smokehouse after the war), the feather beds ripped open and emptied out the upstairs windows, all food in the pantry taken, the smokehouse emptied, and finally all livestock driven away. Even though Aunt Hattie was a staunch Scotch Presbyterian, she had a hard time accepting her niece's marriage to a Presbyterian missionary. Why? He was from New York State.

On the other side of my family, it was another story: My mother's people lived on the south side of Cumberland River in Montgomery County; the planters and slaveholders lived on the north side. This made all the difference. In the hills and hollows of Palmyra, there were no plantations and certainly no wealth. Grandma Wickham was a Unionist. When the Confederate conscriptionist came, she hid her sons in the rag barrels kept for carpet-making; she willingly cooked for the Union soldiers who impressed her for a night's lodging; she was an Abolitionist, counseling relatives and neighbors; and when the Union was being restored, she was one of the first in the county to make a two-day trip by wagon to Hopkinsville to take the Oath of Allegiance for readmittance to full citizenship in the Union.

So was the dichotomy of my childhood allegiance, giving me a background of understanding as I search in my final years for some glimmers into a more faithful allegiance, for "these things that must needs be."

It must be that "he had loosed the fateful lightning of his terrible swift sword." The PBS historians made this point. Without the resolution of the Civil War, we would have been a fragmented nation, slavery would probably have been entrenched even into this century, and the liberty—imperfect though it is—that we proclaim never would have been heralded, world-wide. The Emancipation Proclamation yet reverberates. His truth is marching on in Russia, Eastern Europe, China, South Africa, and in the longings of all nations. Being dragged screaming through history, we are often too dull and too blind to see His day is marching on.

I have strived to be the blessed peacemaker, have prayed for peace, protested for peace; but after World War I to make the world safe for Democracy and World War II, the war to end all wars, Korea and Vietnam to rid us of the Communists, and finally Desert Storm, I know that these things will be, man being as he is, and even must be, as Christ said. Surely the desolation of Iraq holds the promise of the terrible swift sword: this nation's ultimate liberation after centuries of despots.

J. Glenn Gray in his book *The Warriors*, attempts to fathom the mystery of why men go to war. He makes the point that it is recorded in holy scriptures in The Revelation that there was war in heaven causing the Devil and his angels to be cast out upon the earth. There is some great warfare beyond our knowing, some struggle for righteousness that causes the nether region around us to seethe in its agony. St. Paul writes in Ephesians: "For we wrestle not against flesh and blood, but against principalities, against powers, against the rulers of darkness of this world, against spiritual wickedness in high places." This struggle must declare that if man is ever loosed from these death angels of war, unshackled from these powers and principalities, it must be by divine intervention, "beyond the human, in the nature of being itself," unto the coming of his kingdom.

> *He hath sounded forth the trumpet that shall never call retreat;*
> *He is sifting out the hearts of men before the judgment seat.*
> *Oh, be swift, my soul to answer Him*
> *Be jubilant my feet!*
> *Our God is marching on.*
> **The Battle Hymn of the Republic**

MARCH 1990

> *Yes, the Body of Christ has many parts.... and whether one member suffers, all the members suffer with it.... and these members of the body which we think to be less honorable, upon these we bestow more abundant honors.*
> **1 Corinthians 12**

Several years ago I broke my little toe on my right foot, smashed it against the leg of the couch rushing to the telephone in the dark. This little member, black and swollen, suffered on pillows, in hot water, in cold water, wrapped and unwrapped; and my whole body agonized along with it, especially when I decided to wear a decent shoe to a wedding. I came home "Diddle, diddle dumpling, my son John ... one shoe off and one shoe on." Never before had I been aware of this "lesser member" until it wracked my whole body. Now I pay it due reverence with a special massage each time it gets a bath to see if its crushed state is still retreating, forever aware of its importance in my body. This lesser member has been bestowed its "more abundant honor" serving me well with its reminders for the welfare of my wholeness in the dark. It knows from its crushed state that I am one body, one spirit.

So are we all members in this Body of Christ: some little toes, some backbones, some feet, some hands, some tongues, and here and there a brain or two. You who would earnestly give yourself away to Christ will know your place. It will feel right, you will experience joy and fulfillment; and you will relax with your ordained role as a hand, or a foot, or a backbone, or an ear. The abundant riches of Grace have given us each our unique gift or for some fortunate few, many gifts, and this benevolence is not going to expect our little toe to be a brain. St. Paul reminds us that the lesser members of the body, which we think to be less honorable, should be bestowed "more abundant honor." My unrecognized little toe demanded it. So it should be within our Body, the Church.

I remember well at our country church a young man, illiterate and crippled with rickets, who always laid the fires in the stove in the winter, came early in the morning to get them going, swept up around the stove, and in the summertime made sure the *Tarpley Funeral Home* fans with Jesus-and-the-little-children were on each seat and the songbooks in proper distribution. These were lesser-member feet, fumbling and deformed, yet part of our Body and we suffered with him. He said the Lord had called him to preach, but, alas, he found he was not a head; however, his faithful service counted for greater honor because "comely parts have no need of honor." Had Jonathan Edwards himself appeared at our church with his powerful gifts of expounding the scriptures, his sermon would have paled in the shadow of this lesser member's gift with its double burden of ignorance and disease.

Our only offense to the Body of Christ is not using our unique gift, or being unhappy with another member who is not like us or maybe too much like us—a hand wanting everyone to be a hand; or a mouth not wanting anyone else to be a mouth; or a head which does not respect another head. This body has aches and pains. Let us respect hands in service, backbones in business and finance, heads in meditation and study, ears to hear our deepest wounds and confessions, and feet to stand ever faithful, undergirding the Body with patience and faith. "They also serve who only stand and wait."

May our tongues speak only praise and thanksgiving with words of honor for all members of this Body, weak or strong, for "strength is made perfect in weakness."

Unorthodoxy and Questionable Theology

JUNE 1989

Wives, submit yourselves unto your own husbands as unto the Lord—Husbands, love your wives, even as Christ also loved the church and gave himself for it.

St. Paul

An old aunt of mine, hearing that her son-in-law was stepping out on her daughter, was inundated with advice from her sister about the advisability of the couple's getting a divorce. The aunt's terse response was this: "Ella Sue should kill that low-down, low-lifer. Divorce is not scriptural."

So in the month of June with its fairy tale hopes for this glorified institution of marriage, I mull and muse that if it endures for more than a few months, murder and divorce will from time to time seem a reasonable way out, and our hope of glory rests in the fact there will be no marriage nor giving in marriage beyond the resurrection.

Some few couples appear to maintain a life-long love affair, and I use the word "appear" because beneath the facade of a great love can lodge great hate, unrecognized and certainly unresolved. Or it can be one partner's total dominance, dependent on the other's submission, thus keeping an unfair peace. The couples who do realize a union of wedded bliss and eternal devotion have to be those mature persons who understand St. Paul's idealistic admonitions for a happy marriage. Who has ears to hear such selflessness? Certainly not I.

From my vantage point and from the testimony of many friends, I find the majority of us wrestling with this most difficult of our earthly relationships: the making and keeping of a marriage; or, conversely, knowing when the relationship is impossible and letting it go. There is pain, death and resurrection in either alternative.

It is ironic that an institution that our hormones make us yearn for so badly is the most difficult place to find harmony for our insistent hormones. As one dear to me has said, "Marriage is a lifetime sentence with no time off for good behavior," and Oscar Wilde wrote, "Divorces are made in heaven."

According to St. Paul, the burden of the marriage is on the husband's shoulders. He has to love his wife as Christ loves the church. Who wouldn't love a man like that! He would die for you and say you didn't know what you were doing when you murdered him; you couldn't do anything so bad he wouldn't take you back seven times seventy, even to not balancing the checkbook or locking the keys in the car sixteen times; he would love you just as your are and not try to improve you or make you over and no "if onlys and why didn't yous"; he would suffer all the little children you produced and die for them too; and when there was sickness or you were no longer slim and sexy, he would be more faithful than ever. This is the love that will not let you go. We wives must only obey this man, submit ourselves unto him, and love him as unto the Lord—with all our body, soul, and mind. Easy? To you, St. Paul, who pen such great lines, but we must remind you that you were never married. Couldn't you stand any more thorns in your flesh?

Christ does love us, the Church, in this manner; but we, both husbands and wives, are unfaithful lovers of so gracious a bridegroom. Our humanity overwhelms us as we struggle in this finite world of prejudice, pride, and paradox. Our chosen gods are worshipped differently, our bodies and souls grow in different directions: out, around, and beyond, and we sit in frozen non-communication, unforgiving in holy deadlock.

So what will it be: murder, divorce or maybe a fool's paradise? Or do we take up anew the mature struggle to keep our relationships as best we can by St. Paul's prescription?

After forty-three years I shall continue the journey with a husband who most of the time has loved me as Christ loves the church, even though I have not submitted myself unto him. As we approach our 50th year and the eventual end of this earthly relationship, I mull and muse what in the heaven we will work on in the way of complex puzzles in the hereafter. All that singing around the throne and treading the streets of gold may get deadly dull without some marriage and giving in marriage. When St. Paul's not watching, maybe we can indulge in some alternate after-life styles.

Unorthodoxy and Questionable Theology

AUGUST 1988

> *I set my bow in the clouds, and it shall be a sign of the covenant between me and the earth. When I bring clouds over the earth and the bow is seen in the clouds, I will remember my covenant which is between me and you and every living creature of all flesh; and the waters shall never again become a flood to destroy all flesh.*
>
> ### *Genesis*

In those last days there dwelt in the land of Asu a man called Haon, who honored the Lord. Now the Lord came to Haon and said, "Forty thousand years have I kept my covenant with the sons of Noah, with the cattle of the fields, with the fowl of the air, and with every creeping thing upon the earth; but every imagination of the heart of man is only evil and I repent that I made my covenant with my servant Noah. His sons have grieved me to my heart and I wish to blot them out of my sight."

Then Haon of Asu answered the Lord saying, "You have put your bow in the clouds as an everlasting promise that you would never again destroy all flesh; and you gave your promise that while the earth remains, seedtime and harvest, summer and winter, day and night shall not cease." And the Lord God took counsel with himself saying, "I have placed my bow in the clouds and I shall hold fast to my covenant with man even though his heart is only evil and his greed consumes him."

So in those last days the sons of earth took their ease. They saw the bow in the clouds and boasted in the covenant of the Lord and laughed when Haon called them to repent of their evil. They answered Haon saying, "The Lord God has given us dominion over creation to subdue it and has commanded us to multiply and replenish all the earth."

Therefore, man broke the mountains apart, ran the rivers behind great barriers and chose their paths, felled the trees of the great forests, and laid the fields bare with burdens of grain. And then he said unto himself, "I will build cities with such great towers that they shall reach the clouds, and I shall use the wealth of the earth for my ease. I shall make such machines of burden that they will take me over land and sea and, yea, even into the heavens and beyond the heavens." And man saw that all his creation was good and he rested in his great cities.

The Lord God looked down from the firmament of the heavens and smelled the smoke rising from the mighty forges of man and felt the heat upon his face and he said, "My covenant is sure and I will never blot out man as long as my bow is in the clouds, but he is burning the clouds where my bow makes its covenant, and he will destroy himself." And the dry winds of man's creation began to blow. The heat from his machines filled the sky, and the clouds which in the past had borne rain and the bow of the covenant were dry shadows over the sun. There was a great drought in all the land. And man was afraid. The fields perished, the waters dried up, and all the creatures of the land no longer had food or drink. In the great cities the dwellers came down out of their high towers and clung to the edges of the dying rivers. The heavens were as brass and the sons of Haon pleaded with the Lord for a flood to come again. But the Lord had made his covenant and the great floods were sealed in the fountains of the deep and the windows of the heavens were closed.

And the Lord came again to his servant Haon of Asu. Now Haon and his sons were mighty forgemen in those last days and skilled in the ways of man, and the Lord said unto Haon, "The end of all flesh is before me. You shall build an ark that shall split the heavens and it will bear you and your sons and your sons' wives. You will command it to take in frozen vessels of glass the seeds of all flesh both male and female and seeds of every living plant. And you will command the ark to float beyond the heavens above the realm of time and then it shall, when I command you, return to the face of the earth to see if there is water for my new creation."

So Haon did as the Lord God commanded him and he and his sons built the ark and stored thereon in frozen vessels of glass the seeds of all creation both male and female. And the day came when the Lord commanded them to be lifted up from the earth and they wept to leave the dry plains of Asu.

It came to pass that after the time was fulfilled the ark was commanded to leave its place beyond the heavens and to return to the face of the earth, where it was told to come to the mighty Father of Waters and to dip its iron hands into the flow of the river. The ark came to rest on the mighty river, put forth its iron hands, and, lo, in one hand it held a skull of a fish and in the other hand a crushed vessel bearing a word of man: Budweiser. The heart of the ark told Haon and his sons there was no mighty river for its frozen seeds in the vessels of glass. And they commanded the ark to pierce the heavens once again.

And the Lord God said to Haon and his sons, "Get you out of this firmament to a place I shall show you, and I shall make my covenant with you. This is the token of the covenant which I make between me and you and every living seed that is with you for perpetual generations: "I do set my cooling winds in the caverns of your new earth and when you feel their breath upon your face it will be a sign to you that the fires of your folly shall never destroy all flesh as long as my breath is in the winds. And God blessed Haon and his sons and said with them, "Be fruitful and multiply and replenish the new creation."

So Haon departed as the Lord had spoken unto him.
II Genesis

NOVEMBER 1986

When Desmond Tutu, the new Archbishop of Cape Town, agreed to meet with President Botha of their country, he received not only criticism from his fellow South Africans but from many of those who sympathized world-wide with his cause. But Archbishop Tutu pointed out that the grace of God includes President Botha as well as all other people and races and "whether we like it or not, President Botha and I are brothers."

This statement began my meandering musings. The more I mused the more I meditated on the unutterable, incomprehensible, infinite proportion of God's grace and how we in our blindness have limited it. How soon we are to write off those not of our opinion, our race, our religion, and certainly not of our social stratum. The barriers are myriad. As I pondered Tutu's inclusiveness and reread in the gospels those whom Christ included and those whom he finally excluded from his kingdom, it was those who, themselves, were excluders. These stumbling blocks would negate the good news of Christ's unconditional acceptance. Thus the Pharisee. Their name has become synonymous with the self-righteous, those bound in narrow ritualism, the judges of what is acceptable and good and what is unworthy. Oh, the Phariseeism in all our hearts! I hear Christ's resounding woes down the centuries: "Woe to you blind guides. Woe to you scribes, Pharisees, hypocrites! because you shut the kingdom of heaven against men." It would be better, he suggested, that a millstone be tied around their necks and they be drowned than to keep these little ones from the grace of God. These are woeful words.

Our exclusiveness comes because we are blind guides. Our Phariseeism has not been exorcised because we cannot grasp the depth and breadth, the magnanimity of Grace. This grace we have limited in our hearts as well as our institutions. We have established it and disestablished it, reformed and deformed it, schismed, inquisitioned, denominationalized, and Hell-fired it, and made it into a cheap substitute while we attempt to pull ourselves up by our own "goodness." We do not have eyes to see.

Through the jumble of blindness I hear: "God so loved the world.... My house shall be called a house of prayer for all the nations... In My Father's house are many rooms... I have other sheep that are not of this fold; I must bring them also... Come unto me all ye who are weary...." More inclusive words cannot be uttered.

What shall we do with our exclusiveness? Where do we stand as we perceive the world from our *Wasp*, Southern, affluent vantage point? Does this grace include China, India, all of Africa, the Middle East, and Communist Russia? Is the good news for the Buddhist, the Hindu, the Shiite, the Shintoist, and all those dark and slanty-eyed people and those with rags on their heads? Bishop Tutu says "So."

My fundamentalist background says "No"...unless they convert to our way and our tradition. May my audacious hide fry in Hell, but I must at last take issue with some theologian's narrow-pinched exegesis of these words of Christ: "I am the way." His way is the one of total acceptance. "I am the truth." His truth is all men are brothers. "I am the life." His life is the abundant life of joy, given in loving service to others. "No one comes to the Father but by me." He and the Father are one and he who has seen him has seen the Father. Wherever his way, his truth, his life lives, there is the living Christ made flesh. St. Paul tells us that it was for him that all nations were created, and he holds them together waiting for the time when he will be more fully revealed to all his creation. May our eyes be opened to the coming of his kingdom, his redeeming of all.

SEPTEMBER 1986

You know you've hit the bottom of the barrel when you start mulling and musing about used car lots. Anyway, one has me in its thralls. Driving along Fort Campbell Boulevard admiring the plastic flags that flutter over beautiful downtown New Providence, I was captured by this flash-arrow sign: *Any Offer Excepted.* I knew in my vitals if I mulled around enough there could come forth some profundity from the muses, so the message has to be that my life is just one big used car lot and any offer is excepted.

Unorthodoxy and Questionable Theology

If I sat there on the lot, I'm sure I would be suffering from radiator fatigue, muffler burn-out, and scorched valves. Something is always breathing on me demanding that I go fast, get it done, and pour on the gas. I'm on fast cruise control; any offer of relief from the pressure on the pedal is excepted. "Well, they expect me to go fast, I've always done it, and that's the way Mama taught me to do it. I can't slow down because if I do someone will see how I'm only spinning my wheels and going nowhere in particular; and if I make enough noise with my cut-out muffler no one will notice the turbulence under my hood or what a little fuel I have. Don't suggest I park under a shade tree or cool my tires in the creek because I know what a fine, faithful car I am. Goofing off and fun are not my line."

But when I am finally settled in the lot and look out between the plastic flags of *Doug's Used Cars*, I ogle the low-slung, long-nosed, well-serviced sports cars going by, and I suffer piston ping. I need some lubrication. I need some oil to ease my rust. When they screech in to the *Pickle Works* or the *Belle-Aire Country Club*, I remember the exception I took to being driven to a Turkey Raffle for Retired Teachers. Any old crate knows that's gambling, but maybe I was too strict about where I laid down rubber. Looks like there might be more joy and honesty at the *Pickle Works* than in some of the pickle-faced meetings to which I have hauled many a sinner. Speaking of sin—oil must be sinful because it makes you feel good. I except that too. I don't need any oil.

The worst part, however, of being on the used car lot is that my lot is confused. I've been from a little old lady to a callow youth to a Fort Campbell taxi-driver, and I wound up not knowing whose I am or was. I've tried to please them all. I haven't even claimed my spare tire as my own. The little old lady was most demanding and I had to have my entire route planned for her, and when I didn't report in with clean spark plugs—then I did have exceptions. Once I rebelled, blew a tire, landed her in a ditch, and spilled all her double-day coupons. When she traded me off to a high school junior, then I longed for the safety of the little old lady's garage.

The junior cursed me, kicked my tire, but then offered me a trip to *Six Flags Over Georgia*, but I was afraid to go. To be safe I let my universal joint go. Military life was all excepted. After sixteen months, 60,000 miles, and greater Fort Campbell through my back doors, I got all four tires flattened in an imbroglio at *Frenchy's Place*. I gave up. I have been sitting here twelve months eating on my own crank-case grease. I'm trapped.

108

Unorthodoxy and Questionable Theology

"Two hundred fifty dollars! He must be crazy. I know I am not worth that much. I will make exception to any offer over $150.00. But I know him and me too—*Any Offer Excepted.*"

AUGUST 1985

Jesus said he had come to fulfill the Law and give us abundant life. When I think back how we children were drilled on the Ten Commandments, memorized them for gold stars on our record, and were admonished over and over again that they were inviolate, I question whether we were in the Christian dispensation of Grace or still under Moses' command. I would lean toward the latter. "Honor thy father and thy mother" was given special emphasis. This was the one chosen to keep down any sort of sass or uppityness in general and included respect for all aunts, uncles, great uncles, cousins twice-removed and any neighbor over eighteen. After a few feeble attempts at rebellion, one became most careful lest one run afoul of the law enforced by a peach tree limb. To protect ourselves from dishonoring our elders, we cast ourselves into the role of "people pleasing" which included many a devious and dishonest means to protect our facade: We washed and went to meetings when we didn't want to go; we kissed sour-smelling uncles and anxious aunts; we said poems at the missionary society; and we tortured the truth into fantasy in our conforming to the Law. Elders were an omnipotence to be served, and we hung our dependency needs on Mama and Daddy and other authority figures of questionable divinity.

Herein lay the route to the servitude of the wrong master, one who didn't fulfill, but led to resentment and bitterness, rather than to life.

I mull and muse over this dependency, this people-pleasing that I hooked into at an early age and find myself yet in its tentacles. This need to please nags that you aren't doing enough and makes it difficult to say NO. You must be all things to all people. I'm not into dishonoring parents or, as Greek mythology would have it, killing them; but rather into looking at the dependency, the uncut umbilical cord that we take into our adult lives. With our clinging, we attempt to save our lives rather than lose them, outward, with a search for freedom. It's the good girl vs. honest girl again.

This is scary stuff. Who isn't afraid to give up old securities? Who isn't afraid to look at parents as poor mortals in need of understanding and forgiveness? The crucial psychological battle, therefore, is against

Unorthodoxy and Questionable Theology

our dependent needs and our anxiety and guilt as we struggle toward freedom. This on-going conflict is between the part of us which yearns for growth and change and the part that wants to stay in a safe place. What are the choices? It is a matter of staying with the same old people-pleasing games or searching for ourselves as persons of worth in our own eyes and not in the eyes of others. It's a matter of what gets priority—our safe place, or the unknown that calls to us. In Jesus' words, it is the search for the pearl-of-great-price; it is the search for our true selves.

> Do not think that I have come to bring peace to the world; No, I did not come to bring peace, but a sword. I came to set sons against fathers, daughters against their mothers, daughters-in-law against their mothers-in-law; a man's worst enemies will be members of his own family.
>
> ***Matthew 10***

JUNE 1985

This morning Tess and I were up and out just before sunrise. Tess is our Schnauzer who holds the record for being the sassiest dog on Pollard Ford's Road. I, marveling at the majesty of the sunrise, the unutterable mystery of creation, was called from this moment of praise by Tess who was frantically barking at a lizard she had found under a rock, and she insisted that I come see this prize she found so worthy of her attention. Then suddenly in a shining arrow out of the horizon rose a mighty jet, flashing silver and silent, leaving its contrail in the glory of the sunrise, piercing straight into the vastness of the unblemished sky; and I, but not Tess, found the lizard lost in the presence of God and in the knowledge of the ingenuity he had given man, the height of his creation.

Tess, still tormenting the poor lizard, who was only seeking the first rays of the sun, made impossible any more profound musings. But after I came inside and stood at the sink still seeing the morning out of the window, I began to see us all as Tesses. There is a faithful sunrise every morning, a flashing jet of creativity to ride into the heavens, praises to pour out of our deepest need to know our creator, and arrows of hope to hold us on the journey through the unknowns of life—yet we spend our days barking at lizards under cold stones.

Unorthodoxy and Questionable Theology

MARCH 1984

> *During supper, Jesus, well aware that the Father had entrusted everything to him, and that he had come from God and was going back to God, rose from the table, laid aside his garments, and taking a towel, tied it around him. Then he poured water into a basin, and began to wash his disciples' feet and to wipe them with a towel...*
>
> *After washing their feet and taking his garments again, he sat down. "Do you understand what I have done for you?" he asked. "You call me Master and Lord, and rightly so, for that is what I am. Then if I, your Lord and Master, have washed your feet, you also ought to wash one another's feet. I have set you an example: You are to do as I have done for you."*
>
> ***John 13***

Having been reared in the literalist, fundamentalist, Calvinist persuasion, every time I read about Christ's washing the disciples' feet I can't understand why, if it's in the Book and the Lord said, "Do it," we didn't do it. Only our Brothers-in-Christ, the Free Will Baptists, practiced the rite of foot-washing. We strained for every fragment of information about baptism, particularly the right amount of water, and split hairs over the Lord's Supper to the exclusion of all Christians save the ones in our local congregation; but no preacher ever mentioned washing feet or dangled us over the fiery pit if we didn't get them washed, even though the Savior of the World had admonished us to follow his example. Strange indeed!

Then when I look back over the two-thousand-year history of the liturgical church, why was there never the Sacrament of Holy-Foot-Washing? I can see so many marvelous possibilities for ceremony and symbolism: the blessing over the Podos Font, the proper raising and lowering of feet, the prayer after the washing of feet, and the glorious vestments for girding on the towel. All this rich humility lost forever. Sad indeed!

Mull and muse I must, and forever I arrive back at the same square with the same questions and answers. Foot washing seems again a matter of pride. Baptism is no humiliating problem. Either you put on a long white robe and wade out for a discreet ducking or you have a bit of water splashed about your brow. Same with Holy Communion: Either you pass the grape juice around or parade your reverent body down the aisle. But wash feet! There are problems both for the washer and the washee. When my mind scans over the communicants at

111

Trinity, my pride trembles at the picture of my pouring out a pan of water, unlacing shoes, removing socks, and washing some august foot. Dear Lord, deliver me from presenting my 10 1/2 set of pinkies, unleashed from their shoes and stockings, for a public ablution.

Christ asked the question, "Do you understand what I have done for you...?" and I don't. If I did I would be more than willing to wash anyone's feet, and probably more blessed, receive the washing. This was the lowliest servant's task, and here the King of Glory humbled himself for our example. If we, as his body, are to be great, we must be servants and gratefully wash any foot as a symbol of our servanthood.

"...But, dear Lord, you had a long flowing robe and sandals when you laid aside your garments. Please reveal one thing to us ladies: At a foot-washing, how do we manage pantyhose?"

MAY 1983

Salute one another with a holy kiss—

Romans 16

When we first started *Passing the Peace* at Trinity, I had a hard time with this greeting. Finally, I went inside myself and mulled around my murky emotions to see why I was uncomfortable with this addition to the liturgy.

First, anything new I don't like: new shoes, new ideas, and especially anything new in religion. But little did I know until I did some studying that the Peace was from antiquity; in fact, it was part of the Eucharist for the first century church, and the members were required to be in love and charity before they partook of Christ's body. They took literally Christ's commandment that they love one another, and they declared to the world through their love that they were Christ's followers. That was a dangerous declaration in first-century Christendom.

The second reason I was uncomfortable with the Peace was my dealing with those emotions common to us all. Way down deep we fear that we aren't worth much, that we are not attractive and lovable, and that we can't let anyone get too close and see how we really are. Here I had to mull and meditate and admit to the same old trap of putting up facades and trying to make myself worthy and good.

Unorthodoxy and Questionable Theology

It's uncanny how all my meditations, wherever they might meander, come back to the good news of the gospel, to the unmerited grace of God that accepts us as we are, forgives us, makes us worthy, and gives us the gift of love for each other. When we have received this grace, how comfortably the Peace of God rests as one forgiven and joyous sinner turns to another. It might be with a "holy kiss," or a "I love you," or "Peace be with you," or "forgive me."

Can the world look at us and know we are his disciples because we love each other?

Relatives and Acquaintances
Some Here and Some There

AUGUST 1989

The effectual, fervent prayer of a righteous man availeth much.
James 5

My mama tolerated no "strong language." That included "gosh, golly, and darn" not to mention, or even think, four letter words, cuss words, or taking the Lord's name in vain. This abhorrence was ground into my being. However, dear Gentle Reader with the need for truth in reporting, there is the necessity for one "strong language" in this *Mulling and Musing*; and if you, like my mama, are offended by such, particularly in the church paper, please read no more.

For those of you whose virgin ears have already been assaulted, I shall recount to you the effectual, fervent prayer of a righteous man. This man was Mr. Tom, our closest neighbor, when we moved on Pollard Road in 1952.

He must have been seventy, his hair in forty seasons of birds' nests, his teeth no longer considering corn-on-the-cob, his wise old eyes tired from too many years in the fields, and his clothes a scare-crow collection that sufficed, in layers, both summer and winter. His house sat up a sharp, rocky path on the last corner before our farm, well hidden in summer by horse weeds and Queen Anne's Lace. His two unpainted rooms with lean-to and front porch, crowned with a 'V' crimp roof, reigned over a scattering of small, discouraged outbuildings, a wood pile, a weedy garden, and a cistern. Like Thoreau, Mr. Tom had taken to the woods, and he, too, marched to a different drummer and a different fiddler.

When we first became aware of him across our west pasture, it was the sound of his front porch fiddling. On long, hot afternoons his music filled the cicada and dry-fly summer symphony with its melodic line and drifted, both heavenward and earthward, in its varied themes. There were toe-tapping hoe-downs as well as old hymns whose "power in the blood" and "gathering at the river" caught our ears through the late afternoon's breathless haze. In winter time, his front porch door always open and the fire blazing inside, Mr. Tom's fiddle haunted the afternoons in a different mode, lonely and austere, in ice and snow.

We were to learn that Mr. Tom was sufficient unto himself with his music, his front porch meditations, the meager bounty of his small fields, and the treasure given into his earthly keeping: *the Book*. When the fiddle was laid aside, the Bible was taken up. How well Mr. Tom read or understood I do not know, but he touched the Book with a trembling humility and squinted at its pages with eyes of wonderment as though he held in his hands the mystery of God's grace, revealed, on Pollard Road.

He was a man of few words. His dog's name was *Dog*, and his mule's name was *Mule*. From life he asked only the simple and the necessary. He seemed to sense creation's economy and oneness and his existence as part of this wisdom. His acceptance of his finiteness in the face of the infinite was the clothing of his soul. About once a month he rode with me to the store at New Providence for flour, meal, a side of bacon, a can of "coal oil," and a box of stick matches. He had a potato patch and a few hills of pumpkins, cut some hay for *Mule*, and tossed *Dog* odd corn pones off the front porch. His life was one that you instinctively did not intrude upon or desecrate with offers of help. The beat of his drummer and the music of his fiddle seemed more than enough for this unwashed, untutored Thoreau.

But as to all the human family, a time came for Mr. Tom when he was not sufficient unto himself. Earthly and heavenly aid had to be called upon.

It was a windy, threatening March day with rain forecast, but the ground dry enough to work. Taking advantage of this hiatus in the wet weather, Mr. Tom was burning a small plant bed for cabbage and sweet potato plants. The wind changed suddenly to the southeast, and his fire got out! Down the hill from his house, northwest, across the pasture, and into the woods which overlooked the cut of the Tennessee Central Railroad, it raced. Here a great, high-stilted wooden trestle spanned a quarter mile ravine. With its creosote permeation, this was supreme kindling wood. Hearing his calls and seeing the smoke, all of us neighbors in earshot arrived with shovels and wet burlap sacks to fight fire, but our feeble efforts in the face of so great a conflagration were futile and the flames, undaunted, marched in unrelenting lines toward the trestle.

Mr. Tom was distraught. He knew well the worst consequence of the fire he had started. Pulling his all-season felt hat low over his eyes, he stood apart from us, leaned heavily on his shovel and implored the God of Moses at the parting of the Red Sea and the God of Joshua at the standing still of the sun. "Oh, Lord, if you will only let it rain, I'll be the most thankful son-of-a-bitch in this county."

And it rained! It poured down. The fire stood still and died. The fervent prayer of this righteous man availed much. Like the publican in the temple, Mr. Tom went down to his house justified. "Lord have mercy on me a sinner. Lord have mercy on my SOBness."

JULY 1993

I know whom I have believed and am persuaded that he is able to keep that which I have committed unto him against that day.
St. Paul

Mama said Cousin William Stonewall Wickhams had a "kink" in his brain. "He has absolutely gone off on eating and religion." When I reminded her that these were old family failings since we all ate too much and were bent on being "religious," she rebutted, "I would never go off eating 'poke salit' stalks, mullein blossoms, and drinking snake root tea while I waited for the Lost Tribe of Benjamin to get back together. He hasn't even planted his garden—just sits around in the sun reading some fool preacher's books."

Cousin Willie had committed himself. Straining his words through clinched teeth and blinking his pale eyes like an over-exposed owl, Willie expounded the final and only *Truth*. Furthermore, a bit of aboriginal sun-worshiping was compounded into his dietary laws and his Judgment Day pronouncements. Every body part had need of the sun: the open mouth, the ear drums, the under arms, and other discreet places where the sun never shone. All this sunning was made more potent at high noon when the ultra-violet rays could penetrate deep and far. The rays heated the juices of the body to course more effectually to each member and the absolute deepest heating was made standing on one's head, in full bloom like a sun flower.

Cousin Willie's schedule was a scandal for the denizens of Shiloh. He would stay up late at night to catch The Reverend Alcott's radio broadcast from the West Coast. This latter-day prophet foretold the wrath to come, the ones to be saved, the ingathering of the Twelve Tribes of Israel, and the ultimate reign of those who followed his teachings. The English were the Lost Tribe of Benjamin. The Stone of

117

Scone, which is under the coronation chair in Westminster Abbey, was the stone on which Jacob had his dream. It would accompany its people to the New Jerusalem. The English would inherit the earth, the Reverend's blood being of that stock; and Cousin Willie fancied his corpuscles the same.

Bleary-eyed in the late morning after sleeping on so much *Truth*, Willie would rise, drink several intestinal teasers, point his gyroscope at the sun's zenith, and get his blood flowing in the right direction. Then it was gathering time.

Nuts, fruits, and roots were a must. Reverend Alcott demanded a return to basics, to Eden, to the fruits of trees and vines. So off Cousin Willie would go in the afternoon, after giving his body to be burned, for anything in season. In the spring it was berries; in summer all sorts of fruits, including paw-paws, which he dried; and in the fall he was squirrel-busy with nuts: black walnuts, "hickernuts," and some acorns whose acid counteracted bloat in both humankind and cowkine.

Down in Willie's cellar was a nut-cracking assembly line. Two great metal blades zapped off each end of a black walnut; a whop with a hollow-headed hammer brought the walnut meat out whole. The hickory nuts were more tedious. At the end of November there were sacks and sacks of dried nuts, fruits, and wild herbs as well as jars of bubbling elixirs that only Rev. Alcott, Cousin Willie, and the Ghost-of-Tribes-Past anticipated.

Cousin Willie stayed his commitment to Eden-eating and *Paradise Restored* until he was suddenly, one night, cast out—maybe West of Eden—where he could no longer make his food by the sweat of his brow. The Reverend proclaimed for his followers—*Fasting*—beginning that very night. Faithful to whatever teaching promised him eternal health, salvation, and restoration, Willie refused all food, not for days, but for weeks, accompanied by great drafts of purification circulated through his system by solar power. He became so weak he could no longer point himself toward the sun. He had to brown, pancake style.

After a series of these fasts, Willie's nervous system collapsed and he couldn't raise his arms to feed himself. *The True Believer* was a shattered and pitiful shell with not even a "kink" left in his brain. At length, he joined the Tribe of Benjamin, even though unassembled; and the Stone of Scone is waiting for the next coronation, if there be one.

Relatives and Acquaintances   Some Here & Some There

With anguish I look back on Cousin Willie. What are my "kinks"? What are my commitments, my true beliefs as we race through space on this maddening planet? Are we not all anchored by our "Truth", our sacred places, our panaceas, our pride in our tribe, and our never-ending quest for acceptance and belonging? We remember Jim Jones, David Koresh, and Reverend Alcott.

To whom shall we go?

This question was asked by Peter in the last desperate hour before our Lord's arrest. Many of his disciples had already deserted him, and Christ asked the twelve, "Will you also go away?"

Until this very moment, Peter's reply rings clear to our call to commitment. "Lord, to whom shall we go?" Peter's great affirmation follows: "You have the words of eternal life and we are sure that you are the Christ, the Son of the living God."

May our search for Truth rest in this credo. May Cousin William Stonewall Wickham rest with his tribe in Abraham's Bosom. There is room for all.

NOVEMBER 1987

Now therefore ye are no more strangers and foreigners, but fellow citizens with the saints and the household of God.
St. Paul

One blustery March afternoon five years ago I was curled up on the couch in my favorite reading position when a sudden knock came at the door. Standing there was a young Japanese man, barely five feet tall, with a broad grin on his face who pronounced, "I see you have Paulownia tree." Wide-mouthed and eyed, I responded, "We have what?" and he repeated the pronouncement, "You have Paulownia tree."

Now if you are as ignorant as I was about this mysterious tree, it is the one I always called *Catalpa*. This tree, considered quite a nuisance at times, insists on growing in unlikely places: in the cracks of sidewalks and against abandoned buildings. Supposedly it was the tree of *A Tree Grows In Brooklyn.* You see it all around with its great heart-shaped leaves, its pale violet display of blooms in the spring, and its mass of sticky seedpods that hang on from one season to the next. It seems about the least promising tree growing. But not to the Japanese.

It is a native of the Orient and got its name honoring Czar Paul I of Russia, and the seeds came to this country as the Chinese and Japanese used the seedpods to pack their delicate china. The seeds found a hospitable home in the Eastern United States and have flourished here for many years.

The Paulownia wood has properties peculiar to this tree: It is almost without weight but unbelievably strong and weather resistant. There is a certain reverence for the wood in Japan. Every household that can afford it has at least one piece of furniture, usually a ceremonial piece, made of Paulownia. The stringed instruments of the Geisha houses and Japanese clog sandals are made from this special tree. Therefore, as the Oriental supply was depleted, the lumbermen of Japan turned to the USA—thus, Tasio Kioke standing on my steps.

Something about Tasio drew me to him at once: his bounce, his radiance, his reaching out to me as a fellow human being. My old stereotyped World War II JAP was threatened. Since my husband wasn't handy to talk about "Paulownia tree," I invited him in, and with space limiting many fascinating details, I will simply state we became fast friends, and he spent several nights in our home.

Whence this joy that emanated from Tasio? I was about to turn Shintoist when in the course of his telling about his life and his asking about mine, I brought out pictures of our children, one of them being a picture of our oldest son's wedding at Trinity. Tasio studied it intently looking at the hymn board in the background. With a breathless inquiry he asked, "Are you Episcopalian?" and when I told him I was of that persuasion, he in a great explosion of a shout: "I Episcopalian too!" With this revelation began the recounting of his long day's journey into light.

Born to typical working class parents, Tasio had risen fast in the Japanese business world because of his academic record. The importers of Paulownia wood hired him because of this record and his excellence, to them, in English. When he got to Paducah, Kentucky, where the Japanese lumber company had its headquarters, he found that his English was anything but excellent, so he enrolled in an English class. There, to do the expedient and assure his citizenship in the States, he married an American girl—here Tasio found looking into his past almost too painful—whom he later abandoned along with their child. His confession to me was summed up: "I was so bad, so bad," On a lumber buying trip to South Africa, he found himself seated by a Catholic priest, who during their long flight over the Amazon Basin, brought about the light of change in Tasio's life. Not wanting "to be with the Pope" as he expressed it, he came back to Paducah and joined the Episcopal congregation there, found his wife and child, put his family back together, and became a strong arm in the congregation.

In the fall of that same year we were invited by Tasio and his wife for dinner. There we saw their new son and Tasio as star hitter and first basemen on the church's team. His was a life of amazement at the grace he had known. When he compared his life in Japan and the years spent in being "so bad" with the joy he now knew, all he could say was "miracle, miracle." This little Japanese man in his openness and honesty brought home to me the fact that joy can only be ours through honest confession and actively searching for our real selves. Tasio at our last correspondence was still on this quest.

P.S. We sold many "Paulownia tree" for several thousand dollars—a grace, an unmerited gift from our woods.

APRIL 1995

And then my heart with pleasure fills,
And dances with the daffodils.

William Wordsworth

Seed catalogues are the tabloids of gardeners. With my feet propped up in front of a winter fire, I dance through fields of painted daisies and potentilla, build tall trellises for many varieties of clematis, dig deep beds for begonias and dahlias, and plant straight rows of gladiolus and zinnias in front of a vegetable garden—all catalogue perfect with nary a bug in sight. When my shins get too hot, the memory of the July sun crawls up my back and I turn to the reality pages. Zinnias I can do and glads I can do because my husband plows them when he cultivates the vegetables. If weeding can't be done on a garden tractor or clipping on a riding mower, that's too bad. His hand does not fit a hoe and his feet prefer wheels. In his time, he contends he has plowed his share of rows looking at mule rosettes.

Several springs ago, *Breck's* Catalogue came through with an auspicious offer: a half-bushel of assorted daffodils, only $49.95—to be paid later—and to be delivered at the correct planting time in the fall. Their "Finest and Best," exactly what the "imaginative gardener needed for naturalizing." Now "naturalizing" meant that you planted these bulbs, at random, on the lawn, in the pasture fields, or anywhere you felt like dancing with daffodils. So charming, and so easy. I dropped the pay-later card in the mail.

"Women and their fool ideas." You can imagine how this flinging of daffodils agreed with my mechanized man since he trails a twenty foot mower behind his biggest tractor when he is clipping pasture, not to mention his having to mow around clumps of daffodils in the yard. If you cut the leaves off the bulbs before the tops die down, there are no blossoms the next year. Therefore, all my flowers cower under the eaves of the house, sit high in movable pots, or rest between tree roots too big to be sliced by a riding mower. Where might the expected half-bushel of daffodils find refuge?

In late September, the UPS man hurried to our front door with the order and rushed away before I could sign. Maybe he was afraid he would be "naturalized." He didn't have to be in such a swivet because the box sat and sat and sat and languished by the back door while we gave it the silent treatment. How to keep those bulbs in their proper place was a mystery that only the master of the house could solve, and I resolved that I would walk around them until the Second Coming before I would make any suggestions for their final resting place. Now, that's communication!

One rainy morning after Thanksgiving, I saw my husband long-leg it by the kitchen window, rain gear on, the biggest crowbar he owned in hand, with a painful, yet delighted, look on his face. He had found a place. Forget the proper bed, the mulch, the bone meal feeding—just get those bulbs of contention into the ground.

The cattle had already eaten all the *Blaze* climbing roses off the barbed wire fence along the driveway, but they won't as much as sample a daffodil; and too, you can't run a mower under a fence. Elementary. With this flash of brilliance, my husband began to make holes under the barbed wire with the crowbar, dropped a bulb in each hole, and the half-bushel was planted and firmed with a good stomp before you could say "ouch" from barbed wire. This was a half-hour project that restored daffodil communication for many a spring to come.

Last Saturday, I had a Daffodil Party, and invited dear, dear friends to have a sandwich and dance with the daffodils. This we did. With buckets and scissors, we cut hundreds, which seemed to leave even more. Sunday, I brought them to Dorothy Conroy Hall for our Chili

Dinner. I trust your heart danced a bit with these undaunted miracles of faithfulness and ever-multiplying beauty. To be picked is all they ask.

Also, daffodils go to show that some things don't have to be communicated to death. Guess who has planted a long row down to the cattle chutes?

OCTOBER 1994

Be not carried about with divers and strange doctrines.
For it is a good thing that the heart be established with grace.
Hebrews 13

MIGHTILY, WE WELCOME YOU
THE REV. DAVID MURRAY
AND KATHY MURRAY

Mullings and Musings puts out banner headlines and Trumpets your coming with its tallest M and M's! But I shall begin on a negative note: Let us beware of Aunt Lucyism.

Aunt Lucy was carried about with strange doctrines, the last one being the Russellites. She began a Baptist, found their wives fanned too much and their preachers sliced the butter too thick and finished off whole fryers. She did a scandalous thing—she became a Methodist. But, alas, there was no perfection there. The preacher didn't preach; he just talked, and their baptism was white-wash. His wife was such a senseless woman that she kept a small suitcase turned upside down on her living room table and it stayed there all the time. "Why didn't she put it up and why did she keep it upside down?" Aunt Lucy had not entered the world of portable typewriters.

Too, the preachers's wife's hair wasn't right. Lucy detected some drugstore tampering in the "rinch" water. However, her worst sin was slovenliness. "She can't fasten her shoes worth a hoot. The straps across her insteps stand up like croquet wickets and her dress placket is always unsnapped." The instability of the mucous membrane of their children's noses will not be mentioned here.

Presbyterians were too snooty, the Campbellites too narrow, the Nazarenes too noisy and the Episcopalians worse than Catholics; therefore, Aunt Lucy found a dislike for all churches, their diverse doctrines, and the human race in general—never knowing it was she, herself, who

123

was her own judge and jury. Aunt Lucy established herself in bitter isolation.

So be forewarned, David and Kathy: Check your shoe laces, all fasteners, and wipe your children's noses. Chicken is inexpensive now and so is butter, giving you license to slice as thickly as you like. We won't watch. We know your coming is a good thing, established with grace. Our thanksgiving enfolds you.

The second M: Mercifully we pray that we love each other, accept each other, forgive each other, all confessing our humanity with its blindness to our faults. May we not be carried away by petty preferences. Give us a vision of constructive support beyond negative criticisms and attempts to fit David and Kathy into preconceived molds. God grant us grace to rise above such mockery of freedom. May we let them be who they are— forgiven sinners like you and me. Let us hear the Gospel anew. Each morning is a gracious gift to put behind our yesterdays and be Christ's body in this world today. Let us be about this good news, "for it is a good thing that the heart be established with grace." Again, Welcome, David and Kathy.

JULY 1994

Sufficient unto the day is the evil thereof.

Matthew 6

Uncle Ben Weems' philosophy of life was cynically simple: "Ah, I'll tell you—life is mean and the days are evil. You've got to take chances to stay ahead of trouble." Seizing each trouble as it came, he took chances with wives, but with no doctors, no insurance salesmen, and certainly no lawyers. Sufficient for him was the knowledge that he had accrued as he made his way through the late 1800s to the 1900s.

His book knowledge was impressive. Coming through the Cumberland Gap from the Tidewater of Virginia, Uncle Ben's family settled in Athens, Tennessee, where he graduated from Tusculum Presbyterian College. As a child, I knew no one with such a library. In two massive bookcases there were leatherbound volumes including Gibbon's *Rise And Fall Of The Roman Empire*, the complete works of Shakespeare, tomes of Civil War history, Greek mythology and tragedy, medical journals, writings of Supreme Court justices and two shelves of Victorian prose and poetry. To most of the citizens of

Palmyra, this collection could be paper to start a fire in the cook stove, but to Uncle Ben it was treasure. He looked down on local ignorance.

Evil days came early to Athens. Uncle Ben's first wife died leaving him with two small daughters; whereupon he placed an ad in some rural publication for a wife. Now this was a real chance! Cousin Rosie Shelton, who lived at Shiloh on East Fork Creek, answered the ad in hopes of ridding herself of her spinsterhood. Uncle Ben loaded up library and daughters, came to Palmyra in hopes of finding a mother for his children. He wedded Cousin Rosie without courtship or ceremony—just a ride down the creek to Squire Fessey's place.

"She knew my situation," he explained. This chancy romance produced a child, causing Cousin Rosie to depart this mean life and left Uncle Ben again with his two daughters and an infant son.

To stay ahead of trouble, Uncle Ben came into my life. He took a chance on my Aunt Ada for this third wife, and she became the mother of two more of his children and gathered his brood under her ample apron. To compound the problems of those days, Uncle Ben was injured in a logging accident that left him crippled in one foot. I see him yet, sitting on the front porch of their listing farm house, reading, forever reading, and smoking his pipe, which, during his great agitations, would turn its fiery contents upside down and singe a cascade down his front. He argued, agonized, and arranged ahead of time for impending evil.

Peeping from underneath his perennial felt hat, he would squint his black eyes and clamp his teeth on his cob pipe and smoke out the latest scams of the day.

"If you fool with these doctors long enough, they'll kill you. 'Practicing' medicine is right. I'll take my chances on dying, untampered, without them practicing on me." And he did. After a few more pipe tampings and firings, Uncle Ben would take on the insurance industry.

"Now, I'll tell you—if they can take a chance, I can too. Why should I pay them to take a chance for me? I'll take my own chances." Not one penny of insurance did he ever buy and to my knowledge he never had a fire nor lost a mule.

But certain lawyers were lowest on his list of public vultures. There was one in particular in Clarksville, famous for his bilking of poor, uneducated people, that at the very mention of his name Uncle Ben lost all perspective and laid down a home-spun, smog-alert of expletives.

125

He took a chance on his own lawyering, wrote out his will, had neighbors witness the document, and it was valid in probate court. Preachers also weren't high on Uncle Ben's list—particularly unlettered ones whom the Lord had "called"—so when Cousin Rosie's son married a lady Holiness preacher, his will was adjusted. He didn't believe his grandchild had developed properly having been nursed on fire and brimstone milk. "Now that boy was asking for trouble. There's no excuse for marrying a stomping woman preacher," he fumed.

Uncle Ben smoked and read his days away, and left us a legacy of warnings. Most of us have not thrown the dice of chance as he did, but I never pay an insurance premium or visit a doctor or lawyer that his sayings do not surface. What I do hear from him is the inevitability of evil days; there is no way to avoid trouble, and you should steel yourself as best you can against the time that shall come. What Uncle Ben did not leave me, however, was the acceptance of evil and evil days as part of being alive and the grace to give thanks for the teaching of tribulation. He smoked and fussed and cussed and never pondered above the cloud of tobacco. He was eternally anxious about tomorrow.

I should not judge Uncle Ben for his anxiety, for I, too, am anxious about tomorrow. Who does not borrow trouble? But I can hear the promise, "I am with you always," and that means in the midst of and at the dark, murky bottom of the evil days. When St. Paul asked to be delivered from his troubles, the reply for all times sounds its glorious affirmation: "My grace is sufficient for you." And that is for all our days, good and evil, from here to eternity.

DECEMBER 1993

> *Do you not know that a prince and a great man has fallen this day in Israel?*
>
> **King David**

When I am shattered with sudden and unexpected grief, lines and images that have been hidden in my memory come forward and hold me in their keeping. Tom Cowan's death evoked such lines and pictures. I see him at this moment, as clearly and as alive, as I saw him standing outside the church the Sunday before his death. He was waiting for Mary Louise. A prince and a great man stood there.

I greeted him, "Hello, Tom," and he gave me his shy, sideways smile as if we shared some secret joke. His approving, "Hello,

Charlotte," will live with me. Forever will he be there, forever in his dark suit and white shirt, forever handsome and dignified, forever unbowed in the prime of his princely years. His picture is indelible.

John Keat's poem *Ode On A Grecian Urn* came in my grief. Here the poet held the urn and saw there, carved in marble, lovers who would ever love, youth who would ever be fair, and melodies that would ever be anticipated. But the line that rang clearest was this one: "When old age this generation shall waste, Thou shall remain..." This unchanging picture of Tom remains with me as we go toward whatever wasting and insults of old age our generation must endure. Oh, that each of us might leave behind so clear and dear a picture! This generation shall not waste him.

A prince and a great man. Both appellations belong to Dr. Thomas Wynne Cowan. I knew him as a great teacher, one knowledgeable far beyond my understanding of modes and modulations. Yet he was most patient with musical ignorance, and I was not intimidated to sing as best I could. For his memorial service, a generation of students and choir members came to honor his memory with the lessons he had taught and to raise up their Alleluias to call his name "blessed."

As we sang, I heard anew a line from The Fallen Prince of all time—"I go to prepare a place for you." As we read from the book of Ecclesiasticus last Sunday, this place shall certainly be one where praises are sung for famous men, ones who are the composers of music. Tom Cowan's *Gloria* precedes him to the place prepared for him. Each time we sing his compositions at Trinity, I shall see him there among us, this Communion of Saints, as we sing his hymn of praise.

Then at the Eucharist, his setting of the Sanctus rings out:

Holy, holy, holy Lord, God of power and might,
heaven and earth are full of your glory.
Hosanna in the highest.
Blessed is he who comes in the name of the Lord.
Hosanna in the highest.

Until we sing the Sanctus together in the heavenly choir, a prince and a great man awaits us.

APRIL 1993

Behold, God will not cast away a perfect man, neither will he help the evil doers; Till he fill thy mouth with laughing and thy lips with rejoicing.

.   ***Job 8***

My grandmother was a *Fun*damentalist. She, like my daddy, loved a practical joke, a good story—often quite spicy—and both of them could spot phonies from Port Royal to Kirkwood with a special eye for shyster preachers. I do believe they went to church for their general amazement and amusement, which filled their mouths with laughing at the foibles from the pulpit and the pews.

There appeared at Little Hope Baptist Church one revivalist hungry for more than fried chicken. Announcing early on that the Lord had sent him to blot out the vanities of the flesh at Little Hope, he, like, St. Paul, condemned elaborate hair-dos and only approved of modest coiffures, parted in the middle and severely bunned at the back. Anything more was of the Devil. Now my grandmother was considered quite a beauty in her day, her hair being her joy and crown; and the fiery brother's eyes flashed often into her pew with much desire for her immortal soul or mortal otherwise. She once warned us girls, "Remember, preachers have all their principal parts." A wise grammar lesson.

Thus grandmother's preacher story began: "That old farce bragged that whatever page he opened in the Bible that he could bring his fingers down on a verse that would be the very text that someone in the congregation needed to save her soul. 'The Holy Spirit guides me.' He flopped open the Bible, squinted down at the page where I knew he had his finger already fixed and read Matthew the twenty-fifth chapter, the seventeenth verse, one of those red-lettered Christ verses, 'Let him which is on the housetop not come down...'"

Grandmother heated up, "That old Bible baloney salesman looked square at me, did a few hmmmms, some chicken-stuffed grumps, pulled his galluses out, snapped them a time or two and announced his text: *TopKnot Come Down.* I may be adding a letter of the alphabet but the Spirit is speaking to some sinner here tonight."

Grandmother always told us children, "I was never vain about my beauty," but she did pile her thick chestnut hair high on her head, put the curling iron down the lamp chimney, and made a most appealing row of ringlets across her forehead and dangled careless curls in front of her ears and at the nape of her neck. This was worldly stuff! Almost more than the Lord's anointed could bear. Also she "rooged" her cheeks and "chalked" her face, the sign of the harlot, according to this preacher, along with the topknot that wouldn't come down.

"Harlotry and vanities of the flesh do not see the resurrection of the righteous, only the condemnation of the damned," as my grandmother was pinpointed.

She waited her turn after preaching. With a twinkle after the passing of those many years, she ended the story, "I told that preacher my hair had already been resurrected and if I am a harlot, you are worse to be lusting after harlots; and if you don't quit looking at my legs through my petticoat when I am carrying my lantern and getting up on my horse, there isn't going to be enough of you left to resurrect." She said Cuddin' Lula Highsmith agreed, "Glory to God for you, Mattie." So much for Little Hope's sexual harassment and women's lib.

Grandmother's *Fun*damentalism has carried me far. It has carried me away from literalism and legalism into the freedom of love and grace. I bless this gene that comes from her. This legacy has seen me up from many deaths - deaths almost too dark to face in the early morning's light, death of dreams and hopes, death that took hold of my physical body, the death of relationships that withered in anger and bitter unforgiveness, and the death from doubt—to curse God and die.

Easter is about rising, a levitation that defies earthbound gravity and causes one to come up out of death; and surely the word levity has the same etymological root. From out of the depths of my darkest of deaths, there has come a spark, a light, a resurrection of laughter from a place beyond my knowing. The Biblical account of Christ's resurrection and his first meeting with his apostles has a somber and mystical note. But if the writers of these accounts could have gone back some seventy or eighty years to the actual scene, I can imagine the joy, the tears, the laughter, the forgiveness, and the fun that they would surely have recorded.

The Christ who is our salvation and who is living in us has a sense of humor. He has gone before us and is preparing a place for us, and like Brer Rabbit in the *Tales Of Uncle Remus*, I'm sure we will find our "Laughing Place" there.

DECEMBER 1992

> *He shall cover thee with his feathers, and under his wings shalt*
> *thou trust.*
>
> ***Psalm 91***

My great Aunt Ada lived at Shiloh, which is south of Palmyra. Off Old Highway 13 to Erin, down a snaking gravel road that followed East Fork Creek, then through a ford in the creek, up and down a young mountain road, and finally another ford of the same creek until we came to a wagon track through the woods — to Aunt Ada's house we came. Aunt Ada was considered my grandmother on my mother's side. When my mother was eight, her own mother was ill and lived away from her four small children.

This was quite an expedition: Mama would write in advance of our coming because our *Model T Ford* could not go beyond the last ford, and Aunt Ada's husband or son would have to hitch up the team and wagon and meet us at the final ford where we loaded ourselves and our gifts into the wagon bed. It was a bone-rattling and rutted ride for at least a mile; but at the final turn up a long hill, our first glimpse was of Aunt Ada, regardless of the weather, standing on the front porch of her old barn of a farmhouse, dressed in a long calico dress, her all-enveloping apron, and woolen shawl pinned around with a cameo pin. She was a story-book grandmother.

The austere and simple life was hers. She rejoiced in her cellar filled with dried fruit and canned vegetables, in the smell of new lye soap and clean clothes, hog-killing, great ricks of wood for the cookstove and heaters, a good dip of snuff, a baby calf and the cow being "fresh"; and she had an obsessive yearning after fresh feathers, feather beds, new pillows, and long bolsters for the head of the bed.

On one Christmas visit when I was about fifteen, Aunt Ada with her gray hair pulled back unusually tight and her grayer eyes bright with Christmas cheer, took me aside for a confidence only for my ears. "You have always been my pet. You know that, don't you?"

"Yessum," though I really didn't know.

She continued her confidence, "I have something special for you, something for you to keep always and it isn't store-boughten. Store-boughten things don't mean much because there hasn't been any heart put in them. I try to give things that I treasure in my heart." With this

130

she opened her treasure closet and presented me a brand new feather bolster with its stripes shining like gold, frankincense, and myrrh. At the time I was insensitive to her vicarious joy in giving, but now I know she delivered to me a gift of incalculable price, one whose feathers have softened me from heart to heart.

Bolster is the right word. How many times during my forty-five years of housekeeping has not this gift been the treasure for the right spot. First it kept all the babies from rolling off the big bed when they were infants. Then when I wanted to dress up the guest room for special company, I would bolster up the regular pillows and put on the crocheted spread. In the winter it was a warm bedfellow to my back. With the coming of grandchildren who just have to sleep with Granny, it goes down the middle of the double bed so poor Granny won't get kicked all night. I take it to Nashville for visits and have promised to hand it on to our granddaughter. Then when I read in bed, it bolsters me up just the right height until my reading falls on my face. All who have been sick during the years have been propped-up for their chicken soup; and to get its usage absolutely current, our choir director, Nancy Slaughter, who is having minor surgery today is coming to our house for recovery. Yes, the feathers are ready.

Aunt Ada's gift symbolizes her gift of her self to me. She made me know myself as special, taking me aside and declaring me her favorite. God in his grace has declared each of us special, his favorite; and if we could accept our specialness, rejoice in it, and give it away, that would be our acceptance of God's gift that came for us two thousand years ago. We are cushioned, we are bolstered, we are loved with all our foolishness and failure, we are forgiven, God is with us and none of these priceless gifts can be "store-boughten." This grace is the free Pearl of Great Price.

May all your feathers be unruffled at Christmas. Peace and love to all.

JULY 1991

Come unto me all ye that labour and are heavy laden, and I will give you rest.

Matthew 11

My grandmother committed suicide. The relatives near and far hush-hushed this dark deed and an undercurrent of judgment coursed across the family. "Mattie's going to Hell. I'm not going to cry because she killed herself. God won't forgive anyone for doing his work," and on and on it went. I was eighteen at the time and I mulled and mused that for someone who had been a bright light in my childhood this eternal roasting was most inconsiderate on God's part. But who would dare voice such radical theology before tight-lipped and corseted aunts who warmed their hearts on hellfire?

My poor, dear grandmother. She was eighty-two, had breast cancer that was beginning to erupt to the outside of her body, and was, for all purposes, blind. Her only daughter was visiting her from Florida, and Grandmother, thinking this an appropriate time, found some insect killer with chloroform, placed this in a box of cotton, put her face in the box, covered her head with her blankets, and we found her the next morning. Now my questions—was this a great sin or an act of bravery? Is her pitiful, corrupted body being eternally tortured because of this iron-clad Will-of-God that my aunts espoused?

Having many years to ponder my grandmother's death, I give courage its final dues and the Will-of-God gets it place as grace given.

What we must come to respect is The Agony called Living. It can become too great. I know; I have suffered from severe depressions, maybe inherited from my grandmother. The suffering of body and spirit can be so intense that you will do anything for a few moment's respite—alcohol, pills, drugs—and the ultimate respite is suicide. And mark this down—there is never self-destruction unless suffering is greater than the spirit can bear. This is where I must wrestle with the Will-of-God. I asked for strength to bear my suffering, and God in his grace gave me strength. By the same token, if he had not granted me this grace and I had taken my own life, I would still have been in his will; and I thereby, offer this understanding to those who by God's grace and their hands find his rest. One dear to me has said that she has prayed for strength to end her life. God in his infinite mercy must have a special ear for such suffering. He heard my grandmother.

So Grandmother and I thumb our noses at blue-nosed relatives, and for whatever part of me is her, I give thanks. Till this day, I hear my father and her closely harmonizing some bawdy ballad like "Old Aunt Sis" or being nice and singing "Amazing Grace." From her, Daddy and I inherited the drive-'em-crazy-gene of singing-while-we-work, as well as a life-long love of music. When Grandmother came to visit, she always wanted the Victrola cranked up, and we children had to place her favorite record on the turntable because she couldn't see the needle. She basked in the sound of some uncertain tenor singing these lines through his tin funnel:

Lay me where sweet flowers blossom
Where the dainty lily blows
Where the pinks and violets mingle
Lay my head beneath a rose.

So Grandmother, I lay your head at peace beneath a rose. "For I reckon that the sufferings of this present time are not worthy to be compared with the glory which shall be revealed in us."

MARCH 1991

The light of the body is the eye: If therefore thine eye is single, Thy whole body shall be full of light.
                                                                      Matthew 6

Dorothy Ann Russo and I have discovered a great legacy. It is a gift of the *True Eye.* This eye gives you complete confidence. It liberates you to tackle any job, takes down the mole-hill mountains, clears the path of any anticipated failure, allows you to size up a situation in one bold glance, and puts intrepid soles on faint-hearted feet. There are no instructions too complex or measurements too intricate that the *True Eye* cannot eyeball them correctly. It demands no hedging around—hemming or hawing—just, "Do it!!"

Now this is a pearl-of-great-price, this single eye. I beheld it first-hand and have adopted it, however imperfectly, for my liberation and, lo, have passed it on to Dorothy Ann, one who gathered immediately to her bosom such an expeditious gift. How our lives have been simplified.

Miss Gloria Powers—Mrs. Abbot Powers—late of Kirkwood, was the possessor of this gift. She first came into my infant focus as I became a regular Sunday visitor in her household of ten children, rang-ing in ages from full blown beards to unblown noses. Here there was delight in disorder and order in chaos.

Miss Glory's confident true eye matched her size and her general bearing. From underneath her tent dress, cut butterfly, peeped cascades of corpulence that draped from her elbows and knees. Despite her face-lifting hair-do screwed to the top of her head, her great jowls shook with good humor and her voice, resonating on a bass line, quaked the pots in their stacks and tinkled the glasses. Her blue true eyes overlooked a W.C. Field's landscape, adorned at its end with her "seeing" glasses. Yet there was an elegance of lightness in her steps as she wove between the cook stove and the flour bin with a battalion's worth of biscuits. Her true eye measured the crowd, sifted several sifters of flour in a dishpan and made a hole in the center where she judged in lard and buttermilk. As if by magic, the biscuits were perfect.

All were welcome as we children made havoc through the house, jumping from the rafters in the attic and perusing old trunks for dress-up. There was never heard a discouraging word of "cool down, be quiet, or straighten up your mess." She said children needed "imagination." My first exposure to dancing—that worldly pleasure—was from the Powers' parlor Victrola playing, "Yes, Sir, That's My Baby" while the grown children did the Charleston. Miss Glory had fringed the girls' skirts to accentuate the shimmy and, despite Baptist disputation, declared dancing part of "imagination."

After Miss Glory had fed the majority of the Intermediate Sunday School Class of Kirkwood Church, she blocked out Pandemonium, arranged her folds into a split hickory rocker, split just for her, and put on her "reading" glasses. Here she feasted her true eye. By Kirkwood standards she had a literary turn. She vowed that no one had any sense until they had read books. Her children's names reflected the scope of her eye: There was Brandon, Iris, Enoch, Beatrice, Hester, Arthur, Tess, Susana, Silas, and finally, Val Jean.

Miss Glory's husband, Mr. Abbot, was a small Pa Kettle of a man who looked to her for the final word on any subject. One wondered what small part he played in the creation of these ten children since he called her "Mama." When there was a calf to sell, she would true eye it and without a moment's equivocation name its price; when there was an acreage to let, she immediately knew its terms; when the tobacco went to market, she set its price per pound and stuck with it. Within her household it was the same. Miss Glory could sit in her chair, eye a space, and cut wallpaper to fit; she could hold up dress fabric in the air and cut gores for skirts and enlarge armholes; in one afternoon she could cut and sew a change of clothes for every younger child in the household—all with her true eye. The marvel of it all was that her eye never seemed to fail.

As I look back on Miss Glory, I know she early came upon a great truth: the imperfection of perfection, or maybe it should be the perfection of imperfection. She knew nothing could be perfect and you had to go on and do something, not be frozen in total paralysis trying to have everything just right. I would say she thought seventy-five per cent was most acceptable and with ten children she would probably accept sixty-five per cent. Her true eye told her the windows didn't have to be clean or the house dusted to have company. A relaxed good time and plenty of biscuits were much more important. Too, she knew someone had to have leadership and a clarity of confidence to bring that big family through the depression; and since Mr. Abbot had neither, she made sure her children had an example of a single eye that filled the whole body with light and joy.

Dorothy Ann and I now can put our true eyes on an undulating dress hem with utmost confidence, and there's no waistline too tight that we can't let it out—not to mention entertaining with all the dust nicely rearranged. We are understanding the *True Eye* and the truth is setting us free. Thank you Miss Glory, for this glorious gift.

APRIL 1991

> *A man may be a heretic in the truth; and if he believes things only*
> *because his pastor says so, as the assembly so determines, without*
> *knowing other reason, though his belief be true, yet the very truth*
> *he holds becomes his heresy.*
>
> **John Milton**

In March I wrote of Miss Glory and her professed *True Eye*. In April I mull and muse about another of my Great Emancipators, Mr. Louis Francis Strange, also late of Kirkwood. He was our mentor of broader ideas and wider horizons, one who challenged our self-righteousness and small-mindedness, not caring one Amen what the assembly determined. He laid my foundation for a "faith-to-live-by."

Mr. Strange we called him, and "strange" he was for our kirk in the woods, certainly strange in his uncommon dash of haberdashery and his delicious abandon of country orthodoxy. He was a Spanish-American War veteran, ramrod straight, exuding a military air, a rarity

135

indeed in the environs of Guthrie, Kentucky. Whether he rode up San Juan Hill with the Rough Riders, I do not know; but he longed to return to the Caribbean and the light from other climes never left his eyes. Being a veteran gave Mr. Strange an impressive advantage: He had a pension. Now if you got any sort of "check" during the thirties, you were rich; and as we knew, riches often equated privilege—privilege to dress well and privilege to be your own man. Mr. Strange did both.

I can see him yet. He was thin, not tall, but he always wore a tall hat: a high panama in summer, a five-gallon felt in winter. Since my father, uncles, and most male Kirkwoodians had the indestructible blue serge suit, how well I remember the snap of Mr. Strange's pinstripe, replete with vest half-circled by a great golden chain and fob, ajingle with exotic coins from the Spanish Main, or perhaps from Long John Silver himself. What a tingling moment when he would suck in his breath, sigh, look out across the churchyard, and casually bring out a bejeweled watchcase and pop open its face. "It's time to highball," he would announce, which meant it was time to go home from meeting. Then the treasure returned to the pinstripe.

His eyes were small, dark, and scrutinizing. His voice was the same. He pierced you with his glittering eye and querulous voice and you leaned in with eye and ear. "What are you going to make of yourself?" was one of his stilettos which left us speechless but reminded me that Mr. Strange expected us to amount to something. At the time we couldn't imagine what, but I never forgot his expectations. He spent the majority of his "check" on his only son's education, valuing this legacy above all others.

But the time I remember Mr. Strange best was on the occasion of his being ordained Deacon at our church. He had been delayed for some years because of the suspicion of unorthodoxy; but being "well-off" and the coffers needing his pocketbook, he was finally asked to sit for his examination. What an afternoon that was! Congregated were assorted preachers and hoary deacons who were invited to administer the doctrinal quiz. Mr. Strange was put in a chair facing two rows of these Grand Inquisitors. All the hair-splitting doctrines were dusted off, particularly the ones that separated us from the Methodists, the first being baptism by immersion: "Do you believe immersion is the only true form of Baptism?"

"I don't know about that." Always he prefaced his responses with his doubts. Then he added, "I never heard Christ making any noise about it one way or another."

136

When the doctrine of "Closed Communion" came up, which meant that only members of that local church family could have the bread and wine, he vehemently didn't know about that. "You mean that if someone walked into your home that wasn't of your family you wouldn't ask them to have anything to eat? I was taught to welcome strangers. The Bible tells you to." (Silence from the jury)

Finally the big question, the Calvinistic doctrine of predestination and the "security of the saved," not being able to "fall from grace" came around. "I don't know about that." Skewering the judges with his piercing eye and his voice bitter with disgust, he added, "You preachers don't know either. You can read both ways in the Book. You had better be studying about loving your neighbor and quit trying to teach fly specks. The Lord gave us two commandments —to love God and each other. That's all I need."

The Inquisitors were rather like the accusers of the woman taken in adultery. They ordained him and were gone.

Mr. Strange and my father were best friends and kindred souls. He always longed to go back to Cuba and one day, late in his life, he said wistfully to my father, "Bracy, come go with me. On this trip we won't keep no books." He lived that way—not keeping any books but giving of his resources and wisdom and piercing our small beliefs with "I don't know about that."

NOVEMBER 1990

She walks in beauty, like the night,
Of cloudless climes and starry skies,
And all that's best of dark and bright,
Meet in her aspect and her eyes.

Lord Byron 1814

On the night of September 22, 1990, we saw the best of dark and bright. After ninety years, and on her birthday, she yet walks in beauty and the light shines on in the dark of her eyes and the bright of her smile. We have borne witness to the light, for it has shone for eighty-one years in Trinity's congregation. This beauty among us is our beloved Louisa Conroy.

The dark of her eyes is no chance manifestation. Her Castilian father, Primavito Abelis Rodriguez, brought his flashing eyes by way of Mexico City, Harvard University, Vanderbilt University, to Trinity,

137

Clarksville, where he was priest. There in his congregation was a ray of bright—Louisa Drane; thus, in 1893 Primavito asked Louisa to be joined with him in Holy Matrimony. In 1900 they presented the world the best of dark and bright, the infant Louisa.

Too soon, however, there were clouds in Louisa's life. In 1909, her intellectually brilliant father, enroute to Spain to work on a translation of the Spanish Bible, suddenly died of pneumonia. At the age of nine, she and her mother and four brothers returned to Clarksville to live near their Drane relatives. Since that date, she has been in regular attendance at this parish, making her by far the member with the longest record of attendance. Three generations here have witnessed Louisa's beauty of body and spirit, and we count ourselves blessed to have been included in her queenly reign of ninety years.

Her family reign began in 1931 when she caught John Conroy after he had chased her for twelve years. He loved only Louisa. He proposed when she was nineteen, but being an early liberated woman, she went into the working world as a physical therapist at Mayo's Clinic and then to New York as a pocket-book saleslady at Saks Fifth Avenue. With the crash of '29, Louisa came home to John, was married, and immediately increased Clarksville's population by two: John McClure Conroy and Louisa Drane Conroy—Mrs. Wade Hadley. Her kingdom now includes ten grandchildren and seven great grandchildren.

Ah, the power of Beauty! Louisa has been given its secrets: her regal posture, her model-thin figure, her classic profile, her dramatic hands, her crowning of white hair, her hat at just the right tilt, her clothes in eloquent harmony, her jewelry never overstated, and her high heels. Her neighbors vow she takes out her garbage in high heels and with more style than they could ever muster for a ladies' high tea. Hands down, she is Clarksville's quintessence of style!

So that we might give homage where homage is due, we need to know Louisa on the inside—see how she rules her kingdom, where her values lie.

Her reign is, according to her daughter, Louisa Hadley, that of a benevolent despot. Her values are so firm, so ingrained from childhood with civility and correct deportment that there is no deviation. Good manners, proper attire, appropriate table conversation, and genuine kindness are absolutes. She never fussed, never allowed a scene, did anything to keep harmony in the family; and in the long run ruled them all, "played us like a fiddle," especially her husband, John.

138

From Louisa's philosophy of life, there are more absolutes. "Beauty, truthfulness, and goodness are embodied in a loving harmony, a gift from God. There is a reciprocity of reflections between the body and spirit, the body being the temple of the Holy Spirit; and this temple must be maintained in its very best order and in its very best attire. To be unloving or untruthful on the inside or to be disheveled or uncouth on the outside would be to dishonor both body and spirit. We are called to do our very best with both our physical and spiritual attire. To do less is slothful." On this foundation, Louisa built her life.

At ninety, she declares with her still-flashing eyes and quick wit: "I've had a lucky life." In thanksgiving for such a "marvelous life" she is devoting her final years to loving everyone, accepting everyone and "trying not to fall around and made a spectacle of myself." She lives alone in her apartment on Madison Street. She feels John's presence as she comes nearer to him, even to knowing his admiration as he saw her decked in her grand jade dress for her ninetieth birthday party. For her, this is the Communion of Saints, John's loving concern surrounding them all. Her life eternal is now.

Louisa, we are persuaded that your lucky life will get luckier as you walk in beauty, here or elsewhere, toward the year 2000. Almost a century's worth of graciousness bears witness to your life's testimony:

> *Beauty is truth, truth beauty—*
> *That is all ye know of earth,*
> *And all ye need to know.*
> **John Keats**

MAY 1990

Like Uncle Wiggly, who needed an adventure to help his rheumatism, Ardell (the church secretary whom you all know) and I decided we must go on one for our Post-Menopausal Mopes. The *Southern Women's Show* in Nashville promised great victory for our retreating hormones and surrendering beauty. At this show there were guaranteed creams and unguents to turn saddle-leather jowls into dew-moistened blushes; hanks of hair that could be entwined into your own to fill out any over-molted pate; great cascading wigs that could be popped on for instant Loretta Lynns or Dolly Partons; and a host of other temptations to adorn the flesh: beads, earrings, scarves, hats, belts, furs, dresses, sweaters; and yes, much food to adorn our flesh further with rolls and dimples, all in the wrong places.

If all the food and fad didn't jostle our systems awake, the maddening crowd did. Saturday afternoon and free samples of food brought out the throngs, who pressed and elbowed into position for ice cream, pizza, peanuts, hotdogs, and every chip to dip for cholesterol. Granny was there in her wheelchair, and Junior was there in his stroller, both lost underneath a forest of legs intent on being the first in line for the *Goo-Goos*. The vanity of the flesh and the appetite of the flesh made space scarce for the feet. So after munching through sixteen lines, Ardell and I said, "Enough." Away to the parking garage and home.

However, adventure was just beginning. We could not let Uncle Wiggly out-do us. With already confused feet and bi-focals, I stumbled over a curb and crashed both my knees on the concrete in the garage. Ardell pronounced me dead on the spot. Then we took the elevator to the sixth floor where we knew our car was parked, but discovered that the elevator only went to the fourth floor because that was all the floors the garage had. We were in the wrong garage! Our hormones began to come to attention.

Next—to take the down elevator and find the right garage—so we pressed the button for the ground floor. The elevator went down and it went down and it went down and it stopped with the first floor about at eye-level. We were somewhere down in the bowels of the garage—Stuck.

Not panicking—yet—we pressed every button for all floors and "Emergency" and "Alarm." Nothing happened. We just sat there underneath the first floor of that cavernous garage with canned music blasting our eardrums. After some minutes we managed, with much prizing, to get both sets of doors parted about two inches, enough to put my mouth to the crack and scream, "HEELLP." This plea from the pit reverberated through the concrete and steel and at last produced a whited-eye and slackened-jaw that peeped down into the depth of our prison. Saying nary a word, he left us and after some time reappeared with a steel pipe to threaten the doors. They were not to be intimidated.

There was a window to the street in the elevator shaft—a saving grace—which at length brought a group of spectators who called to each other, peeped down at our plight, and speculated about our condition. Not being able to hear them, we made desperate gestures, rather like unhappy zoo-inhabitants who refused to swing.

At length, there came another parking-lot attendant, a lady with her "Walkie-Talkie." To whom she made her communication, we were not privy. All we knew was that after an interminable wait our knights in shining armor came to the rescue—the Nashville Fire Department with lights flashing at full beam and siren screaming at full wail. We cheered and our spectator-section cheered! With crowbars, fire axes, and great pronged hooks, they slew the undisciplined doors, ran a ladder down into the depths and, with great gallantry, helped our giddy hormones up to safety.

There is design in adventure. Abraham could have stayed in Ur of the Chaldees; Joshua could have believed the spies and not ventured into the Promised Land; Ruth could have remained in her own country; and Ardell and I could have stayed at home. But we would have lost the lesson of Uncle Wiggly.

You must take hold of life. You must cherish the joy and, yes, the sorrow of the moment. This is the only time you have—right now. Seize this moment. There is always a place for laughter in this absurdity called living, even at the bottom of a stuck elevator. Don't let these liberating moments pass you by. Our creator and the one who keeps us from the beginning to the end wants his creation to know the heights and depths, the full measure of life. He gave us tears and he gave us laughter. Let us purge our soul with both. Let us welcome unexpected adventure.

> *For he brought me up also out of a horrible pit, out of the miry clay, and set my feet upon a rock, and established my goings. And he put a new song in my mouth, even praises unto our God.*
> **Psalm 40**

JULY 1989

> *Those that be planted in the house of the Lord shall flourish in the house of our God. They shall bring forth fruit in old age; they shall be fat and flourishing.*
> **Psalm 92**

My friend Wilmoth is not fat, but she is flourishing. Her sparkling eyes, the optimism in her voice, her infectious laugh, the enthusiasm of many years of loving life and all the persons who have come her way make Wilmoth Chilton Buckley one peach of a fruit in her old age. Old age? She's only eighty-six. Where she is, a young spirit of love and laughter is there. Age is forgotten as we all, be we five, fifty, or ninety-nine, give thanks for Wilmoth and her ministries, still fat and flourishing. Just this past month I have been informed that she is the record

141

holder peanut-butter-sandwich-maker of the *Loaves and Fishes* as well as the newly adopted grandmother of some little girls who have no grandmother near at hand. Her acceptance of everyone is so big that lonely outcasts and little children find joy in her presence; and I, too, when she comes by, find I have a need to laugh, give her a hug, and pass a joke or two.

My daddy said that when folks get old they either turned to pickles or preserves. Wilmoth, we know which jar you're in.

After an idyllic childhood at Pembroke, Kentucky, surrounded by doting parents and two sets of grandparents, Wilmoth abandoned trees and horses for the finer arts: dancing, dramatics, and music. These were to be her life. She was to pass her talents and ministries on to several generations of Clarksville children as well as to a nation at war. She taught private classes and classes in the public school system. At one point in her long teaching career, she organized all the children in the three elementary schools in Clarksville—over a thousand—in one pageant. She not only wrote the pageant, but the music, designed the costumes, directed the whole shebang, which was so big it had to pre-sented on the football field! Wilmoth is afraid of "bragging," but the pageant wasn't bragging—it was an accomplished fact.

Wilmoth's life does, however, brag about its many years of service to the young men and women of our country. For sixteen years, the mil-itary personnel at Ft. Campbell had the good fortune to have Wilmoth for a Social Director of the USO here in Clarksville. How many dances organized, dinners given, cookies requested, problems heard, letters written, service wives soothed, and homes found away from home for these displaced GIs! Children and young people are nearest and dear-est to Wilmoth, and here was a cross section of the whole nation for her to love.

Wilmoth has been a widow since 1956 and her only daughter and grandchildren live in Texas. But she is not alone. Her family is anyone who needs a kind word, a jolly response, or maybe a song or a prayer. She has consistently had Children's Chapel at Trinity, teaching little children to sing while Mama is at church. Without our knowing it, she prays for us as the requests come to the prayer chain. Then she looks after several "old people."

One of these "old people" is a member of the opposite sex—a child-hood friend—who likes to "ride, eat, and dance." Wilmoth helps him with all three. In fact, it was reported that they were seen at the fair-grounds last summer kicking so high that the youngsters stood back and gave them the floor.

As in all our lives, Wilmoth's life has had its defeats and dark valleys; but she says her faith "planted in the house of the Lord" has been the only way she could have made it through. "Defeat, faced with faith and hope, can become a triumph, bringing a special courage."

Approaching her ninetieth year, she, being human, wonders about the ending of her life: "What to do? Where to stay or go? Will I become a burden? Lord, deliver me from a long illness. Lord, please let me keep my right mind."

Wilmoth, our prayer for you is that some sweet night after you have ridden, eaten, and danced, you will lie down in a deep sleep, dream of all the dancing and music and laughter you have known, and dance away in your dreams. When you awake in wonderment, you will be surrounded by all those you have taught and loved, and you will continue what you barely began here. There's a lot of dancing and praising to be done!!

> *Praise ye the Lord. Praise him with timbrel and dance: praise him with high sounding cymbals. Let everything that hath breath praise the Lord. Praise ye the Lord.*
>
> **Psalm 150**

SEPTEMBER 1988

My paternal grandmother was Mattie Winn from Rudolphtown. She had an older sister, Lucy, whose parsimony and spitefulness lived long after her. As children, every bad trait that surfaced in our behavior was attributed to our having inherited Aunt Lucy's disposition. Any selfish response, cruel judgment, falsehood, or too blunt a remark got to be known as an "Aunt Lucy." We dreaded having the inheritance bequeathed to us, for, according to my father and my grandmother, there could be no worse chromosomes swimming around in one's gene pool that the ones Aunt Lucy put awash in her generation. They, however, didn't know about genes and chromosomes; they just called them a "mean streak" or "the work of the devil."

My grandmother held on to hurts with an ever-vigilant tenacity filled with piety and self-pity—good-little-me and bad-old-Lucy. As an old woman, she had never forgiven Lucy for her critique of my father's infant beauty, even though Lucy's acid tongue had long since been silenced by some good shovelfuls of dirt. On the brighter side, though, my grandmother was equally prone to seat us around her and

143

charm us with her infectious fun, her stories, and her store-house of games. But suddenly, in the midst of a hot game of *Hull Gull*, she would get a wounded look on her face, her rouged cheeks would sag under the thick glasses that reduced her eyes to pale buttons, and she would let us in on the unkindest cuts from forty years before: "Do you know what your Great-Aunt Lucy said about your father when he was born?"

"Nome."

"Well, she said he was the ugliest baby she had ever seen! Why, she even said, 'Mattie, aren't you ashamed to bring the baby out to Little Hope?'" (This Little Hope is the same Baptist Church still having hope on Highway 76 to Adams.) When we had finished the game and she had won all the corn, she would reach again into her long-cherished gunny sack of grief and drag out another Lucy heirloom.

"At Edna's wedding (Grandmother's only daughter), sitting right beside me at the wedding supper, Lucy said Willie was the homeliest man in Montgomery County. 'Why, he looks like a turkey egg.'" Now Uncle Willie was a redhead and rather flushed and freckled and would shame the speckles on a turkey egg, but he served to keep Edna from the dreaded state of spinster-hood. Lucy turned the knife when she vowed, "If she had waited much longer, she couldn't have got him."

My daddy didn't care about Aunt Lucy's judgment of his and Willie's facades and her estimation of the plusses and minuses of matrimonial matters, but he couldn't forgive her for her husband's death. Lucy kept a rooming house and was noted for cheating her roomers, as well as her milk and egg customers. When Uncle Harvey couldn't take her abuses any longer, he blew himself into a more restful existence. Lucy's grief was expressed in her mourning the loss of someone to milk the cow.

As I mull and muse over the hurts and griefs that we inflict on each other, the self-pity and depression that possess us, and our wild mood swings from anger to euphoria, I question at length the role of heredity: Does Lucy live in me when I make those most hurtful judgments? Does Grandmother surface in my bouts of self-pity? Does my depression stem from my maternal grandmother, who as a young woman was institutionalized and hidden away for the rest of her life? Have these genes been passed on to my children? Are we locked into being Lucys and Matties?

I don't know. The only thing I do know as I struggle with my guilt, self-pity, depression and anger, is that when my need to be rid of these demons is greater than my need to hang on to them, they begin to loosen their hold and I can hear Christ's call to the Gerasene demoniac, "What is your name?" and when I answer truthfully and name those devils who plague me I hear his other words to the wild man, "Come out of the man, you unclean spirit."

Heredity, no doubt, has its role in our inheritance of demons, but I believe one mightier than Lucy is here. He is the one who will not "allow the demons to speak because they know him," and he unchains us, and we are found "clothed and in our right mind."

JANUARY 1988

> *...And God said to them, "Be fruitful and multiply and fill the earth and subdue it...and have dominion over every thing that moves upon the earth."*
>
> ### *Genesis I*

My mother-in-law took the Lord God literally. She was fruitful and multiplied, but above all she had dominion over and subdued every living thing that moved upon the earth of Rossview and greater Montgomery County. This included all animate flesh, its occasions and organizations: her children, her husband, in-laws, grandchildren, neighbors, household pests, the family cat, the chicken house, all birthdays, anniversaries, Mother's Day, Father's Day, all holidays, Country Women's Club, Kirkwood Home Demonstration Club, Kirkwood Community Club, County Women-of-the-World, Farm Bureau, Rossview Ladies' Aid, PTA, County Fair, various card societies, all drives (heart, kidney, and rheumatism), all annual picnics and bazaars, all quilt-chance raffles, plus the spiritual directorship of the straying communicants of Grace Chapel, Rossview. Each of us living things—be we biped, quadruped, domestic, civic, churched or unchurched—was expected to fill its place in creation as it was ordained by this ninety pound *Bishop Of Rossview*.

The Bishop, fondly known to us as Mary-Jim, had an urgency in her nature, a souped-up psyche set on fast-forward that subdued all around her. If she were not president or otherwise organizer of the above mentioned, she set up a puppet regime which she directed with an iron determination that somehow seemed her right. She had been endowed with a hysterical spontaneity for immediate problem solving. With whoops of laughter she and only she knew how to get jobs done, and any anarchy was quickly subdued. We knew dominion when we saw it—and that included the family cat and me.

We were in attendance to the Bishop on *Roll Day*. Now *Roll Day* was the baking and freezing of dozens and dozens of rolls for all organizations and celebrations. Had the entire complement of Ft. Campbell suddenly bivouacked on her front lawn she could have furnished every man in his regiment a half-dozen hot, buttered rolls within the hour. On *Roll Day*, her staccato heels punished the linoleum and rattled the tea cups—back and forth from the flour bin to kneading board to stove to cooling boards. Kitty and I were standing by to see how we fitted into this flurry of flour.

He meowed around our legs, tickled us with his twining tail, and enjoyed the warmth of the kitchen while I offered what paltry assistance I could to one so intently organizing the flour and pans. Now Mary-Jim believed in flour—not some little five-pound, throwaway sack you could hold in the palm of your hand, but a great sack of *D And F* which was put in a cavernous bin in a venerable kitchen cabinet with a bread kneading place on top. This bin had a weight in the bottom and you pulled it out and it flopped back in again, suggesting it might bite your arm off if you weren't careful. With this copious supply of flour on hand, she was ready to begin. Mary-Jim put on her apron, got out her biggest mixing bowl, found the sifter with the reel inside, got out a great stack of pans, kicked the cat out of the way, pulled open the flour bin, peered in among the rolling pin and the biscuit cutters, gathered her skirt around her in a mighty flamenco, and let out a S C R E A M that made the original hole in the ozone. A mouse was in the flour! Creation was in chaos! Without missing a step, the Bishop assigned Kitty to his rightful place in the hierarchy of the universe, pulled out the bin, dropped him in, and let it fly shut. There was a muffled thumping and bumping inside; and when to Mary-Jim's satisfaction enough time had elapsed for this subduing, she released her skirt, pulled open the bin, and there, wild-eyed and changed from gray to white, was Kitty with the poor squeaking, floured mouse in his jaws. Mary-Jim rejoiced in this triumph and deposited both outside the back door for Kitty to do his final dominion. Order had been restored in creation.

What moral can I muster for the New Year from the late *Bishop Of Rossview*? It must belong to the mighty bishops of this world. They would do well to attend: *Roll Day* is at hand. You have been imbued with power. Use it. Don't pussy foot around. Throw your kitty in the flour bin lest the master of the house find you not using what you have. "That which you have may be taken away!"

SEPTEMBER 1987

My husband's brother Jim is with the State Department, his present post being The Hague in the Netherlands. We visited him in July. Right across the street from Jim's house was this beautifully kept churchyard, containing a most respectable Dutch Reformed Church, whose bonging clock raised me from my bed on the hour and the half-hour, and whose bell on Sunday morning raised me from my breakfast chair. Just as salmon have to spawn, there is some inexorable urge that calls me to the assembling of myself come Sunday morning; so with the bell ringing its ten-minute warning, I ran upstairs, put on *The Dress*, fuzzed up my hair, made a swipe with a lipstick, and joined the Body of Christ.

The Dutch language is long on consonants, and I was short on understanding and certainly riddled with language barrier. With a bulletin in hand I made my way around left end and sat down by a carefully groomed man who eyed me either with amazement or disdain—or maybe both—as I tried to find the page and puzzle through the order of service. First we sang. I found the page but no familiar tune, no word I knew, and as far as the singers were concerned, there was no choir, no song leader, no visible organ, not to mention fervor and zeal. Seldom have I heard more discouraging words. If only we could have stood up, gotten a good puff of air in our bellows; but we sat. After the hymn, I realized there was a prayer because heads bent forward perhaps five degrees and the man up front punished the consonants with a bit more emphasis here and there, probably at omission and commission. Another hymn, derriere still unmoved. Next came a dour report by a little man whose doom-edged presentation spoke to me of portents to come: of famine, plague, pestilence, and persecution. No response from the congregation, no clearing of throats, no uneasy squirming, and we contemplated the silence with due respect.

Then the sermon—all thirty five minutes of it. The minister jarred the consonants in what I presumed were long passages from Scripture, in lengthy exegeses from Calvinistic theology, and, finally, at about the thirty-minute milepost, in poetry. I could tell by the meter. Just as he was winding down, he dropped his book of poetry in mid-rhyming couplet which delighted my tickle box no end. (Maybe in my ignorance I didn't recognize this was for dramatic effect for some fallen hero or life snuffed out suddenly.) Not a smile from anyone, no one twisted around in his seat for hopeful relief, and the minister didn't retrieve his book. It lay, abandoned, as though it were outcast for social impropriety. When he had punctuated his last gargle, I felt we would get to stretch since I had heard how frugal the Dutch were, and I was sure they would stand in praise for their version of "Praise God from Whom All Blessings Flow." Not only did they pass the plate, they passed two, all done in dead silence and you guessed it—seated. I mused that the two plates were to keep the left hand from knowing what the right hand was doing.

There was another gesture toward heaven and then we sang. I knew the tune! "God of Grace and God of Glory"! I sang in English and I didn't care, especially when we came to the words "on thy people pour thy grace," because in my judgment I was truly with people who needed the grace of God to set them free from being too dressed up to smile or get up and down. I pondered our passing the peace at Trinity and thought about St. Paul's instructions to greet the brothers with a holy kiss, envisioning myself reaching over to my well-groomed friend and hanging one on him. Finally, after an uninterrupted hour of being absolute pew potatoes, we were released from our seats with a tip toward the Almighty.

Going back to my Baptist background, I was hopeful some good brother or sister, someone from the greeting committee, would extend the hand of Christian fellowship. I no doubt didn't look like a Christian because I got neither hand nor fellowship. Outside I saw a lone man standing by the walk. I gave him a smile, told him who I was and why, because I refused to be among God's people without any semblance of community. He understood English and was gracious. With this last attempt at brotherhood, I mulled my provincial way back across the street, judging my neighbor, all the while thinking if I were black in South Africa, I would be in favor of Apartheid in order to keep my religion safe from the Dutch Reformed Church where I had felt no welcome, no praise, no joy, and at last, the most condemning lack of the Christian community—no love.

> *By this all the world will know you are my disciples, if you have love for one another.*
>
> ***John 14***

OCTOBER 1987

Now you are the body of Christ and individually members of it. If one member suffers, all suffer together; if one member is honored, all rejoice together.

St. Paul

Mulling and musing about the Body of Christ and what it means in our personal world and the world universal, I continue my summer travels. From my Dutch Reformed brothers and sisters in the Netherlands, we made our way into France where I joined the Catholic Communion in Brittany.

Our daughter's in-laws have a summer home on the western-most point of France in a small fishing village, St. Pabu par Ploudalmezeau, where I made my usual Sunday commitment to the Church, this living Body of Christ. The small church, austerely granite on the outside, sat in the middle of the village where the cows graze to the seaside and the sea creatures can be caught in bucketsful when the tide is out. On the inside, the church welcomed us, filled almost to capacity with the saints of God and harbored also a few of his personable flies which buzzed up and down the long windows in search of their place in the kingdom. Farmers and their wives, fishermen and net-menders, keepers of small shops, boatwrights, the village postman, the summer people—all could be assigned a place among the faces that were this people of God. And there were children! Noisy and agitated ones who reminded us at once that "of such is the kingdom of heaven." After the preceding Sunday with my seated brethren, I relaxed into the reality of this body where an encompassing and humble acceptance was in the air.

We did our ups and downs in responses, hymns of praise, and certainly for the *Doxology*. Some I could understand; some I couldn't but the spirit was there. A most earnest young man played the organ, two rosy-cheeked young ladies read the lessons, and the congregation, standing, sang in their native Celtic language. The gospel, read in French, was the Parable of the Sower. I could follow the gospel reading since this passage is so familiar. I couldn't follow the priest's homily, however, but I sat and mused over the seed on my barren ground and how the birds of anxiety and the world-too-much-with-me devoured my seed, not to mention my collection of weeds. I'm sure the good priest made all my good points. After the offertory came the communion of the people with our going to the priest who gave us only bread. I wasn't about to get into any interior theological hassle about not get-

149

ting any wine, so I took the bread gladly, meditating that Christ was looking on our hearts and if we took a moon pie in his name and tried to be his presence in the world that would be a fitting remembrance of his sacrifice for us.

A microcosm of the joys and burdens of us all was represented in this body: a fragile old lady, bent with too many years, leaned upon a younger woman for support; a younger man in rough work clothes whose hands, stiff and swollen, held the hymn book with reverent care; a young couple, probably summer people, who showed off two beautiful daughters; a social worker who had two rows of under-privileged children she had brought from Paris for a seaside vacation; young people who suggested the hope and faith of a new generation; a resigned priest who blessed all he surveyed; and I, a stranger from another culture. We were members of one body in this place.

The awesome bequest of being the Body of Christ! We—all these fumbling mortals—the Body of Christ? The very idea is mind-blowing, but when you get right down to it, we're all that's here to be the presence of Christ. The Spirit is here but I mean the nuts and bolts of the body to do the teaching, the preaching, the praising, the healing, the forgiving, the listening, the loving, the accepting, the cooking, and yes, the paying. There *Ain't* nobody else. Sitting with my frozen Dutch brothers or standing with my Catholic ones, I know the Body is we, and we are called to be his presence where we are—not in some exotic, far-off place. To the measure that this member, our very selves, becomes unloving, to that measure the body is weakened. It is strong as we open ourselves and are empowered by the spirit of Christ to make his body strong. May we go from strength to strength.

JANUARY 1987

> *Let us love one another and laugh. Time passes and we shall soon laugh no longer—and meanwhile common living is a burden, and earnest men are at siege upon us all around. Let us suffer absurdities, for that is only to suffer one another.*
>
> ***Hilaire Belloc***

The cold of January and the burden of common living call for some winter levity lest we take ourselves too seriously. Time was I did just that, but time, again, has compromised the absurdities that abound all around; and rather than dying of mortification, I have tried living with merriment. It's better for the liver. Therefore, on this bleak day indulge me a few moments to tell you a warm summer's tale.

My brother-in-law, Paul Edwin Peale, a scion of the illustrious family of painters, had alerted me that his oldest brother, Augustus Peale, whom I only knew by reputation, was to stop at our house on his way from his home in Natchez, Mississippi, to Paul Edwin's home in Chicago. Not having met the old bachelor uncle whose blood I understood coursed true and blue, I wanted everything proper and in its place.

Uncle Augustus had spent the night in Memphis, and not knowing his penchant for waking the chickens and telling the rooster to crow, I was not ready for his 9:00 a.m. call from the Holiday Inn where he was to get directions to our house. Just as I came in from the garden all prickly with okra leaves, green beans, and honest sweat, the phone rang. The grand uncle had arrived. No time for a bath—only a wild jump into something decent and ladylike. The Holiday Inn is only four miles from Pollard Road, Box 551. With a cool summer dress with a full skirt pulled on, a swipe with a comb and a lipstick, I was ready. Just then I looked down at my legs, eternally white and sunless, and did a quick draw-on of panty hose. With this last act of presentability I heard Uncle Augustus' faithful Plymouth at the door and rushed out, my southern hospitality at full gush.

Initially we greeted each other with great enthusiasm, noting all the mutual favors on both sides of the family; but by the time I had Uncle Augustus unloaded and on his way into the house, he became more and more mumbling and stumbling and by the time I got him to the front door, he had an owlish-frozen grin on his face, his neck seemed unable to turn, and his eyeballs stared straight ahead. He stood rooted by the front door. Why this paralysis?

Now already visiting me from the Tidewater of North Carolina was my aunt, Mrs. Ada Livingston McBryde Austin, who always did the proper thing. When she went across the street in the afternoon and sat on the front porch with a neighbor, she put on her white gloves. She never saw the sifted flour on her shoes. She knew the correct protocol for any situation. With this knowledge, it was she who unglued Uncle Augustus. Coming out to greet the guest, she looked me over and looked the rooted uncle over and asked me, "Charlotte, what kind of skirt do you have on?" With that, I felt around and behind...Horror of horrors—I had my full skirt tucked in the top of my panty hose and had been all the while flashing Uncle Augustus Peale!

Mark Twain would say, "Let's let the curtain of charity descend on this scene." The ascending curtain of this comedy of error, however, was a liberating scene, one to rid us of useless pretense. Uncle Augustus immediately unfroze, my proper aunt got suddenly unproper, I gave up my gush, and we all sat down in the living room with great whoops of laughter. An absurdity of living had pierced through to that place where we pretend we don't make such miserable blunders; and the blunder itself was the agent for our enjoying and suffering each other. Soon it was "Uncle Gus" and by the time he left the next morning, it was plain "Gus." From that time forward, it was an annual visit, Christmas cards, and great boxes of pecans from his favorite orchard. Uncle Augustus accepted me as a fellow blunderer, one who bears all things.

So ends this winter's tale.

DECEMBER 1996

I do not give lectures or a little charity.
When I give, I give myself.

Leaves of Grass
Walt Whitman

Miss Sula's Christian name was Ursula, but it was southerned to Ur-su-la; then we neighbors got it down to its final inflection, "Sula."

At Kirkwood, this Miss Sula and her husband, Mr. Rufus, lived down the road from us where he practiced the ultimate in parsimony while she practiced the ultimate in loving their only daughter, Grace Marie. Caught between parsimony and pampering, Miss Sula used many devious ways to see that Grace Marie's world came first; and this world was our sweet benefactor of "cream candy," which was ours each and every time we came to play.

"Now, you know I'm not much of a cook, but I think I can fluff up the sugar sack a bit." Thus began Miss Sula's treat for the afternoon. Evidently, Mr. Rufus kept a close eye on the level of the sugar sack, which in our childhood was purchased in hundred pound bags and stored in the pantry along with a barrel of flour. With fluffing expertise, Miss Sula would stir the sugar around, take out a few cups, and see if she could rearrange the sugar bag to deceive Mr. Rufus' ever-vigilant eye. She was good at these deceptions, for I never remember once her failing to produce this basic recipe for our afternoon treat.

152

Cream candy was simply sugar, milk, butter, and a splash of vanilla, cooked to a soft ball and poured to cool on a platter. Then it was cut in squares. Often, it was grainy with undissolved sugar, but to us children who ate anything sweet, it was superb. One Christmas, while her kind eyes twinkled and her prized gold tooth shone through a triumphant defeat of stinginess, she presented us her one culinary delight. "Now you know I'm not much of a cook, but it's Christmas and I stirred the sugar sack pretty hard." Each December we had our treat, and one year the candy was Santa Claus red, laced with food color and served on a Sunday platter.

Now Jeff, the hired hand, suffered also for our benefit. He declared, "Miss Sula's pie is so sour you have to put your fork in your mouth to keep your jaws from locking." Pie was especially lean around Christmas since Mr. Rufus' Scrooge disposition was on red-alert because of "too much tom-foolery in the kitchen." Miss Sula suffered for our sake when she ran afoul of Mr. Rufus' narrow control over her pantry and endured his no-control over his acid tongue.

This recounting of Miss Sula's gift giving is an account by which we can measure our giving. She gave us what she had, what she could glean from her kitchen, because she loved her daughter and loved. us. She gave despite suffering her husband's wrath. She gave like the widow with the two mites, out of her living. She gave herself.

In our present day frenzy of mega-gifts and gift-swapping, we have lost sight of true gifts. How we give is infinitely more important than the gift. Unless the gift is given in love, and often with suffering, as with Miss Sula, it is no gift at all—just a cold exchange of things.

With the gift of the Christ Child, unconditional love and sacrifice were made known to us. God loved us so much he gave his most precious possession and he told us that we must be like him and give ourselves away.

"Now, I know I'm not much of a cook," but may I and all of us fluff up our sugar sacks this Christmas and put some sweetness in the world. "Bah, Humbug" to you, Mr. Rufus. Thankfulness to you, Miss Sula. Merry Christmas and my love to all of you.

FEBRUARY 1997

> *...Nature made them blinder motions bounded in a shallower brain.*
> *Woman is the lesser man, and all thy passion matched with mine,*
> *are as moonlight unto sunlight and as water unto wine.*
>
> > *Locksley Hall*
> > *Tennyson*

In January, after Cousin Abel had stripped his last barn of dark tobacco, he came a-courting to Grandpa Winn's house. The sap was rising and Cousin Abel's frustrated testosterone was telling him he needed to grace the world with his brain, his sunlight, and his wine. He was looking for a wife, both utilitarian and fertile.

Now Grandpa's daughter, Aunt Bess, had been on the market a few years and had been passed over by the neighborhood swains who went to adjoining communities for wives, and her "shallow" brain did not delude her. If she wanted a husband, she must take Mr. Swift's offer. Nature had not blessed her with much to please the mirror. Her untamed hair, parted in the middle and oiled into submission, was screwed to the top of her lesser intelligence while her eyes, rimmed with latent rebellion, squinted behind small, oval spectacles. Her nose and full lips reigned over an equine face whose expression was the old political slogan: "Don't tread on me." The family album showed her a formidable figure, a head taller than Mr. Swift, and endowed with powerful arms and legs to bear burdens and children.

Mr. Swift, as Aunt Bess always called her husband, was of the old St. Paul school and considered himself quite a scholar. All his readings were to bolster the male ego and to keep the women in their proper places. " I suffer not a woman to teach, nor to usurp authority over a man, but to be in silence;" and, of course, "wives, obey your husbands." Cousin Abel knew all St. Paul's anti-women verses and assigned Cousin Bess to her role of mute, uncomplaining childbearing and household drudging. While she was occupied with presenting him with four sons with high I.Q.'s and two daughters with lesser brains, Cousin Abel continued his domination of the household, forever memorizing St. Paul—chapter and verse—blaming all ills on Mother Eve, and immersing himself in John Knox's *The First Blast of the Trumpet Against The Monstrous Regiment of Women.*

After the sixth child was born and another in the oven, Cousin Abel branded Aunt Bess's role in the household as "concubine." This was too much! What seethings had been going on under her smoldering

Vesuvius only St. Paul knew. But the eruption reverberates in story across our family until this day.

Bess broke the churn-dasher over Cousin Abel's magnificent cranium; settled scores with a full set of his mother's best china—which she was never allowed to use; turned over a week's washing, soaking on the back porch; burned his books—both Calvin and Knox—in her cookstove; and as a final statement—went out and jumped off the chicken house several times in an attempt to abort number seven. "Concubine, indeed!" For three months, Aunt Bess took her pregnancy to bed until she presented Cousin Abel with yet another brainy son. After that; no more. Cousin Abel took himself mostly to barns and woodsheds where he contemplated his authority from afar, and a cold silence shadowed his sunshine and wine.

In later years, Cousin Mettie Winn told the denouement of the Bess and Abel Story. It was the *Ladies Home Journal* that brought Cousin Bess and her daughters to life. She read this quote from Grover Cleveland: "Sensible and responsible women do not want to vote. The relative positions to be assumed by men and women in the working out of our civilization were assigned long ago by a higher intelligence than ours."

Too long Aunt Bess had heard this hogwash. She grabbed Beulah and Norene with their moonlight brains and joined the Suffrage Movement with fire and vigor like the Pankhursts of England. They only put the horse and buggy up after the Tennessee Legislature cast the two-thirds vote that ratified this nineteenth amendment to the Constitution. Bess and her daughters had found their brains and the sunshine.

This verse from Paul's writings saved him from being burned in the cookstove: "There is neither Jew nor Greek, there is neither bond of free, there is neither male nor female: for ye are all one in Christ Jesus." For our Christ never once, under any circumstances, put women in their "place." As he went about his ministry, his responses toward all were forgiving, uplifting, and liberating. Paul, in his epistles, placed sour notes into the good news of unconditional love and respect.

As you look down from the ramparts of glory, St. Paul, we uppity women—be it for good or bad—cut our hair, wear flashy clothes, speak and pray in the churches, get divorced, and obey our husbands when it suits us.

Perhaps I should be obeying my husband more since he has financial brains and keeps me from living on the side of the road. But somehow my shallow brain has more sunlight since I have been liberated by Aunt Bess's generation. Women may be the lesser man, but we have what the greater man has always been seeking—moonlight and wine!

APRIL 1997

Have you not a moist eye? A dry hand? A yellow cheek? A decreasing leg? An increasing belly? Is not your voice broken? Your wind short? Your chin double? Your wit single? And every part about you bloated with antiquity? And you call yourself young? Fie, fie!
Shakespeare: II Henry IV

Mr. Dick Polk called himself young. His yellow cheek was rouged, his increasing belly was corseted, his mousey hair moussed and combed over, and his decreasing leg rode high in a buggy behind a fast horse. He was longing to make a fast move on any lady acquaintance who didn't hide when he wheeled his buggy into Kirkwood society. When two unclaimed school teachers came to the community, Mr. Dick sprang into action, which included stoking the stove, dusting the erasers, filling the water cooler, and hanging around all day if it were PTA day. Greater love hath no man!

I can see him yet, squinting around the tin jacket of the pot-bellied stove, his gaunt cheeks a-shine from the rouge pot, clasping his old hands together again and again in anticipation of whatever his senile dreams might be. He was the laughing-stock of the countryside and the bane of all women, young and not so young. Poor old fool. He died in his buggy, riding after his lost libido, a burden to himself and all around him. Fie, fie, Mr. Dick.!

In contrast, Granny Ross, Dorothy Ann's mother, grappled with the reality of her years. She summed up her anguish with the succinct words: "Old age is *Hell*, just *Hell*." She refused to let the mantle of her years rest anywhere and raged bitterly at her compromised physical independence. Her mind, however, was ever independent. She doubted all cut-and-dried religious dogmas and debated all unanswerable questions which could only be answered by a leap of faith. Granny did not choose to leap. Her ever-questing mind pooh-poohed the poet Browning and his sissy lines of "Grow old along with me, the best is yet to be." She lived by the lines from Tennyson's *Ulysses*: "Something ere the end, some work of noble note may yet be done, not unbecoming men who strove with gods."

With these words, Granny Ross began her noble work. She was a student of Greek and Roman mythology and during her last years, she went to the public schools with many a tale of the gods and heroes. With wide-eyed wonder, the elementary students knew Ulysses, Theseus, Perseus, and the gods of Olympus. To this day, these middle-aged students recall this legacy left them by one who challenged her years and refused to yield her unique gifts of mind and spirit. At ninety-five she came to the River Styx with her existential questions still unanswered. She left us a rare example of intellectual curiosity that did not accept a cheap faith but wrestled nobly with the gods—"to strive, to seek, to find, and not to yield."

As I approach three-quarters of a century, what shall it be for me? For us? Shall we be Mr. Dick or Granny Ross? Some of these answers are in our hands and some in the hands of our genetic make-up. We do not know our end. The scary part is that we may not be aware of our actions and responses. If our future behavior could be viewed from where we are at this moment, we could be horrified by what we have become. As we remember our relatives who have traveled this final way before us, we vow, "I shall never do that. I will never be like that." But we have no guarantees. We can not foretell the ravages of time on body and brain. Incoherence, incontinence, and immobility may be ours. Why should I be favored not to suffer these indignities?

The loss of independence is the cruelest reality of all. This was Granny Ross's Hell. Lo, all these years we have been in control!...And here at the end of life...dependence! We will hate the ones who take our independence—our cars and checkbooks—and the hand that feeds us. As Christ said to Peter, "When you are old you will stretch out your arms, and a stranger will bind you fast and carry you where you have no wish to go." These words sound like a nursing home verdict rather that a prophesy of execution. There are times when there is no say-so in our situations. Relatives do what must be done for the good of all. What we Christians bring to these anguished times is our dependence on a mercy that is our lasting independence. We give up these unknown days to an omnipotent and omniscient love that knows no beginning or end. God rest Mr. Dick, Granny Ross, and all of us.

157

Sheep, Goats and Others
of God's Creation

FEBRUARY 1995

> *Many bulls have compassed me; strong bulls of Bashan have beset me round.*
>
> ***Psalm 22***

I have known personally quite a few bulls. When I was a child, Daddy warned me against Old Scamp, a dirty-yellow Jersey with keen horns and a mean, dirt pawing temper. "Never trust a bull," he told us children as he cracked Scamp around the ears with a tobacco stick. Neighbors brought to our barnyard lowing cows, tugging at their halters, because we had a "male" or more genteelly—"a gentleman cow." One of my childhood mysteries was being banished to the house as my father introduced Scamp to his latest captive conquest.

When we began farming and my husband had brood cows, I was introduced to short-horn bulls, no-horn bulls, Angus, Hereford, and various exotic blends as we bred for length and breadth and bone and on and on for attributes to increase the nation's cholesterol. These bulls did not compass me round because they free-roamed among the herd and beset the latest heifer, hoping to find romance on the range. However, Daddy's words of warning stayed with me through the years until, in my old age, I got at ease and trusting of bulls. As a result, a strong bull of Bashan almost bashed me.

We got a new neighbor down Pollard Road who had dreams of being a cattleman after his retirement from the Army. Off to the market he goes and comes home with twenty cows and a two-thousand-pound Angus bull. From the very start Angus had no idea of staying at home—probably the reason he was on the market—and he always made a dash for our place. Why, I don't know. We only had steers, which, City Reader, are bulls who have had an operation. We would herd him home, his owner patched the fence, Angus promptly flattened it again, and back he came for his visit. Our new game for the fall season was *Pen The Bull*.

On my way to the mailbox one Saturday morning, I saw Angus eyeing our steers and eating honeysuckle in the fence row. "Here we go again." I called my husband and we started our usual routine of getting this philanderer down the fence to a holding pen and then calling our neighbor to help us get him home. This morning, Angus wasn't his usual docile self. He seemed to resent this intrusion into his honey-suckle and honey-filled ideas. He did a haughty snort, turned on his massive round steaks, bounded a ditch, lowered his head, and charged me! And I had no cape, only a scream that must have awakened the heavenly host of guardian angels because just as his massive head was on a bee-line collision course with my vitals, he veered to my left. I could feel his wind rush by.

To quote David again after his encounter with the bulls of Bashan, "I am poured out like water, and all my bones are out of joint; my heart is like wax; it is melted in the midst of my bowels...and my tongue cleaveth to my jaws." And if I might be so bold as to add a verse to Psalm 22: "I clingeth to a fence post and jello dost overcome my extremities." Too late the warning, "Never trust a bull."

After my heart glued back together and my knees firmed up, I began to mull and muse this chronicle of bull. One of the prayers of my seventy-two years is the one that all persons my age must pray: "Please, Lord, may I not be a burden in my last years. Please, Lord, let my brain outlast my body. Please, Lord, no nursing home for me. Let a rock fall on me—anything." And here I just blew the perfect answer to my prayer and a news-worthy one at that. No ho-hum dying in bed, but headlines in the paper: Bull Overcomes Local Cowgirl. Rather than accepting this clear answer to my prayers and offering the neighbor-hood some notoriety, I scream and implore heavenly intervention, hastily calling out my guardian angel who must think me totally ambivalent about my requests. Surely I was saved for some yet unknown purpose—maybe to reflect further and separate the transitory from the transcendent.

After Angus and Christmas and New Year, I take stock: Surely it's not how big my bank account is, or my house, or my car, my wardrobe, or my diamond ring. Such earthly matters pale into unimportance as I muse over my years. It is how big the capacity of my heart has become in treasuring those immeasurable gifts that are mine: children and grandchildren, a good husband, an ever-growing circle of friends, and finally, the greatest gift of all—the sure foundation that I am accepted and cherished, here and now and always, by a loving God who has saved me from both the literal and the figurative bulls of Bashan and has included me in being his presence in the world. What glorious knowledge.

"I will disclose thy name unto my brethren: in the midst of the congregation will I praise thee."

P.S. Our neighbor sold Angus the week of this episode. Thanks be to God!

SEPTEMBER 1985

> *A voice is heard in Ramah, lamentations and bitter weeping. Rachel is weeping for her children; she refuses to be comforted for her children because they are not.*
>
> *Jeremiah 31:15*
> *Matthew 2:18*

There is much weeping and lamentation in our cow lot this morning. The calves have been separated from their mothers, then run up a loading chute—amid waving sticks and loud threats—and trucked away to market. Behind are left these inconsolable Rachels, these mother cows, endlessly walking the fence, calling in low, hopeful bellows and then in high, hysterical trumpets for their children who are no more. This will continue all the afternoon and through the long night. Their calls in the night are the most desolate. They refuse to be comforted.

The cow's anguish is real. In her bovine soul, where she suffers her relatedness to all creation, she must sense her role in the "groaning of the creation." She has been called on for a sacrifice too terrible for Treblinka, Auschwitz, or Dachau: Her child, who has only eaten grass and milk, will be eaten by the Great Carnivore. He will pack her child into a truck for a long trip to market, shout and prod it into the sorting pens, subject it to a long, hungry day on the auction block, and once again load it for a cross-country ride to a feedlot in the high plains of Texas. In a restricted area it will be offered the richest of feeds in order to put on pounds and more pounds. When it is layered with the right amount of fat, it will be sacrificed to the national corpulence.

My husband and all the practical-minded farmers will count these mullings and musings as pure drivel. But drivel we must have and starry-eyed ones who sympathize with cows. The cows, too, may have their final retribution: Their force-fed children will block arteries, stop hearts, and, in general, wreak havoc with their *Choice* and *Prime* cuts.

Poor Rachel-cow, continue your weeping and lamentations for your children and all the children of creation. Remember, we have been promised a better time and a better place where the food chain ends.

The wolf shall dwell with the lamb, and the leopard will lie down with the kid, and the calf and the lion and the fatling together—They shall not hurt or destroy in all my holy mountain; for the earth shall be full of the knowledge of the Lord as the waters cover the sea.

Isaiah 11

OCTOBER 1989

Fear not, thou worm Jacob, and ye men of Israel; I will help thee, saith the Load...

Isaiah 41

The worm Jacob was found in our yard, and he wrestled with angels. He was having his sabbatical retreat on a Paulownia tree on the Sunday afternoon before Labor Day amid a great insect hunt being carried on by the Marshall grandchildren. In their boxes and jars these angels had grasshoppers, woolly worms, butterflies, pumpkin bugs, and crickets, when suddenly one of the granddaughters spied Jacob! What the opening of King Tut's Tomb did for the world of archaeology or how the first fires from the Hope Diamond electrified the world of precious stones—this was Jacob's impact on our budding entomologist. And old ones too.

Never! never in my most grotesque imagination could I have dreamed up this worm. On first seeing him, I thought he was a fake to make old grannies jump, but when I saw his angry horns, both fore and aft, and his snapping mandibles, I knew he was a Jacob who would wrestle man or angel. And he was big enough to do it! Imagine the biggest hornworm you ever saw—we call them tobacco worms—multiply him at least four times; give him vicious horns, head and tail; add angry spots here and there; and endow him with a mean disposition that you would only trust a stick to test; and that's the best word picture I can give of Jacob. Only seeing would be believing.

After Worm Jacob had been wondered at by old and young alike, he was given a home in a box amid leaves for fodder and taken to his Peniel—Columbus, Ohio—where his final wrestle would be with "Show and Tell." One of the grandsons in kindergarten was so empowered by Jacob's mien that he forgot his shyness and stood, proud and undaunted, before his class and explained, "This is a special worm found on farms in Tennessee." Jacob survived his testing and is safely in their backyard living under a bush waiting to pupate and emerge next summer. We trust he will be no longer crippled and will be renamed.

Joe Dickson Allen, who writes the nature column for the *Leaf Chronicle*, said this huge larva was probably one commonly know as the "Hickory-Horned-Devil." He had never heard of one this big. This horned-devil in the adult stage is the glorious and spectacular moth known as the Royal Walnut, one of the Imperial Moth group. My encyclopedia shows this ugly worm in all its glory.

So fear not, thou worm Jacob, for you shall be royalty; you are renamed Israel. And let all of us men of Israel take heart from your stage in wormdom. Horned-Devils may know more of the spirit of love and forgiveness than those soft, safe cabbageworms in the garden who haven't wrestled in the dust and haven't been crippled by some overpowering ugliness. The Lord has promised he will help us, metamorphize us.

Out of our ugliness in the dust into the beauty of velvet wings in the heavens, we spread out trust in one who redeems all of his creation. "Blessed be the God of Abraham, Isaac, and Jacob."

SEPTEMBER 1995

> *In the sweat of thy brow shall thou eat bread...cursed in the ground for your sake.*
>
> **God to Adam - Genesis**

God's curse on Adam has been in full blaze this summer. The sweat of my brow and other parts of my anatomy, pointed sunward in the butter beans, cry out for release from so steamy a way to earn my bread. Butter beans, like green peas, should mature in the gentle spring and not wait until 100 degrees to swell their pods; but they dawdle along until butter bean-starved friends and relations converge at the crossroads of the world on Pollard Road.

Who needs the spa or the health club when there are two long rows of butter beans across the garden? The sauna, the aerobic workout, the vascular stimulation and buttocks-tightener are all rolled into one. In this upside down position, the blood courses to the brain, encouraging the mental processes while sweating away foggy thought patterns and petty irritations. God intended a curse, but, alas, the blessing of the butter bean patch—for my sake.

Sheep, Goats & Others of God's Creation

But the blessing of the okra patch is brought into question. Surely God had a good laugh in mind when Adam streaked the okra in his fig-leaf apron. Not only does the plant insist on making hundreds of pods over many weeks, but the hotter and dryer the weather, the more fruitful the plant. With curses intended, God gave it leaves to nettle the okra-plucker with an itch that makes the 100 degrees seem cool and causes its victim to break into a mighty tango, tossing sweaty garments aside in wild abandon.

Five okra plants would be enough—but what to do with a whole row across the garden and a half bushel every other day? Visiting foreigners, especially Frenchmen, "Yuk," and "Urp," and gasp, but we sweaty natives let it slide gently past our epiglottises and slither through out vitals; or we fry it, crunchy and brown, in a black skillet, a reward for the sweat of our brow.

In defense of okra—it is a noble plant. When frost is imminent, the golden days of fall are waning and the okra stalks are as high as a giraffe's ambition, they stand there, still bearing, and festoon the barren garden with their stately shafts. "And God saw that okra was good," and blessed it.

Sweating the brow is part of God's wisdom for his children. "Cursed is the ground for thy sake." To have a hamburger, Adam had to grow grain and hay for his steer, herd him from pasture to pasture, slaughter and skin him at the right time, and then pound the flesh into edible portions. To have a bun for said hamburger, Eve must go out with her scythe, harvest the grain, grind it with a mortar and pestle, knead it into bread, chop wood for the oven, and finally bake the bun. No burger-bellies or bulging buns for these two.

The curse for our generation is "No Sweat." The beguiling snake once again whispers to us: "Take your ease; everything you will ever yearn for is in the markets (two for the price of one); eat and drink and satiate your hunger with this bounty; God's curse on the ground, I now negate. Your bodies will stay strong and lithe as you rest on your couches before your Cyclops."

In the far away hearing of our ears the echo of Isaiah's question sounds through this din of consumption. "Why do you spend your money for that which does not satisfy?" Our inner hungers cannot be assuaged with food. The sweat of our brows and the curse upon the ground for our sake must be endured until we find food for our empty selves. Then we will know our true selves and our worth from the God who made us for his own, in his own image.

Sheep, Goats & Others of God's Creation

SEPTEMBER 1994

> *There is a power, whose care*
> *Teaches thy way along that pathless coast-*
> *The desert and the illimitable air,*
> *Lone wandering, but not lost.*
>
> > ### *To a Waterfowl*
> > ### *William Cullen Bryant*

Our dead-end road is an easy dog and cat dump-off. On our driveway last Sunday afternoon, I came upon an earthbound creature, "lone wandering, but not lost." The illimitable air, seared by the afternoon heat, was alive with phantom dancers; and the desert was an entanglement of honeysuckle vines, fescue stools, blackberry briars and trumpet vines that cascaded down an embankment into a roadside ditch. Added to this setting was our new dog, Ginny, who was doing her most threatening barking and snapping, synchronized with the wagging of her splendidly plumed tail. The lone wanderer was a tiny kitten. Arched to its utmost, each hair standing at terrified attention, spitting its desperate courage at this woolly dragon, it held its spot.

I stopped the car just short of this scene, which gave Ginny even more bravado to bark and dance around so small a threat. When I reached down for this kitten, Ginny, in her jealousy, had to give it a nudge with her sharp nose, which sent the kitty scrambling up my front. At least it was accustomed to being held, and it nestled into my arms and into the car as Ginny ran alongside with a litany of protest. The "power whose care teaches the way along the pathless coast" and roadside had led us aright so far. But the power was not finished.

I had been to the Parish's New Member Committee meeting at Ann Ross's house, where her cat, Ashley, charmed us with her antics. Ann's other beloved cat had died some time ago so a spark went off in my brain: "Ah ha! Miss Ann has her Ashley, of *Gone With The Wind* and I have either found Scarlett or Rhett, (I had no idea which, since cat anatomy has always been a mystery to me) and she needs this wisp of a kitten who has recently survived the burning of Atlanta." Its Persian fur was pure soot with tinges of flamed orange and scorched yellow. Its eyes, blue, not green like Scarlett's reflected the terror of its burning on the wayside desert.

Depositing the now known Scarlett with our cats, Snowball and Tiger, who gave her only sniffs and solemn, condescending stares, I began to search along the uncharted coast for a refuge for Scarlett.

Sheep, Goats & Others of God's Creation

There is a power who cares. I am persuaded of this certainty, and the entwining of circumstances and coincidences is too overwhelming to be deemed blind chance.

Monday morning, I called Ann with the good news of another cat, giving her my best sell. But "No," she was going away, she had Ashley under control and didn't have time for training a baby. But she knew someone. This someone needed a kitten to go with her barn cat who was wild and needed a calming influence. Barn Cat, or B.C. was Hazel Irwin's kitty that had been raised away from two-legged animals and scampered away at their appearance. "Yes," she would take Scarlett. "Oh ye of little faith." The way along the pathless coast was charted.

Scarlett must have had a communication from the power who had cared for her during her wanderings, even though her tiny body was still famished and dehydrated. After a night's feedings, she nestled against me and purred her thanksgiving when I put her in a basket to take her to her home. Imagine a roadside cast-away one day and a cherished kitten in the household of Hazel and Ed Irwin the next! That's nine lives that will be filled with care beyond any cat's longings, even Garfield's. And I hear Scarlett has been renamed "Miss C"—my very own namesake.

So what do we make of this cat tale? It rings pollyannaish in light of the multitude of creatures who perish, flattened on the roadside. It questions with bold cynicism the benevolent eye that watches over creation as daily the holocaust of unwanted animals is carried out. Is this power that teaches the way averting its eye?

William Cullen Bryant was in his teens when he wrote *To A Waterfowl* and his most famous poem, *Thanatopsis*, a meditation on death. His poetry reflects his Calvinistic heritage, his unswerving faith in the universality and ultimate redemption of all creation, the care of the power who from "zone to zone" guides our certain flight. The zones are beyond our knowing. We walk by faith in the "Will of God" for the redeeming, the unfolding, the answering of questions that are as old as the wanderings of Adam and Eve. From the beginning "the creation has groaned and travailed," but one kitty last Sunday was redeemed.

Dear unlost kitty you are found.
Your glorious liberty is here.
Welcome home, Miss C.

Sheep, Goats & Others of God's Creation

MAY 1994

> *My flesh is clothed with worms and dust; my skin is broken and loathsome.*
>
> ### Job 7

Poor Job. He had all the curses except one—chiggers. God in his mercy did spare him this torment. But not me. My flesh seems to be a chigger retreat that has been advertised for its cuisine, its discreet dining areas, and its extended hospitality. As soon as frost is over and weeds show their leaves, the dining room is open for the summer. At this moment I have the first guest of the season, his accommodations being somewhere south by southwest of my umbilicus.

No doubt I inherited this delicious gene from my mother. To her last day she relived her ride from Atlanta to Clarksville on the *Greyhound* with Georgia "red bugs" nestled in her corset. Now my mama had a real corset, the kind you put on by exhaling, shrinking in, and hooking a stalwart row of hooks in the front after having laced the back with enough string to rig a schooner. All around, there were steel stays that held up this garment and forced the decolletage up under the jabot. Thus gusseted, she boarded the bus after having made a prolonged visit to my brother's garden. These "red bugs," which mama declared more virulent than Tennessee chiggers, found their ideal spot since she said they had to have "something to prop against" to get themselves dug in and truly at home. There were thirty-three by her count, all of whom dug in their heels against her steel corset stays and feasted across half-of-Georgia and the full width of Tennessee.

The denouement of her story was the agonizing ecstacy of release, the exultation of thankful flesh when she finally got home, got that corset off, and could scratch!

Through the years we have amassed a catalog of repellents and cures. My father favored kerosene and tight-legged britches. I was told to eat garlic and ate enough to repel the Italian army, but I got chiggers anyway. Bacon grease and salt were used after the attack, as well as baths in vinegar water or baking soda. Loose fitting garments with nothing under them were recommended so the chiggers wouldn't have a bracing point. If you see me streaking the butter beans, you will know this is the latest in chigger-rid. However, all I have ever found effective is scratching. This scratching is only for home, that divine place where you scratch where it really itches.

Sheep, Goats & Others of God's Creation

The marvel of chiggers is in creation's design—even its sense of humor. This tiny mite can cause torment, and I can't even see him. An elephant, I understand, is a kind and benevolent creature, and causes me only wonder and admiration. God called all his creation good and there must be a good purpose for my itchy friends. It must be to put me in my place—the crown of creation brought down from its mighty seat by a mite. As I back up to the doorjamb to scratch under my shoulder blades, I perhaps could hear chigger-chat, if I had ears to hear: "This old gal doesn't taste too bad. She has a bitter twang at times and gets too high and mighty. That's when I give her a good one under her lower right flab. She tries to scratch me off but I hold my territory. We chiggers have rights to places where no others dare go. Get out your nail polish, your *Off*, and your garlic, and we'll show you who is the miteiest in creation."

NOVEMBER 1993

> *Behold, I show you a mystery; we shall not all sleep, but we shall all be changed.*
>
> ### St. Paul

Mystery has come upon me unaware, and I have been changed by its revelation. The first time I saw a male peacock strut his stuff it was as if all the Sultans of the Arabian Nights had suddenly in one royal flash cast at my feet the jewel caches of their empire. I stood before creation, stunned and incredulous, an Alleluia stuck in my throat. From what mind did such a creature come among us, scratching in the trash piles of the barnyard? How could this mystery be? These sudden transports through the unknown, I call my "peacock experiences."

I had such an experience this past weekend. This time it was butterflies.

Callaway Gardens at Pine Mountain, Georgia, has the largest glass-enclosed butterfly conservatory in North America with more than a thousand butterflies, all free and fluttering by. In your hair, on your arms, or hooking rides on your clothing, they seemed "buddyflies" and delighted the children who had them as passengers. But the magic was their wings. I stood like Job, silenced at the edge of mystery. Where was I when God painted these wings and breathed them across the air?

They were from the rain forest of South America—some as big as saucers; others smaller than a dime. Each was a kaleidoscopic wonder.

Sheep, Goats & Others of God's Creation

In this high, glass-enclosed world with its rain forest temperature, the butterflies were at home. One as big as my hand, settled on a branch so I could look into the "eyes" on its wings. They were great sorrowing eyes as though they had fluttered by the horrors of the Holocaust or seen the hunger of little children through the ages; however, the wings were set in such crimson and golden filament as to make Scheharzade's veil seem modest. At length the vision settled into a pan of rotting fruit, sipped its lunch, and winked its winged eyes. Peacock experiences do come down to earth.

Then there were the striped and polka dot butterflies. The black and white ones seemed to be creation's attempt at gene-splicing—the zebra into the butterfly. The polka dots were for the fast lane. They zipped down your face in clown suits, a carnival of neon, buffoons to contrast the black satins who clung among the damp leaves, occasionally unfolding their wings. Here was another mystery: butterfly personality.

In glass cases their life cycle was ongoing: the egg, the larva chomping away on leaves, the pupa encased as if dead in its chrysalis, and at last the freed beauty flexing and drying its wings, ready to explore its world and start a new cycle—the mystery of procreation.

The older I get the less I know. This must be the beginning of wisdom and the taking hold of the "beyond knowing." Peacock experiences are more frequent; and I am surprised by them often as metamorphoses become unclear and passages blur into one another. Beauty arises out of trash piles, rotted fruit, and shriveled cocoons and wonder passes over this world's reality.

"Behold I show you a mystery." In life we are in death; and in death we are in life. We are being changed. From our birth we spend our appointed time as greedy caterpillars and after we are sated, we encase ourselves in the hard shell of our own chrysalis and seem to die. But life is always there. We are redeemed from our encasement. We are glorious flying worms, dust of God's creation that have known the ultimate metamorphosis. We are not asleep but have passed beyond mystery into a place where we shall know as we have been known. Alleluia.

Sheep, Goats & Others of God's Creation

FEBRUARY 1993

Oh, Death, where is thy sting?
Oh, grave, where is thy victory?

Tess, our Schnauzer, of whom I have mulled and mused muchly, died December 28th. The sting of death is with us. How vacant the bed where she lay, how empty her pan and bowl, how bereft the household of her bark; and how aware I am of our mutual mortality.

In the twinkling of an eye, the veterinarian let her go gently. My husband said there was instant release, away from the sting of her persistent pain and blinded confusion and into the peace of humane ending. Relaxed for its returning, the still warm furry ball was brought home to me.

In a trunk in the attic I found an old bedspread—a thick, white one with fringe—that seemed a fitting burial garment. We shrouded Tess well in several folds of this cozy old coverlet, loaded onto the truck an axe, the posthole digger, and a sharp spade; then the cortege processed to her favorite fence row and stopped underneath a great walnut tree. There we buried her where nothing could disturb her returning to the basic elements, back into the hands through whom all things are made.

With Tess as my example, my wish is that I be granted the same graces as she, even though they be a scandal to all current standards and mores. If my departing be too painful for human endurance, may some noble hemlock be my potion. Spare the dignity of my departing the indignity of tubes and machines.

When my breath no longer comes, may hands that love me wrap my husk in some comforting old blanket that has served the family well, find a suitable box, and nestle me into the good earth. If my going be at night, bury me soon after sunrise; and if by day, find my spot before the setting of the sun. May such words of comfort be read over my spot that all shall rejoice and be glad.

Oh, to be kept away from strange halls and hands and pink-velvet plush. Let no set smile be pasted on my dumb lips nor painted blush be on my bloodless cheeks. Allow no prying eye to invade my defenseless face to comment on its naturalness or otherwise; and lastly, let no sad dirge be piped across my discarded bones.

When time, alas, has reduced my elements into the stuff of creation, may the roots of some stalwart oak or delicate dogwood pierce my heart and take such sustenance that acorns will be a banquet for the squirrels or the blossoms of the dogwood be so radiant that the springing world of birds will sing a sweeter song. This autumn I shall look for a special crop of walnuts under Tess's tree.

"Oh grave, where is thy victory?" St. Francis of Assisi gave us his answer. He was convinced of the brotherhood of all creation, respecting all creatures, however lowly, and once preached to the sparrows, reminding them that their Father's eye was upon them, knowing when they fell. He was confident of the redemption of all of God's handiwork, the re-creation of all mortal dust, the promise of the one who declares, "Behold I make all things new."

When the walnuts fall and the acorns flourish and the birds sing, rejoice for Tess and me. We shall dance and jump and bark and sing among the stars when we behold the glory that is to be revealed in us. Our death is swallowed up in victory.

AUGUST 1992

The Lord is my shepherd, I shall not want.
Psalm 23

I have an earthly shepherd; I shall not want for instruction into the shepherding of steers. For you, gentle reader, who do not know the difference between bulls and steers, steers have had an operation. My husband, with my most able assistance, has just delivered two hundred and six of these potential steaks to the feedlots on the high plains of Kansas. This man, who is a mind reader of recalcitrant bovine flesh, has me trained well. He has implanted into my genetic make-up the instincts of an Australian Blue Heeler dog and the thought processes of rodeo steers. I can nip heels and outthink the wiliest longhorn; therefore, there's no stampede too thunderous nor steers too rebellious that I can't head them off and lead them in paths of righteousness.

First, there is the business of getting steers to lie down in green pastures. It sounds easy, but they must cross the road. Since cattle only see in black and white (*Drover's Journal*, October 1972) the double yellow stripes down the middle of the road look to them like two long ditches and these stripes must be painted out or there is no setting hoof across to greener pastures. The correct herding toggery is a must. The steers are accustomed to my husband's blue jeans and denim shirts which means no white clothes and no uncovered white locks or it's stampede

171

time. Therefore, at roundup I am swathed in blue denim and my crowning glory pinched beneath a *Guthrie Feed Mill* cap. First ironclad instruction: Never drove in white.

Then there is the problem of leading by still waters. Time-of-day is a prime factor in droving. Ferdinand likes to come out early, fill up his first stomach with about two bushels of fodder, and then retreat to some cool bower to leisurely belch up his cud. He won't move easily from this contentment. Get him early and hungry, invite him to a new pasture, and he will run over you rather than having to be driven. The heat of the day makes all cattle seek the shallows of the creek or deep shady places, away from flies. Forget high noon as moving time by any sort of water. Next instruction: Be cool; drove early.

Sometimes the heads must be anointed with oil for pinkeye. Steers don't like to be rounded up, corralled, and run through the chutes to the head gate, especially the rodeo type. They have been hemmed up, roped, and turned loose until they can find the remotest corner and highest bluffs of your pasture. You must outthink them. Hanging from the highest precipice on the bluff land, I await the mountain climbers when my husband starts the herd toward the cattle pen. Doffing my cap and shaking my hoary head, I send this outwitted stampede off in the right direction. Remember: Always be bullheaded.

After the cattle are together again, my Australian Blue Heeler genes come into play. I can sense the steers' flight pattern—how close I can come and at what angle. You instinctively know after you've done it long enough. Cattle not only see forward as we do, but sideways and backwards having eyes on the sides of their face and heads rotating on long swinging necks. You creep and crouch along just so close and no closer, all the while anticipating the exact right time to move them on. Absolute silence is a requisite of a good stock dog. Resist the urge to bark and nip heels.

From time to time steers gather in groups in secluded spots, refusing to go anywhere. They will only mill around. They must be ruminating about restoring their souls and their boredom with two-hundred-and-six others of their kind. My husband-cowherd says leave them alone until they decide to stop their contemplation of things that might have been. Allow steers time to discuss their operation.

My earthly shepherd has trained me well. I have learned there are boundless skills to be mastered by the human family with none so lowly that it is not without honor. The simple shepherds at Bethlehem were the first to hear the tidings of great joy for all people. Those of the lowest degree were raised to the highest of heralds. Thus, I proudly take my rod and staff and slog through the cattle pens, knowing full well that in all the days of my life I have never wanted for any blessing and I shall dwell in the house of the Lord—both here and now and through the valley of the shadow of death—forever.

MAY 1992

Rachel is weeping for her children; she refuses to be comforted for her children because they are not.

Jeremiah 31

Our Collie dog, Taffy, was a Rachel in her time. Each spring she presented the farthest corner underneath the house with at least eight puppies and sometimes more. No restraints could keep her from romance and its fruitful folly. The hayloft wasn't safe. We didn't know dog-Romeos could climb ladders. The corncrib wasn't safe because Taffy and her suitors could eat planks. In desperation one season, we tried the safety of the back porch and lost the foundation of the house. Romance always won out. Just after the puppies' birth, Taffy was a doting mother, spending long hours in tender nursing and grooming amid all the infant whimpering. But when the puppies were about six-weeks old, chewing and tumbling and playing, Taffy would retreat from this entanglement with several still hanging on. Anywhere she went, here they came and grabbed on again. There was no respite. Her long, silky hair was frazzled and her underside pawed bare—a martyr to motherhood.

In the meantime we took a census of all dogless domiciles and at length found the puppies a home, the selling point being that Taffy was "registered." In fact, the word got around of her puppies' worth as watch dogs and stock dogs which erased all question of questionable paternity. Taffy didn't seem to mind at all to see the crowd dwindle, but on the final day when the last puppy was given away she went into such a state of mourning that she refused all food. Lying on the front porch, she put her long nose between her front paws and lay there motionless, day after day, following our movements with her sad eyes. Her children were not. She would not be comforted.

At length, I experienced Taffy's suffering. Our older son was getting ready to go away to college in Atlanta and I said to myself, "This isn't going to be bad at all; some women are so silly and sentimental about their first one leaving home. He'll be back in a few weeks."

Sheep, Goats & Others of God's Creation

About two days after he left I put my long nose between my front paws and stayed on the front porch of grief two weeks, weeping for him. When our only daughter left, I was better prepared; but, still, with her being the only girl and the world so wide and wicked, and her enjoying some of its wiles, my grief followed her. The telephone bill tripled. But when my baby left, I could be comforted. He only went as far as Cookeville and he had a car. He could come home!

So what did Taffy learn and what did I learn from motherhood? We know for sure joy and grief are its rare mixture. We know that we were frayed and frazzled, dazed and befuddled; but we shudder to think of the void in our lives without the lessons that have issued from our very own bodies. We pity the childless. My children have made me into what I am—they mothered me. They have taught me humility, charity, and, yes, some patience. I have learned to live by Hope, and I continue to cling more closely to this virtue above all others. And finally my children have helped me understand grace. They were my unmerited gifts, miracles that only the God of unimaginable creativity and love could bestow.

So on Mother's Day, Taffy and I are comforted for our children because our children are, and our little children have led us.

FEBRUARY 1991

And he shall separate them one from another as a shepherd divides the sheep from the goats.

Some people of our parish and some also across the diocese have a lofty question. Our revered limestone church has a magnificent front facade with its heavenward spire and its double-entry doors. But the back of the church? Why the door to the outside? It's fifteen feet off the ground, beautifully red, without steps, leading off into thin air?—a mysterious exit.

It's really quite simple: Anyone grounded in the scriptures and the ways of flocks would know. There is a door into the sheepfold for sheep, so there must be a door out back for stray goats. Rather than trying to herd the goats out the front, it is easier to corner them in the sacristy, judge their goatiness, and cast them into outer space. At Trinity, this door has been sadly neglected.

According to our church historian, Richard Gildrie, this door was given its first usage in 1892 at which time a nanny, bleating in the choir, was forcibly ejected on the fifth verse. Then in 1902 some strays got in the wrong pew, made some bla-a-a-tant mistakes in the liturgy while their kids gamboled up and down the aisles. Later one old billy got to leaping too high with some ewe lambs of the flock; and then in 1912 other goats, coming from a backward fold, praised the Lord out loud. And their wool! It was a mess—all unshorn and turned loose in the wilderness. Immediately all these were judged unworthy and banished out the back door. Since then, however, the vestry has clamped down on such swift judgment because many in the sheepfold felt some nagging kinship with these errant goats and sympathized especially with the old, rheumatic nannies.

In 1991, however, with the advent of the technological age, some prize-winning sheep felt we must be more discriminating. The installation of sophisticated electronic sensors can detect goatiness in a billionth part, leaving no question to the final separation, sounding an alarm which can dispatch a goat out the back door in the twinkling of an eye. So, *Beware*, all ye goats!

Those coming for communion, unworthily, or not properly baptized—too much or too little water in some alien watering trough—will set off the goat buster. "Out, out, spots and blemishes." Then there will be the-truth-and-nothing-but-truth sensors. In this sheepfold, wedding parties will be much at risk. Some prospective mothers-in-law who answer to "Who gives this woman in marriage?" will activate this alarm and will be grabbed in mid-utterance in all their mother-of-the-bride finery, and cast out. Uncertain brides and grooms of the flock who promise to "love and cherish" will be whisked away by their cathedral trains and tuxedo tails. Certainly the confessions of sin will cause a thunderous goat stampede. Before the line "we are truly sorry and humbly repent" rather than ringing a four-alarm abandon-pews, the goats will jump, en masse, clogging the rear door of the sheepfold, forgetting the empty space below. I, myself, am looking into air bags, parachutes, and padded underwear.

So dear Sheep and Goats of Trinity and the Diocese, if the explanation does not answer your lofty question of our high and exalted rear door, I shall refer you to the final authority of doors and the sheep and goats thereof:

"Verily, verily, I say unto you, I am the door of the sheepfold—and he that cometh unto me I will in no wise cast out."

These words from the Good Shepherd have given us sheep and goats and hybrids gracious comfort, and the vestry has voted to put a slide out the rear door.

Sheep, Goats & Others of God's Creation

MAY 1987

Who is that coming up from the wilderness leaning on her beloved?
Song of Solomon

My brother lives near a small lake in Atlanta where wild ducks make their home. The lawns of the houses all around go down to the edge of the water which means that the only nest sites are in the shrubbery and flower beds of the yards. In one of my brother's prize azalea beds, Mr. and Mrs. Duck had chosen a spot to build their romantic bower. The nest was protected on one side by a birdbath, on the other by a most glorious *Pink Glory* azalea and was undergirded by a handy bed of fallen leaves and pine needles which, mingled with the down Mrs. Duck had plucked from her breast, made the perfect camouflage. She nestled so close to the ground in her speckled nest with her feathers blended into the fallen leaves that, if it were not for her lone shining eye, you would declare this just another accumulation of the April wind underneath the *Pink Glory*.

I stood and stared into this shining eye—this stoic, omniscient, unmoving eye—that seemed to fathom the love of the Creator for the rightness of his creation. Mrs. Duck knew she had found her place. She sat there hour after hour with her eggs at her downy bosom awaiting the time when her progeny would break out of their crackled prisons; but more immediately, waiting for the long shadows when Mr. Duck would arrive and escort her from her dry egg-sitting duty to a joyous reunion with her beloved and the water.

They rose from the edge of the azalea bed on wild wings and away to the lake where many a tail-up and bob-down made for a good supper. As the shadows got longer and the time to return to the nest drew nearer, they paddled their way to an inlet at the foot of the lawn. Here amid the most intimate and inquisitive quacking they spoke of private things as they circled and dived and reveled in their duckhood. Each delighted in the other. Gone was the dull matron with the down-plucked breasts. Here was a slick flirt tantalizing her beloved with her best diving form and her wet body. Mr. Duck took at length a perch on a fallen log to treasure every movement of her presence, while she bobbed in the security of his total commitment to their place in creation.

As the sun was setting and the light growing late, we sat on the carport to watch their returning and their parting. From the lake's edge, through the undergrowth, onto the open lawn they came, cautious step

176

after cautious step. Mr. Duck was a sentry par excellence. His high arched neck and searching eye were ready for dog or fox or whatever preys on baby ducks and nests. With a quick jump-of-a-flight over the azaleas, Mrs. Duck soon settled back into her shining eye position, but Mr. Duck stood, a feathered statue, like a guard at Buckingham Palace. He did not move! Only after he was convinced that all was well for the night did he suddenly, on a great flurry of flight, wing away from his beloved into the dark.

Mr. and Mrs. Duck's mutual cherishing and domestic tranquility testify to a union that pales the disordered ones we know. The creator gave them a precious gift we struggle for and often never find. Oh, that we could do what ducks do and lean on our beloved in the wilderness.

OCTOBER 1986

Our Schnauzer, Tess, has been the terror of the backyard. We have a long generation of cats, progeny of Dorothy Ann Russo's cats, who have moused with us for many years. When they have their kittens in the barn and then bring them to the smokehouse where all the cats are fed, they must run the gauntlet of Tess. She is ruthless with kittens. One shake of the head with her rat-killing instinct, and that's the end.

One of last year's females, thin and calicoed with a long, long tail, had her first pregnancy this summer. When I surveyed this most unpromising mother, I committed her litter to their fate as they crossed no-kitten-land since their mother seemed so small and defenseless when compared to our other three females.

About three weeks ago the middle of the morning was shattered by a sudden explosion of hysterical barking, the kind that you know there's something at bay. Remembering that Tess was abroad, I rushed outside to see if I could rescue some hapless kitten when this yelping, insulted, bloody-nosed gray ball of fur tumbled from the brambles around the smokehouse and hid behind my feet—Tess in full rout. Who but poor stringy-tailed Calico spat through the brushes, hot-eyed with every hair standing, in full and furious pursuit. The three other females were peeping out through the rat holes under the door, six incredulous eyes stunned at this scene in their domain. Goliath had fallen.

Stringy Tail and her lone kitten have had a peaceful September. Tess leaves the back door like a cartoon character with her leg-wheels spinning, but when she rounds the corner of the house and the mother cat

177

takes her station, there is a wide Tess diversionary action on the other side of the shed. The little yellow kitty nestles against its mother and if cats can smile, that kitten does. The other females have taken courage, not losing as much fur diving through cracks or surrendering their dignity up a tree. Stringy Tail's eyeballs and arched back are all that is needed to send Tess to dig for her mole or smell out the groundhog population.

Since one mother cat has claimed her own, a benediction has fallen on the barnyard. The birds seem to congregate more, the cucumbers and beans have decided to bear their fall crops, and the turnip greens are making turnips even though the rain has been sparse. One creature of creation has blessed us by claiming its space, its right to be, its inheritance. One small spot of courage has not only made the cat's lives better but has made the bully satisfied not to bully. Blessed are the pussycats for the smokehouse is theirs.

JUNE 1986

Since I am a lover of birds, I have a small St. Francis of Assisi, made from Red River Block's best concrete, standing guard over the yard. The ironic twist to this guardian saint's position is that this happens to be the favorite roosting place for our sassy mockingbird. He, in his exuberance over the prospect of a new nest of babies, flies up and down, joyfully singing his incredible repertoire, all the while oblivious to this sacred head. You know the rest: Long white tears weep down St Francis' gentle face and his robe is adorned with more than dust. Ever so often the garden hose has to come to the rescue so poor St. Francis can get his sainthood a bit more saintly.

But as I ponder this gentle man, this mystic who knew all animal life as his brothers and sisters, I am persuaded that he would be more than pleased with this scene. A few of God's own insects and seeds, which had passed through this digestive tract to feed his brother mocking bird, would make for a sacred porridge to nourish the unity of the universe. He understood the bounty of all life, the joy of song and new birth, the rhythm of fertilizer and growth, the wisdom of nature scattering her seed, and the necessity of the seed's dying before its resurrection. The joy of the mockingbird was the same joy requisite to St. Francis' order. Their songs resounded to the glory of God and creation.

All St. Francis asked was a bit of food as he tramped along the countryside. All our mockingbird asks is a singing spot and enough insects to feed his babies. So he and St. Francis are brothers. Their joy comes from a simple nest, a joyous song to sing, food for the day, and a oneness with the totality of creation.

Oh, that we might listen more closely to the melodies of our brothers.

NOVEMBER 1984

The Lord God said to the serpent, "I will put enmity between you and the woman and between your seed and her seed; he shall bruise your head, and you shall bruise his heel."
                                        Genesis 3

In the late afternoon, I like to go for a walk. Hanging on to some branches and vines as I ambled down the bluff behind our house, I almost put my foot on a long black snake. He lay there, torpid and defenseless, stretched across my path. In his autumnal state, between the summer's sun and the winter's hibernation, he could only move his head; and he surveyed me with flicking tongue and a cold, glass-eyed acceptance of one who had come to bruise his head. Somehow God's curse on the snake in the garden never made too much impression on me; and as I, standing in my towering position, returned his survey, I felt no enmity between his head and my heel, not to mention our seed.

I found a small stick and gave him a poke. He was practically immobile. Shouldering the awesome audacity of going against one of God's first curses, I felt it was time for some understanding after these eons of bruised heads and heels. A blessing rose up in me and I pronounced the Peace to this fellow creature, this Brother Snake—"May the peace of the Lord be always with you." His flicking tongue and questing eye never left this tall apparition standing over him. His comprehension of this scene in his reptilian eye and brain could have profound meaning far beyond any concept in our hard-domed craniums. St. Paul tells us "in him were all things created" and who knows the mind of the serpent? Who knows his role in the groaning of the whole creation and its final redemption?

God himself said he was the most subtle of the creatures; and when Christ sent his apostles on their first mission, he admonished them to be wise as serpents. So I mull and muse wherein lies the wisdom of this lowly traveler in the dust. Is man, the one made in the image of God who has dominion over his fellow creatures, half as wise? The snake

179

knows who he is: He has wisdom to survive, to keep his kind in perfect harmony within his ordered place. He passes his genes down the ages in a gracious protection for his progeny, which he neither abuses nor abandons; and he does not destroy his fellows. He knows the swing of the stars, the breath of the wind, and the peace of a long sleep.

From the serpent's remote encounter in the garden with man, he must tremble that this prideful creature can be beguiled so easily. From his atavistic wisdom, he must know that this man so intent on being his own God will not only destroy himself but all the Gardens of Edens; and here on a bluffside, he lies frozen at the feet of a member of this species so determined to destroy.

I listened with my heart for his benediction, but I never heard, "May the peace of the Lord be also with you." Maybe, dear *Trumpet* reader, he thought as you perhaps do—"She's gone soft in the head, talking with snakes after too much summer's sun."

JANUARY 1996

> *The cow is of the bovine ilk;*
> *One end is moo, the other milk.*
> **Ogden Nash**

January is our month for tales to chase away the gloom. This January, my venture into bovine genetics, as a presumed expert, should amuse or amaze you; or should, perhaps, be written off as "a tale told by an idiot." But this tale is told by a truthful idiot whose expertise in all things continues to diminish as the years unfold the enormity of my ignorance.

As a preface to my "profound" knowledge of bovine genetics and gynecology, I shall remind you of my Southern Lady heritage, my having been shielded from all procreation activities on our farm, and not being allowed to say the word Bull—only male cow. Queen Victoria and my mama intended for me to be a lady, but when I was told "the gentleman cow" was only getting up higher on the cow to look over the fence," I reasoned the fence wasn't that high.

In the course of human events, I strayed far from Kirkwood. Would you believe Brazil? My own dear brother aided in leading me astray and losing my innocence; but in the process, I became an expert in fields far beyond the lady and gentlemen cows of a gentler time.

Sheep, Goats & Others of God's Creation

My brother headed the international sales division of *US Steel-Chemical*, and one of his most prominent and wealthy customers was one Fernando Cordoso, Secretary of Agriculture for the state of Sao Paulo, Brazil. Dr. Cordoso was born into one of the colonial Portuguese families with vast holdings across the nation. He had dedicated his life's work to upgrading the quality of the country's cattle, horses, and grain corps. Under his study he had experimental cattle plantations, hybrid grain programs, and a far-away rain forest enterprise. This was no small potatoes man.

In the further course of human events, Dr. Cordoso wanted to add to the gene pool of horses in his country, which prompted my brother to send him to Tennessee to look over the Walking Horse situation. You know who got him? Yes, we added many a mile to trucks and cars, visited every stable in Middle Tennessee and some in Alabama and could set our car on automatic pilot to Ellington Agricultural Center in Nashville with vials of horse blood and semen to be tested. These things were my job.

After several months of red tape—both American and Brazilian, tangled, untangled and re-entangled—deals done and undone, and tests finally cleared, several planeloads of horses were flown to Dr. Cordoso, who had long ago abandoned the Tennessee scene. In appreciation of my husband's efforts, he named one of his stables *The Jack Marshall*. I shall not give you my comment of this appellation.

In 1978 and with converging events, I arrived in Brazil. Dr. Cordoso was determined to show me every courtesy, every attention, every educational exposure at his command—and they were legion. Already awaiting me there were my brother-in-law, Jim Marshall, who was stationed with the Foreign Service in the embassy in Brasilia, and our daughter, Emily, visiting her uncle. Dr. Cordoso was ready for us in Sao Paulo. When my plane landed, I was met with chauffeured limousine and a hostess with a long itinerary of sights and sound until Dr. Cordoso could get us all off to one of his plantations so "'Charlie' could understand and review my breeding techniques and genetic experiments." I'm sure he thought I was one of those worldly-wise, liberated American women who knew animal husbandry and the new methods thereof. All I knew was the moo end and the milk end and not to say *Bull*. More ends were in sight!

Dr. Cordoso had his cowboys awaiting our arrival with the herds rounded up in lowing groups along the driveway, all the while giving me technical discourses on this strain and that genetic blend and on and

181

on. I put on a great face of knowing. The last activity of the day, the great culmination of all his efforts to improve the kine of Brazil, was the artificial insemination procedures. The in-season cows had been cut off in a holding pen while technicians with tall canisters of bubbling dry ice stood by with the frozen semen. All was ready.

First, the cows "had to be inspected for any malformation or disease." Promptly the front of old Clara Belle was run into a chute, clamped absolutely immobile in a cow-long wooden vise, a well-lit viewing tube was inserted into the proper place, and I was given this instruction: "Now, 'Charlie' I want you to be the first to look at their tissue. Check to see if it is a healthy pink and if there are any abnormal growths." With this assignment, I came forward, bent over, squinted one eye, and peered down into the most intimate interior of this poor cow. For all I knew, this view could be Queen Victoria's pink petticoat or a dose of Pepto-Bismol. After my inspection, a flexible wand with the frozen semen capsule on the end came from the seething cauldron and added further insult to this cold mating.

Then it was Jim Marshall's turn. He, who stands some six-feet-five inches, folded his frame to the next cow-end and blinked down this same gynecological route. The whole picture was so ludicrous and so dead serious that the three of us—Jim, Emily, and I—came unglued and completely lost it. We laughed, we whooped, we slapped our thighs, and tears of uncontrolled laughter rolled down our faces—all to our host's dumb-struck mystification. The poor Brazilian cowboys and technicians, who spoke only Portuguese, didn't have a clue why we were having hysterics. All were in awe of Dr. Cordoso and probably felt we were insulting him. I'm sure we ruined their long day's work, done for my benefit, and I could not communicate my regrets.

For dinner, we went to Dr. Cordoso's guest house on this manicured plantation. I took our most urbane host aside and explained to him my sheltered upbringing. In the upper classes, Brazilian women are most protected and pampered, and he understood. He had seen me driving farm trucks and helping with cattle so he drew the conclusion that I had great interest in all ends of the cow. I did. But not this much interest!

Dr. Cordoso had a guest register for his visitors, which listed their name, country, and occupation. My entry read: Charlotte Marshall, United States, *Artificial Insemination Inspector*. Dr. Cordoso suggested the title. He has a grand sense of humor, and we have had many laughs about my inspection since 1978.

Sheep, Goats & Others of God's Creation

For the New Year, 1996, this cow tale must reinforce the saying, "To understand all is to forgive all." Who knows from what world others come? How can we judge when we don't know the intricate complexities that formed them? How can we know when our humor is another's hurt. How can we escape our folly?

May God's love follow our foolishness through this new year. May we be kind to our own foolishness as well as other's, letting it rest in God's wisdom. If you have any trouble with the bovine ilk, knowing the moo end from the milk end, not to mention other ends, just call the expert. I know where to look.

Holidays and Hapless Happenings

DECEMBER 1987

We have seen the rising of his star and have come to pay him homage.

Matthew 2

When my children were babies crawling around the Christmas tree and chewing on the ornaments, I started an unsightly, but unbreakable and inedible collection of plastic decorations. There were round Santa Clauses, Santa Claus boots, a one-eyed reindeer, sleighs, multicolored bells, and garish stars in assorted sizes and colors. All this was for the lower tier of the tree. As we graduated up the tree to the breakable and not-so-chewable variety of festoons, nostalgia had me relegate this assortment to the highest closet shelf where it languished until I got grandchildren. Now that puts one in gear. Dragging this twenty-plus year old, tooth mottled collection down off the high shelf, I was told by the Christmas Spirit to have an outside tree, and Santa Claus knew a holly was growing beside the kitchen window. With newly bought outside lights, the stepladder, my younger son who hardly needs a stepladder, we soon had an outside tree whose glories indeed filled the skies! Christmas darkness, K-Mart, and antiquated plastic wrought a miracle.

The light of the next day, however, was not so kind. The miracle of night had vanished as I mulled over these veteran ornaments tossing in the December wind. In the full light of day they were revealed for what they were—plastic pretenders who could only glitter in the dark by an artificial light. Mulling and musing more, I saw the symbolic me in these plastic decorations—and all of us—swaying in the winter wind, wondering who we are, hiding from ourselves on high shelves or in reflected glory in the dark. I have been them all.

I have been the round Santa Claus with my "ho-ho-ho's," the buffoon, who on the inside was quaking with guilts and fears, afraid for anyone to know the real me. I played the plastic Santa Claus to keep everyone laughing so they wouldn't sense my need to cry or my need to confess.

The one-eyed reindeer is mine too. I see with one eye what I want to see. My eye is the true way to see, the only way, and I will not open my blinded eye to any other view; thus, my neighbor is not seen unless he comes into the field of my "right" vision. My blind eye I reserve for my interior—angers too old to see their faces and mistakes too painful to review their scenes.

Along with my one-eyedness are my plastic bells, the cacophony of sound that keeps me from hearing. I cannot be silent and empty myself to hear you . I must clang away and outring your puny tolling. I cannot listen. But if I am honest, my sounding brass and tinkling cymbal is my fear again—I cannot let you hear how lonesome I am and how afraid I am. I must fill myself with noise so I can't feel my pain or hear yours.

Then I hang up my glittering stars to dazzle you with my brightness. I'm going to outshine you. My glitter is just that when I put on the pretense of knowing, of shining forth. My poor star! In the vast totality of knowledge—known and unknown, learned and forgotten, from the Alpha to the Omega—my plastic star shudders in the December night and hides itself among the holly leaves.

Last year when I took the decorations off the tree, I overlooked one small, white star. Later in January as I walked by I saw it hanging there on a back limb. I said to myself, "I'll let you stay. I'll just see how long you can hang there before some big wind comes along and blows you off." It is still there. In my musings, it somehow represents the vulnerability, yet hope, of all small stars who hang on. It doesn't seem to make a big deal of its weak grasp on its limb, its lack-luster in a glittering world, its helplessness in the wind. Yet it hangs on, a strength in weakness, soon to join again its plastic host in their Christmas glory.

Whence the hope of so small a star?—Has it not seen through all the seasons the rising of the morning star and then has seen it again as the evening star when the final light of day has gone? Has it not seen the steadfast star, the North Star, as the Dippers swing around it in their appointed path through the rush of the universe? Has it not seen the bright stars of Orion—Rigel and Betelgeuse—whose lights of the first magnitude have guided sailors from Ulysses to the odyssey through space? Yes—and last Christmas this small star saw the rising of his star, along with all the gathering both inside and outside my kitchen. May all of us who have seen the rising of his star come to pay him homage.

Merry Christmas and Happy New Year. I love you *All*.

Holidays and Hapless Happenings

FEBRUARY 1987

T
> *herefore shall a man leave his father and mother, and shall Cleave unto his wife; and they shall be one flesh.*
>
> **Genesis 2:24 KJV**

For St. Valentine's Day I was attempting a musing, tender and romantic, with hearts and flowers, when suddenly the verb Cleave twanged my heartstrings.

Cleave?...I have heard of a few wife-cleavers in my day who rather than making the flesh one, made it several, whereupon their wives *Clave* to their fathers and mothers. To give the ladies equal time, I personally knew a big, rough, red-haired woman who cleaved her husband with an axe; whereupon, he *Cleft* the door with his exit, and he too *Clove* to his father and mother. The fellow with the cloven hooves must have had an active voice in these violent cleavages. But back to our conjugation.

Get your dictionary and look up these two verbs: *Cleave*. They are spelled the same, pronounced the same, and their etymology is a rare study in linguistics. However, their meanings are 180 degrees apart. One means to divide by a blow, split; the other—to cling to, to be faithful. As I mull and muse the connotations of these homonyms, I begin to see the two *Cleaves* as the verbs on which our relationships stand or fall. We either cleave unto one another, or we cleave one another.

The romantic hearts and flowers and cupid's arrows can play many a deceitful trick on our psyches in the name of love, which is often biology. When the honeymoon is over, the stars in our eyes no longer twinkle, and our beloved is found to be mortal, we crash down to earth as anything but one flesh. We are two unique individuals, cleaved, often already out of love and disillusioned. Our choices are these: Do we take the bare-bone reality of right cleaving and begin the struggle for mutual freedom and support? Or do we retreat into a barren relationship of wrong cleaving with neurotic dependencies? Or do we cleave the relationship? The latter in many cases is the only way out. Some relationships can't work.

But those who survive these cleavages are those who know what to cleave unto and what to cleave. They let go, yet sustain; they give freedom, yet closely cherish. They seek the more excellent way.

May God give us his grace as we cleave unto him and unto the ones he has given us.

187

Holidays and Hapless Happenings

FEBRUARY 1994

Let not a widow be taken into your number under three score years old, having been the wife of one husband...but the younger widows refuse, for when they have begun to wax wanton against Christ, they will marry.

1 Timothy

February is the month for valentines and romance. My grandmother had many a tale to tell of her romances, of widowhood, of slanderous accusations against her during this state, and of her nose-thumbing at St. Paul's rules for the deportment of widows. Romance waxed her wanton twice after having been a "true" widow at twenty.

Grandmother's first husband, my father's father, died when Daddy was two. Greene Oliver had come riding into Rudolphtown, down from Louisville, looking for a farm and a good wife. Mattie Winn caught his eye even though she had been known to do some two-stepping behind Little Hope Baptist Church. But true love would out, and my grandfather married Mattie when she was eighteen.

After his death, Grandmother recalled her desolation, compounded by the expectations of widowhood from church and family. At the beginning of her mourning period, she wore the heavy widow's veil; and after the proper period, she was allowed into a lighter version. Her clothes went from black to gray and, at last, white for summer. How long this decent mourning lasted I do not know; but however long, it was too long for Grandmother who, like Scarlett in *Gone With The Wind*, tapped her toes under her widow's weeds. She came again to live in her father's home along with my two-year old father. They lived there until my father was eight.

Then scandal of scandals! Isaac Oliver had followed his brother to Tennessee and thought that eight years was long enough for Mattie to mourn. He proposed. Little Hope went wild with widow rules. Mattie was almost refused continued membership, not being the faithful widow of one husband. Also, she was riding her horse too fast for ladies, even though she did ride side-saddle. Amid all this furor, she and Isaac rode to Adams, tied the knot, and St. Paul's following at Little Hope cooled off when Mattie and Isaac moved away to Kirkwood.

My father revered "Uncle Ike." As an old man, Uncle Ike's death brought tears in his voice as he recalled his step-father's instructions to

Holidays and Hapless Happenings

him in his eighteenth year. He was to be responsible for his mother and half-sister.

Grandmother kept the second set of widow's rules until my father married at thirty-four and brought my mother into the household. "One house is not big enough for two women and two women can't share one man," she declared. Therefore, she mailed a valentine.

There was a widower about a mile across the fields who could see my grandmother's lamp at night, shining from her upstairs bedroom window. After the valentine, he sent a note: "Mattie, if I can come calling, let your window shade up and down tonight." You know the rest. When Grandmother was fifty-four, I got the only grandfather I ever knew—Josephus King. Being a tobacco buyer, "Seph" moved Mattie into town and bought her a stucco house with a bathroom! The great footed tub provided me my first town bath and water slide. A blood grandfather could not have been more patient and generous; and this same Josephus King was the true grandfather of Howard King, husband of Teena King of our congregation and also the grandfather of Jim Holleman of Conroy, Marable and Holleman.

Despite Paul's letter to Timothy, here was a romance I witnessed that waxed into genuine love. I believe our Christ would applaud the last years of my grandparents' delight in each other. St. Paul could soar so high into faith, into hope, into transcendence, yet descend so low into nit-picking hatefulness. And he did want the women in their place. If he had had a wife, his epistles no doubt would be vastly different, depending on the quality of the relationship. My grandmother would have done him good. Perhaps he would have waxed wanton for widows.

FEBRUARY 1992

Stay me with flagons, comfort me with apples, for I am sick of love.
Song of Solomon

It's Valentine time again and I find myself mulling and musing into my repository of love quotations past.

Aunt Lucy said she didn't have any patience with love. Men weren't worth loving, children were too messy and too much trouble to love, and God was too far away to love; beside, she couldn't love anyone who created such an awful mess and then let it run itself. The worst of his mess was giving out all the lust that made these messy, bad children.

Uncle Bud, who was quite a ladies' man, assured us that love was something you could get farther behind in and caught up on quicker than anything else. No doubt he wasn't referring to the agape variety. My daddy used to say that when you were courting these pretty girls you loved them so much that you could eat them up; and after you married them, you wished you had. From my mother-in-law, the late Bishop of Rossview, comes this simile quoted when she was in one of her whimsical moods:

> *Love is like a lizard*
> *It runs around your heart*
> *Then jumps at your gizzard.*

Then there are the quotes we all know: "Love is blind, it makes the world go round, it conquers all"; and then we blithely quote from the First Epistle of John the most outrageous one of all: "God is love." Stay me with flagons of Jack Daniel! This is a hard saying, one to skew your theological tam and leave you helpless before your pitiful understanding of such a statement.

Then I hark back to grammar school where we cut paper valentines from our *OK Tablets*, colored them with crayons, pierced them with long, pasted-on arrows, and wrote on the inside this innocent wisdom:

> *The river is wide*
> *And I can't step it.*
> *I love you*
> *And I can't 'hep' it.*

Somewhere beyond Aunt Lucy's cynicism, among the lizards at the gizzards, and over the wide, unsteppable river lies the great mystery—the unfathomable love that is God.

Aunt Lucy had her points. We all must admit that we have times when God seems so far away, so unjust, so uncaring that we don't love him. We don't even believe in him. Then there is the lizard at our gizzard. Love has run around our hearts, broken them, made us angry and bitter and literally jumped at our gizzards so we couldn't eat. Apples offer no comfort. What we learn from this leaping lizard is that our form of love is so finite, so fallible that we must accept it for what it is. We all fail each other, cause great jumps at each other vitals, and we are sick of love.

190

Holidays and Hapless Happenings

The river is wide that separates us from each other. We cannot step it without some help. We fall into the river of judgment and bitterness and become Aunt Lucys, soaked through and through. It is only when we have been empowered by a selfless love, an unmerited grace, that we can truly say, "I love you, I can't help loving you, I will love you no matter what comes, I shall always love you." No longer are we sick of love but are made whole in the joy of the greatest of all gifts: the love that is God.

JANUARY 1992

> *And I heard a loud voice saying in heaven, Now is come salvation, and strength, and the kingdom of our God, and the powers of his Christ.*
>
> ### *The Revelation 12:10*

I sit here amid the after-Christmas wrappings, the ash-strewn hearth, the disarranged cedar tree and ponder the salvation and the power that has come to dwell with us. On our tired tree is a symbol of this power. It is a small, half-gourd ornament, painted with an Oriental figure in kimono and streamed with a garish tassel like the ones you see in Chinese restaurants. It is my long-ago Christmas present from Hey Song.

She came into my English class eighteen years ago, a fragile Korean doll with great, opaque eyes sheltered by her ruler-straight bangs. On her dress was pinned this note: "My name is Hey Song Porter." She spoke not one word of English. During my years as a teacher in the Montgomery County School System, I learned to say short, desperate prayers, trusting that they got beyond the overhead-projector. "Dear Lord, not another one! And she speaks no English. All I can give her is your love. Please help me do that." And I drew a chair near my desk for Hey Song.

It was one of these after-lunch classes, crowded with too many turned-off hoping-to-drop-out-adolescent boys. Rebellion lay just beneath the surface, and all my energies went into keeping the lid on this morass of budding testosterone. They didn't know a prepositional phrase from a mongoose, nor did they care. And I was to teach Hey Song English. At this time would you believe I was dragging these scholars through *Romeo And Juliet*? Under the circumstances, all I could do was make reassuring glances at Hey Song, assuring her with yackety-yak motions with my fingers that she would learn English. I found her elementary school readers and let her wonderful intelligence do its work.

Her story is one of the power of love and light and the overcoming of darkness. War left her an orphan in Korea where she knew neither her parentage nor her place of birth. But the power of Christ's love, manifested in Presbyterian missionaries, brought her and hundreds like her into this denomination's orphanage where she lived until her adoption at fourteen.

Darkness was Hey Song's again when she left Korea for the States with an American military couple. What the couple was looking for was an unpaid servant and an object for the adoptive mother's rages. There were two small children in the family who were Hey Song's sole responsibility except when she was in school. The mother was a lady wrestler, on the road much of the time, but when at home she was physically abusive and well-trained in techniques that didn't show the signs of her psychotic torture. Through the school year I sensed something was wrong, but with Hey Song's limited use of the language and being so afraid in her new world, she suffered alone.

By the end of the school year she was speaking quite well, and she asked me to come by her home because her family was moving to South Carolina. As usual, she was alone with the two children. Great tears were in her eyes as she made me a present of pickled cabbage with much garlic, but she found no courage for words. She promised an address, but after that—nothing.

But the power of his Christ is here. One May evening three years later the telephone rang and a soft, Southern voice asked for Mrs. Marshall and said that someone wanted to speak to me; in fact, this someone had asked for a telephone call to me as part of her graduation present. It was Hey Song. In beautiful English she told me she had graduated with honors from high school. The lady who placed the call was her foster mother who had kept her when she was finally rescued from her nightmare of abuse.

More power and strength was Hey Song's. Under the auspices of the Epworth Children's Home (Methodist), she has graduated from the University of South Carolina with a B.A. in Designing and has received her Master of Fine Arts degree. She is working on her thesis for her Ph.D. and her artistic work has high critical acclaim across the Southeast. On a more personal note, Hey Song has a husband and two children, teaches a class in the Methodist Church's Sunday School in

Columbia, S.C. and directs the adult choir. Can this be the tiny waif who appeared in my English class?

To overcome the darkness of war and abandonment and abuse, the greatest of all gifts is here. The grace that was given to Presbyterian missionaries in Korea, to a tired English teacher in New Providence, to a foster mother in South Carolina, to an Epworth Children's Home—all radiated from the strength and power that is come to dwell among us. Oh, that we might fathom its height, its depth, its breadth.

So I put my Hey Song ornament away on a high shelf until next Christmas, but may I keep on the low shelf Christ's love to share with everyone who might come by my class as I learn to use the salvation, the strength, and the power that is for us all.

Love and peace for 1992!

DECEMBER 1990

...and they shall call his name Emmanuel—God with us.
Matthew 1

Emmanuel has come; God is with is, a child has been born to redeem us. These are tidings of great joy. But Christmas Day never comes that I don't relive a horror whose sacrifice of innocence is forever emblazoned in my memory and God seems as though he were never with us.

I was a child—maybe eight—and we were having dinner on Christmas Day with my Aunt Lena. After dinner when all the turkey had been put away, the fruit cake was back in its wrapping, and the final cup towel hung to dry, we heard on the back porch an unearthly wailing, a most piteous lamentation repeated over and over: "Oh, Miss Lena, Miss Lena, my baby's done burned up. Miss Lena, Miss Lena, my baby, Oh, Miss Lena..." Fearing to cling to my aunt, she prostrated herself in a desolate heap on the floor, her agony still too new to be fathomed. "Oh, Miss Lena, Miss Lena..."

In her two-room tenant shack in a field behind the barn, this young black mother had left her baby in a box by the fire while she went outside to gather wood. She had a two-year-old daughter who in her mother's absence was playing in the fire and set her tiny brother's paper box and poor swaddling clothes ablaze. The goddess of the hearth showed no mercy.

Holidays and Hapless Happenings

My mother and my aunt went to the cabin where they found the baby already dead. Unable to find in their grief any "God with us," the impoverished parents stole away in the night, away from this place of their infant son's sacrifice to the inferno of poverty.

For me, the mother's wailing yet rings down the years on Christmas Day. Her wailing has joined the universal grief that echoes through the annals of history from Herod's slaughter of the two-year-old sons of Bethlehem to the mothers who, if we have war in the Persian Gulf, must sacrifice their sons and daughters to *Imminent Thunder*.

Where is the Emmanuel with us? Where was he at the birth of our Savior when all the two-year-old sons were killed by Herod's soldiers? Was he there to hide the mother's eyes when they saw their infant sons impaled on a sword? Where was he when smoke and flame quenched so tiny a breath in a rude box in a tenant shack? Was he there to help thrust the spade into the earth as the father dug a tiny unmarked grave along a fencerow of sedge grass and bramble? Will he be there when *Imminent Thunder* becomes *Imminent Death*? Will he wipe the tears behind the veils in Iraq and behind the sunglasses in Miami? Emmanuel, where are you?

Where?—He lies in a manger in Bethlehem. He is our Imminent Innocence, the birth of our infant faith and hope. He is our elder brother who holds our hand into the mystery of suffering. We must become as little children to fathom such a glory, to hear the tidings of great joy. He has come to live and die as one of us, to hold fast the bottom depths of all horrors, all griefs, all disappointments, all maladies, all mistakes, all estrangements, and finally, all deaths. He has ransomed us from them all. This is truly God with us.

May the glory of Emmanuel keep us in the knowledge that neither fire nor sword "nor anything in all creation can separate us from the love of God which is in Christ Jesus our Lord."

Holidays and Hapless Happenings

NOVEMBER 1989

> *Go out quickly into the streets and lanes of the city and bring here the poor, and the maimed, the halt, and the blind. Go out into the highway and hedges and compel them to come in that my house may be full.*
>
> *St.Luke 14*

Our Lord's table in Conroy Hall is filled to overflowing. We have compelled no one to come in, but come they do six days a week, and our soup kitchen is testimony to the miracle of feeding the five thousand. With each passing month the numbers abound at *Loaves and Fishes*. We wonder about food enough and money, volunteers and tired backs, dishwashing and garbage problems, discouragement and drudgery; but the Lord of the Feast gives us heart. Here we have a microcosm of his people, the ones in the highways and hedges. Among them are the pains, the problems, and the misspent passions of our day.

In the same reading from Luke's gospel, Christ tells us when we make a great feast not to invite our rich friends and relatives who invite us back, but to invite such a group as troops daily to Conroy Hall. With November here and Thansgiving Day on the 23rd, I, in fantasy, invite some of our soup kitchen brothers and sisters into our homes to share our holiday bounty.

The first one on our invitation list would be Miss Lula. She is old, poor, black, and probably illiterate. She has walked many months from Edmondson Ferry Road to be our guest. Where would we have her sit? In her quiet dignity, she should sit at our hostess' right hand with our best linen and silver at her place. She has come out of great tribulation—out from the last bitter edges of slavery, from grinding poverty in some tenant shack, and from racism in all its demeaning forms. This humble lady should be exalted by the testimony of her survival without bitterness and for the praises and thanksgiving she expresses for the small joys she has known. "Blessed are the poor in spirit for theirs is the Kingdom of Heaven."

The second would be the demoniac. Where shall we place him when he accepts the invitation? He appears at *Loaves and Fishes* almost unclothed and certainly not in his right mind. His wild eyes roam over the food for the day, his too-big pants forget to be modest, and the demons who possess him seem to lurk near the surface, ready to torment him. We will place him near the door in case we need help. As Christ in the world, how do we cast out demons in his name and speak healing words at our banquet table? "Come out of this man, you unclean spirit." I don't know.

Where shall we seat the lank-haired young mother with her three-day-old infant? It is reported there is no home, no husband, no finances. The baby entreats with its tiny blue hand, its world, uncharted and unforgiving, as the mother looks with vacuous eyes at the future too empty to be contemplated. Temporarily, we place them by the milk and bread at the warmest corner of the table. This least brethren, denied its place of love and creative nurturing, shall repeat the same pattern of deprivation unless we somehow include it at the great feast. "Suffer the little children to come unto me."

Then we invite the homeless family to leave their battered car at the curb and join the festivities. Where do we place them? Away from the sterling silver! And the messy children at a card table in the corner. The father, a braggadocio of past triumphs and future expectations, tries to mask his failures while his wife holds the baby and stares at a far corner. Too, we will place them away from the center of conversation to drown out the father's bragging, and we will fill the children's plates again and again so they won't start a ruckus in the corner. We have heard and seen enough of this type. We know all the excuses. Through their din we hear, "The foxes have holes and the birds of air have nests, but the son of man has no place to lay his head."

The last guests who are invited in are those murky characters we look at out of the corner of our eyes. They might even be contagious! We will let them form their own group away from the centerpiece, where they can speak in undertones of a world beyond our safe place. What do you do for a fifth of *Thunderbird*, a package of cigarettes, a mind-altering hit, a few moments of intimacy? Here the lepers of our time and the woman caught in adultery judge us. "Who cares enough to care about us? Where are your stones?"

I have a good supply of stones for all except Miss Lula. I, too, am lost and discouraged in the streets and lanes, highways and hedges, trying to compel those who don't grab my invitation. What I must understand is that I am only called to be a faithful servant at the feast; to the Lord of the feast belongs the compelling:

"I come not to call the righteous but sinners to repentance—to seek and save that which was lost."

Holidays and Hapless Happenings

MAY 1989

*Ye are of God, little children and have overcome them: because
greater is he that is in you, than he that is in the world.*
1 John

There is no official Grandmother's Day. So to get a word in for
grannies, I shall usurp Mother's Day, which, as far as I am concerned
has been candied, carded, and flowered beyond any reasonable sentimentality; besides, grannies have been mothers longer than one-layer
mothers. They have gotten down to basics: We know all that teddy bear,
block, and truck clutter will be too soon picked up and replaced by
more complex matters; that sticky hand prints are beautiful reminders
that wash off; rocking chairs and lullabies are the only way to go to
sleep; baths aren't an absolute necessity; chocolate cake is good breakfast food; and that their parents will come get them!

I write the first official Grandmother's Day statement from the perspective of a granny fresh from three weeks' active duty, with stroller,
with a twenty-two-month old grandson aboard. This grandson has
absolutely his own time agenda along with a passion for small, white
rocks, water in any form—preferably mud puddles—and a cuddly,
stuffed Easter rabbit. I write this too, from the novel perspective of
Paris, France. If you missed COM in April, she was mulling and musing by the Eiffel Tower in a sandbox.

Napoleon Bonaparte did us the favor of having his bones trans-
ferred from the island of St. Helena and entombed at the Hotel des
Invalides, a grand hospital and church built by Louis XIV, honoring
disabled war veterans. The grounds of Les Invalides were across the
street from my daughter's apartment and provided my grandson
Charles and me our main strolling and exploring territory. This put our
stroller in the fevered path of tourists from the four corners of the earth.
They arrived in massive buses escorted by impassive guides who gave
their history-laden lectures with resigned determination to an audience
they scarcely seemed to see. The tourists seemed resigned also. Up the
steps and under the great Dome des Invalides to look down on
Napoleon's Tomb, they faithfully followed their leaders. Some were
trying to hear the lecture; the others, not understanding or not caring,
made no attempt to listen. In about twenty minutes, weary-eyed, they
came down the great stairs with too much glory in one day. There were
no smiles, little conversation, and the guides were at last done with
their Les Invalides spiel. There was a ten-minute break before the bus.

Holidays and Hapless Happenings

Now if Charles, out of his stroller, were to be doing his morning promenade by these steps with his Easter rabbit by one ear, there was a sudden metamorphosis, an awakening of spirit in the group. Be they Japanese, Italian, German, Spanish, or whatever, the international love for children was in every bus load. The dead bones of a military genius had no visible effect on their faces, unless to deaden them more; but the light of love beamed in many languages as they admired, took pictures, and tried to ask this proud granny questions. This reaction never failed. I spent many mornings in the park and made a study of the faces when they came down the steps from Napoleon's grandiose resting place. Never once did Charles fail to awaken this spark of joy as he, oblivious to all their admiration, explored his world of wonder among the sticks and stones.

Charles' fascination with stones must have filled some deep, atavistic need of his. He would choose a drainage grate in the park, toddle off to find the right combination of pebbles for two tight little fists, and spend hours chucking them down the drain. Or he would find a bigger stone and go on a long trek to the fountain to see it go "kerplunk." This was off-limits, but try explaining this to a two-year-old! All along these paths were benches where sat hospital patients, old people sunning themselves, young lovers, and, of course, the omnipresent tourists. Again we got the same loving attention. There were greetings in many languages, chuckles under the chin, admiration of the "blue eyes," and kind words for the frustrated granny who held on while Charles fished in the fountain or who kissed the hands that had fallen in the rocks. From the daily visits with my grandson to the Hotel des Invalides, I would say Charles had up-staged Napoleon, hands-down.

The words of the Beloved Disciple came again and again to this grandmother's ears: "Ye are of God, little children. Greater is he that is in you than he that is in the world."

As I mull and muse about Napoleon's career as an emperor, a military genius, an innovator of laws and codes—how different the world might have been if he had understood the power of these words: Greater is the power of love within you than all the pomp and glory of the world. Ye are of God, all you who love, and you will see the kingdoms of this world topple into ashes and decay. All of Napoleon's glory at last crashed around him and he was exiled to die on the lonely island of St. Helena. At his final resting place in Paris, one little child can elicit from the people of many lands a warmth of love that can only be a gift from the spirit that gives all who love their place from God. Thank you, Charles, for letting your granny know you were of this spirit and for lighting up the tired faces that Napoleon's bones had darkened.

My official Grandmother's Day statement is ended thus: Little children, grannies, grandfathers, mothers, fathers, brothers and sisters at Trinity and all Beloved everywhere—"Let us love one another: for love is of God."

DECEMBER 1988

> *He hath put down the mighty from their seats, and exalted them of low degree.*
>
> ***The Song of Mary***

We have heard the Christmas story from the Gospel of Luke until we can almost say it by rote, and we can see in our mind's eye from one season to the next the shepherds with their crooks and borrowed bathrobes. The wise men from the Gospel of Matthew have opened their glittery boxes of gold, frankincense and myrrh until we can recognize their treasures from the past seven Christmases. Mary has looked beautifully calm and beatific while Joseph has stood by the manger, unwavering in his duty, the epitome of understanding and selfless husbandhood. This nativity scene we know too well.

Being raised around stables and people who tended cattle, I mull and muse how it really was, how it was for Mary and Joseph, the shepherds, and the wise men. Matthew and Luke leave us with their bare, beautiful outline; but having brought forth my firstborn with the imminent urgency of the time to be delivered, I muse about how angelic a face Mary presented to the innkeeper and how calmly Joseph steered his donkey to the stable. Luke simply states: "And she brought forth her first-born son, and wrapped him in swaddling clothes, and laid him in a manger; because there was no room for them in the inn."

When I juxtapose this scene to our stable, I hold my breath at the implications. In the winter the stable was warm from the animals' bodies, there was plenty of hay in the manger, but you had better have your boots on to step through next spring's fertilizer. Never in my wildest twentieth-century musings could I envision giving birth amid the pigs' grunts, the mules munching away on their corn, and the mice squeaking across the top of the corncrib door. Yet, Mary laid her firstborn in a manger!

Holidays and Hapless Happenings

Right away, after the Christ Child's idyllic birth, his worshipers came. In Luke they were the shepherds, the lowliest of hirelings. Now, our hired hand around our stable was a cowherd par excellence who knew the treatment for foot-rot, pinkeye, and bloat, and knew how to make the cow "give down" her milk; but his cowherding costume was another consideration. He put it on in the fall with the falling leaves and aired it a bit with the blooming daffodils. The perfume of the stable was the exact medium for his bovine expertise. By the same token, I would imagine the long-ago shepherds abiding in the fields didn't visit the Roman baths in the occupied sector, but abided by night under some sheep skins, watching their flocks in the winter's cold. Nevertheless, these humble shepherds were the first to have the glory shine round about them and were the chosen ones to bear the tidings of great joy! The ones of low degree have been exalted.

In Matthew, the worshipers were the Wise Men, kings from the highest of places. I again bring the setting of our Lord's nativity forward to our stable. These wise men have problems. I can see them coming, holding long robes above the mud puddles in the stable lot, high-stepping over unexplored cowpats, all the while balancing their crowns and treasure boxes as the star stops over the ridgepole of the barn. Then they open the stable door, the warm unfrankincensed air envelopes them, they gather their bejeweled and ermined robes around them, search for an unadorned place on the earthen floor, and "fall down and worship him" at his manger. Then they present their golden treasures in this lowliest of places. The mighty have been put down.

In my musing about what Luke and Matthew are trying to get us to see, I come up with an overwhelming paradox. The order of things has been, forever, turned upside down. The lowliest shepherd is raised up as the bearer of the highest joy: "A Savior is born For All People." There is no one beyond his acceptance, no one is outside of the glory that shines round about us, and all servanthood for love of him is raised up to kingship. The mighty, the wise men and kings, fall down and worship the babe, leaving their treasures and wisdom at his manger. Their kingship is to be found in their servanthood.

The greatest paradox of all is the mystery and majesty of the infant Jesus. The humblest beginning is the mightiest ending. Born in utter poverty and weakness in a stable, he has been raised above all glory, to reign as King of Kings and Lord of Lords. And he shall reign forever and ever! Hallelujah!

Holidays and Hapless Happenings

May the splendor of the Christmas story shine round about us in 1989 and for all time. I love you all.

MAY 1988

...how often would I have gathered thy children together, even as a hen gathereth her chickens under her wings, and ye would not!
Matthew 23

May is motherhood month again. Orchids and accolades to all you mothers as I delve into the storehouse of some models I have known, considering which one would be worthy of a special award on Mother's Day. Taffy, our Collie dog of many years ago, would surely have a nomination for fecundity; but mulling and musing to the very apex, the ultimate superlatives in mothering, I will stay within the two-legged nominees and give the *Cluck and Clutch* Award posthumously to our spectacled hen, Biddy. May her soul rest, unruffled, on the highest roost-pole in a hawkless sky.

She came from a long line of fightin' chickens. She and her game-cock husband—who spent his time crowing on the fence, preening his glorious feathers, or making wise chortles as he clicked his spurs together—had produced about a dozen chicks. While this God's gift to the poultry world exclaimed his wonders, Biddy was all business. She eyed the sky with one eye for hawks and the countryside with the other for dogs and foxes. She was ever-alert. With her brood in tow, clucking and calling, she scratched the leaves and twigs aside under her favorite pear tree in our side yard, hunting for fat grubs and other unidentified squirming protein. The morning was calm except for His Feathered Highness, the sky was clear of any threat, and the scratching was bountiful.

Suddenly, in a cloud of dust, the farm-yard tranquility was shattered. Mrs. Tomlin, the *Progressive Farmer* agent, wheeled in under the pear tree in her *Plymouth*, claiming the shade for her place to park. Now Mrs. Tomlin was an aggressive saleslady who dressed the part. This being the era of hats, she landed with her millinery marvel at full sail, all feathered and flowery and flopping in the following breeze. At a moment's glimpse, Biddy came to a full-fury squawk and lowered feather-ruffle. With one lightning, knock-out flight, she got the hawky hat to the ground, spurred it into the dust, and rebounded at Mrs. Tomlin's bejeweled glasses and marcel. Seeing the chicken-yard crisis out the window, I rescued Mrs. Tomlin and Hat with broomed escort into the house, where we renewed the *Progressive Farmer*, at her spe-

Holidays and Hapless Happenings

cial long-term discount, until 1999 at the rate of fifty cents a year.

Thus, with our literary life secured for five decades, Mrs. Tomlin made some weather and garden chatter, pulled several bobby pins out of, and crimped up, her finger-wave, rearranged the drooping wings and bruised blossoms on her hat, peered critically into her compact, and topped off her dignity once more to sail away. Biddy was nowhere to be seen. Being no ordinary, chicken-brained chicken, however, she had given her hush-and-hide signal, gathered her brood under the front porch, and lay in wait for this hawk-of-a-lifetime.

You guessed it. The scene was repeated, the broom brigade called out again, and as I handed back Mrs. Tomlin's spilled pocketbook and defeated hat into her car, she said neither "Thank you" nor "Good-bye." I never saw her again. Until this day, each month, we faithfully get our *Progressive Farmer*, and I am reminded yet of the protective and possessive mother hen who would have given her very life for her brood. She richly deserves the *Cluck and Clutch* Award.

Biddy and I continued our parallel mothering for a year or two. Her generations matured faster than mine and soon her chickens were so big that when she called them at night to gather them under her wings, she was literally lifted off the ground by her brood. Soon the chickens completely ignored Biddy, who continued calling and clucking in ruf-fled concern. They were trying their new feathers and hunting their own grubs. Truthfully, she was tired of the constant sky-watch and bug-scratch, but she had grown accustomed to her own need to be needed. She hadn't learned who she was beyond her mothering.

Biddy and I had lessons to learn: First, we had to watch for hawks but not be hawky. We had to cherish but not consume. We had to learn the paradox of possessing in letting go. Chickens come back to a com-fortable, loose wing. We had to look to God himself for examples of good mothering. We had to learn that he allows us and our children to make our mistakes, pay our penalties in anguish, and then he welcomes us home from the wild roost poles, loving us all the while as he makes us wiser and more complete. Biddy and I were both bird-brained and chicken-hearted much of the time as we struggled to be good mothers, but we rested in the sure knowledge that we loved our children. That makes all the difference.

Thanks be to God we did learn to let our chickens go. In our letting go and giving up our eternal vigilance, protection, and all our *Wisdom* for the right scratching place for our chickens, we have found them, returned home to roost, but not to stay—free to be who they are, deal-ing with their hawks, under the trees of their own chicken yard.

Holidays and Hapless Happenings

DECEMBER 1986

Thou whose glory is above the heavens is chanted by the mouth of babes and infants—Oh Lord, our Lord, how majestic is thy name in all the earth.

Psalm 8

My mother often recalls the poignant story of my three year old brother's loss of the glory of Christmas: Always, my father was Santa Claus at our two-room school. Dragging out year after year the same grizzled whiskers, the red cambric suit with its missing cotton patches, a long red hood from the annals of our attic, a wide black belt to cinch up the sofa pillow stuffing, and cheered by a dip into my mother's rouge pot, he was the Jolly Old Elf himself. He would have won the rural Santa Claus *Oscar* hands down. Such bounce, such attention to each small child was about more than their wide-eyed wonder could behold. Santa Claus and glory above the heavens were one.

My brother had been labeled "shy;" therefore, my mother cautioned my father not to overwhelm his son with too much ho-ho-ho's and kisses—just a pat on the head and a piece of candy. This Santa Claus did. But when he exited out a window where he said his reindeer were waiting, my small brother with great tears running down his face proclaimed the sad tidings, "Santa Claus kissed everyone but me."

Out of the mouth of this babe and infant came the universal cry of us all: the glory of a kiss from Santa Claus. The majesty was gone from this moment in his life as he reached out for that love that undergirds us all and makes us feel safe and accepted: the love that will not let us go.

My Santa Claus father typified the abundance of love at our command, and reminds me even yet how stingy we are with affirming each other and what qualifications we put on those who "merit" our love. We are afraid of hugs and tears and keep our stiff upper lips, telling ourselves big boys and girls don't cry, are always brave, and don't need kisses from Santa Claus. When we are truly honest, however, we must admit that big boys and girls do cry—if not on the outside, on the inside—and we aren't brave either. I know; I've been a big girl a long time. Another honesty: When we are the most unlovable, that is our statement of how much we need to be loved. We will go to any length for attention: excessive good and pleasing behavior to excessive bad and shocking behavior. The need for love never ends.

Holidays and Hapless Happenings

At this Christ Mass, may we hear the babes' and infants' chant of the glory above the heavens, and may each of you have a *Big Kiss* from Santa Claus.

MARCH 1986

This is St. Valentine's Day, the snow has us beautifully marooned, and I must mull and muse for the upcoming Easter month. Sometimes the mulling is easy; this time it is not. The muse that is now coming to me is a look at the maturation of my concept of love—or perhaps "maturation" is the wrong word—the measure of grace given me that insists that I wrestle with what love is. Through the brightness of the snow and the inward darkness of my understanding ring the words of St. Paul: "Beareth all things, believeth all things, hopeth all things, endureth all things."

When I was child, I thought as a child and my love was the cupid-shot variety. The object of my adoration was Nelson Eddy. For days after I had seen *Rosemarie*, which found Jeanette McDonald in hoop-skirt and picture hat, somewhere in moose country coming upon Nelson Eddy, I would picture myself being crushed in his arms, while we sang these shattering duets, our mouths not two inches apart. Then after the wilderness had echoed and reverberated to my "When I'm calling you U-U-huh-huh-huh-hu-huh-huh-o-oo," Nelson again would give me a blissful kiss behind my picture hat. Then there was a tweedy professor with a pipe that sent incense up to Aphrodite. In his Southern-Shakespearean voice he read Romantic and Victorian poetry better than Nelson sang; and when he read Elizabeth Barrett Browning's "How Do I Love Thee, "I died. Little did I know words like music could transport. He had a wife and too many babies, so cupid's zap was most unfair. But finally, and with many a blow from reality, I have put away some childish things; however, romance has never again been so sweet.

So with Eros seen through the glass, I look deeper into the darkness to what is this thing called love. I don't know. I can only record my musings and offer them for whatever they are worth. But for a better term than trotting out the Greek names, I will call this attempt my understanding of Easter love, the one that bears all things, endures all things.

Too long we have equated right love with right feeling. The need for a warm noble sensation clouds our search for the love that endures all things. Christ, our brother in sorrows, temptations, hurts, angers, disappointments, and guilts, has gone before us; and I muse about how he felt and how sweetly warm were his sensations when he was denied and spat upon. How noble and self-sacrificing did he feel as he sweated drops of blood and prayed to be delivered from his torture? But he knew what had to be done and he set his face toward Jerusalem and his death to endure all things so we might believe all things and have the hope of resurrection. Following his example, is love then doing what has to be done, in the face of unfairness, betrayal, tedium, and seeming hopelessness?

I have seen this Easter love: a neighbor who tended an invalid wife for twenty years who no doubt was tired of the endless bedpans and laundry; another whose mongoloid child sentenced her to a life of never being free of his care; one whose son damaged his mind irreparably experimenting with drugs; and others who have struggled with alcoholic relationships.

So what then is love for all of us who suffer? And all do suffer. In my musing, it comes through the dark glass that love is setting your face toward your Jerusalem, doing what must be done. There doesn't have to be any noble feeling. In your humanity you deliver up your anger, disappointment, and bitterness in all honesty to Christ who has been there, and take up your cross and follow along—perhaps complaining all the way—but anyway following. And in your enduring all things, as surely as Christ has endured, there will arise hope, and oftentimes laughter, and you will, after your period in the long darkness, be surprised by the bright morning of Easter.

JANUARY 1986

I have a January heart. It is dormant, resting after the holidays. It is a time for keeping the fires burning, the water running, the winds from seeping around the doors and windows of our old farmhouse. It is a time for not keeping resolutions. I gave them up when I was left in the winter cold of self-righteousness. I like my January heart; it is left bare of pretense, resting, knowing that it cannot keep its promise.

So what is the gift of a January heart? It is the gift of keeping, of faithfulness. It stays when our fair-weather heart has given up its attempts to be good and do good. It keeps us through the frozen days as we wait for the first warm winds that again empower us to love, to forgive, to grow, to bloom. May our hearts rest in January as we wait for Easter.

Holidays and Hapless Happenings

DECEMBER 1985

As Christmas approaches I am feeling the pressure of my "ought-to's and have-to's." There are about two hundred people I ought to remember in some way; I have to make eight fruit cakes lest my dear late mother-in-law's tradition be violated; I have to get some shopping done or Santa Claus won't find our chimney—all of which is interspersed with the "must-be-done's" like the every day cooking and cleaning. What a trap!

Now I mull and muse about what would happen if I suddenly stood up in rank rebellion and announced, " I just ain't gonna do it no more. I'm tired of all this cooking and decorating and wrapping and trying to please everyone in the four generations of my family. I'm tired of the extra people in the house, the extra church services, the long hours of food preparation, the unpacking of the same frayed and frazzled Christmas decorations (especially the one-eyed reindeer), and, above all, I am tired of the nagging condemnation that I'm somehow not doing enough and that I'm leaving someone out. I feel enslaved by Christmas. I'm on strike."

What would happen? Why, I'd never do it in a thousand Christmases. All this cooking and doing is the way I know who I am in this world: a mother, a granny, a wife, a daughter, a sister, a friend. I yearn to know myself, however, freed from the enslaving law of the "have-to's" and "ought-to's" which demands that my poor body go on and on so I can feel noble and martyred. To be free, I must relax into the "do-what-I-can's" and tune my tired soul to the liberating event of all time: the coming of the Christ.

Good news! I am mortal; I cannot be all things to all people—that's God's place; I am accepted just like I am even though my fruitcakes aren't made. My one and only requirement is to love this Christ and to be as best I can his loving presence in the world. If I can keep my "love-to's" in first place, I will have a Merry Christmas.

And a *Merry Christmas* to you, dear *Trumpet* reader. "Good bless us, everyone."

206

Holidays and Hapless Happenings

MAY 1985

Since May has the day to honor motherhood I mull and muse about this state from which each of us is sprung. If you can find anyone without an umbilicus, it will be Adam and Eve all over again; and I don't believe the Almighty is into mud and ribs these days since the human family does so well with the standard method.

Whether plunged into motherhood by accident or intent, we females down through the ages have kept the gene pool well a-wash, with a bit of help from the males, and have taken no special credit for being mothers since many times we couldn't help it. In our time, however, there has arisen some pious and sentimental notion about motherhood that sells flowers and gives preachers an opportunity to make the congregation give special notice to a group that probably committed mayhem getting their charges ready for church. Needless to say the preacher will not remind these Sunday madonnas that their common mother Eve started the human family's decline, took her husband along with her, and produced a murderer for her first child. No orchid for you, Eve, on Mother's Day.

As I ponder thirty-four years of motherhood with all its comedy and tragedy and endless duties, the words of Wordsworth keep resounding in my musings: "The child is father of the man," and I will add, "the mother of the woman." Who else could teach me so well?

From my children's mothering I have learned the lessons that I must know to be worthy of them. Where else would I have learned tolerance and understanding if they had been all Straight A's and perfect and the roboted extension of my puffed-up ego? or humility? In my judgmental attitudes, only "bad" parents had problems with their children, and I had to learn that children must find themselves away from my mothering, carrying their rebellion into the far country to find out who they are. To warn them of pigsties they could land in was to waste my breath. You must let them go. Gratitude was another lesson—the fact that we made it through another school year, or a love affair gone sour, a mistake too painful to mention, a scene that just doesn't happen in "nice families"—and we were still intact as a family. This is the bare bones of being thankful. And forgiveness. When I come to this one, I was, and am, a slow learner. I had to be taught over and over again not only to forgive the products of my body but my very self. How could one so smart make so many mistakes? Finally I found words of consolation in some of my reading which suggested that it didn't make too

207

much difference the methods you used in child rearing or the mistakes that you made if the child rested in the confidence of your unqualified love. My children taught me that too—love without reservations.

So what credit do we mothers deserve in May when we are recognized? Our honor must lie in the affirmation of hope that we make when we produce children. Life with its tragedy and triumph does and must go on and we add to the unbroken generations with faith for tomorrow. We trust that our children and their children's children, imperfect, as we are imperfect, will be in their time the Children of God.

> *And stretching out his hand toward his disciples, he said, "Here are my mother and my brothers. For whoever does the will of My Father in heaven is my brother, and sister, and mother."*
>
> **Matthew 12**

DECEMBER 1984

When I was seven and by brother was eight he told me about Santa Claus. This was the beginning or our loss of innocence and our introduction into the wiles of the world.

Since we were newly sophisticated and smug in this knowledge about there being no Santa Claus, we decided the thing for us to do was to have a double-barrel thrill—find the presents beforehand and then be presented with them again on Christmas morning. Secretly, we began our search. We tackled the attic first, even the spidery crawl spaces under the eaves; next came the upstairs closets with their remote crannies running into the gables; and then the "dirty clothes" closet under the stairs where we moused our way through soiled laundry, assorted boxes, and empty fruit jars—but no Santa Claus. Finally we narrowed our search down to a tall old wardrobe that stood guard in our parents' room. With its high top molding making a deep recess, this had to be the safest hiding place, and we waited for the all-clear signal when our parents were safely occupied elsewhere. Standing in a chair, my brother held me by the legs and gave me a boost up until I grabbed hold of the molding, shinnnied up the wardrobe, and balanced my middle on the top. There it was! The treasure trove had been found. So announcing to my brother below, I verified the very pocketknife he has craved all year, the Mickey Mouse watch that was my heart's desire, and I rifled through all the presents until our curiosity was content. We came down off our perch to await the big night, the Night before Christmas.

Holidays and Hapless Happenings

Our sophistication was complete. I can assure you there was no big night. Gone was the tingling anticipation in the long half-asleep hours, gone were the visions of sugarplums and reindeer hooves on the roof, gone was the wide-awake shivering in the predawn as we waited for my father to build up the fires—just the same old humdrum sleep in the same old bed. The magic was gone out of Christmas. We were hard pressed to emote any joy as we pulled our deflated treasures out of our stockings. Undone, we secretly shared the sorrow of our misdoings and longed for our shining innocence that was no more.

The years have passed, Santa Claus in an explainable myth told to children as a tale long past. Our feet hurt, politics is rotten, we feel unloving most of the time, and the world seems unrelenting in its cruelty. But into our dead hearts in the dreariest part of the winter comes not magic, but mystery, the birth of true innocence in the form of a baby. "We who dwell in darkness have seen a great light," and the light, despite our doubts and jaded *Wisdom* cannot be put out. So, reclaiming our childlike faith, we once again hear the angels' proclamation and the words of the King of the Cosmos, the Christ child:

> Let the children come to me; do not try to stop them; for the Kingdom of God belongs to such as these. I tell you whoever does not accept the Kingdom of God like a child will never enter it.

JANUARY 1994

> Some trust in chariots, and some in horses, but we will remember the name of the Lord our God.
>
> **Psalm 20**

My husband has put his trust in various chariots and several mules—not horses. He has plowed and hauled with his chariots and has followed the north end of various mules down many a south-bound row. All these trusty servants, both animate and inanimate, have been given their just rewards. After many faithful years, old mules were turned out to pasture, respected and thanked for their straight rows. Our first tractor, an antiquated *John Deere G*, idles its years away, being started occasionally to adjust its valves and pop its pistons. An *International* truck, a 1963 model, is stored in a tobacco barn on another farm where it has languished without a tire kicking for many years. But the chariot most trusted and pampered and still in service is a 1978 *Chevrolet Caprice Classic*! Its long, sleek design, its red plush interior, its adjustable steering wheel, its two remaining flashy hubcaps, and its inimitable paint job make it a gawker's delight.

209

Holidays and Hapless Happenings

The paint formula for this silver gray model seems to have been one of General Motors' worst failures. After about one season, this chariot lost its silver sheen, turned a dull cankered-spoon green, and then deteriorated gradually into a chronic case of rustitus. Therefore its name: Big Rusty. And now another adjective has been added—Trusty Rusty. Like all other horses and chariots that have come under my husband's keeping, the *Chevrolet* has had special care. It wears its yearly stickers as proudly as Douglas MacArthur wore his battle ribbons. Everything works, all the service is done on time, the tires are excellent, and Big Rusty purrs like an *Infiniti*. Press the pedal and Rusty will jerk your neck back and lay down rubber.

The beauty of this car is its ability to serve in its rusting years; and it does all chauffeuring so willingly in spite of stares and insults. My husband says he comes to a four-way stop and suddenly he is given the right-of-way even though he was not first at the stop sign. "See that old derelict in that beat-up car...not one penny of insurance, probably drunk...let him go first out of our way." Poor Rusty was insulted in a local business's parking lot where we had been customers for some fifty years. A note on the windshield read, "If this car is parked here again, it will be towed." Another day I drove in the parking lot behind Trinity and beeped the horn at Ardell (our retired secretary); and she gave a quick glance my way and rushed up the steps into the safety of her office.

Big Rusty, however, has a flip side: shock value in time of trouble. My brother-in-law was visiting us from Washington when he and his chariot were stopped for speeding on Pollard Road. When he stretched out his impressive six-feet-five frame, his Washington driver's license, and his diplomatic credentials, the incongruity of the situation so overcame the partrolman that he let driver and chariot go.

Now the latest to fall under Big Rusty's care are Mark and Melissa Hunter, this couple who have come to us like a special gift along with Julia and Victoria Grace. Their van broke down on the Interstate, and Mark remembered my having extolled the virtues of Rusty. He called to see if the car was available. It was. The Hunter family had the pleasure of its company for about two weeks. They can share with you their new perspective on "you-are-what-you-drive."

Things are not as they appear. Never forget that. My husband is sterling even though in Old Rusty; my brother-in-law, the same. I do not change when I drive this car, and certainly the Hunters were as true and loving as ever during their two weeks with Rusty. Some do trust in chariots and judge by chariots. I must admit that at times my eyes bug-out at *Cadillacs, Lincolns*, and the right-name foreign cars. We are all tempted to put our trust in things that ride us and make us think we are somehow more acceptable because of some fleeting opulence. But ultimately our chariots rust out and our horses die.

For 1994, may we remember the name of the Lord our God, the one in whom we can trust for all our years.

Grace Abounding

Father forgive them: They do not know what they are doing.
Luke 23

At this Easter season I am held by Christ's words on the cross: "Father forgive them." They are as fresh in our time as they were two thousand years ago, and we need to hear them anew and ask in the first person, singular and plural—"Father forgive us; Father forgive me; we don't know what we are doing." Failing to accept this unconditional forgiveness, we deal with our misdoings with self-pity and self-justification. Asking for forgiveness somehow seems too simple, and being Adam's children, we insist we know good from evil.

Once when I was going through a long period of not knowing what I was doing, Dorothy Ann Russo quoted her brother Dan to me: "Self-pity is the neurotic way to work on problems," and this wisdom from Dan has served me well. When I allow myself the luxury of self-pity, Dan's words ring back to me and send me searching inside for the real problem. This self-pity, self righteousness, self-justification—all are my ways of trying to be right; and they send me running away from the forgiveness I need. This selfishness torments my psyche in bouts of anger, blame and vindictiveness. I do believe the kingdom of God and the kingdom of hell are within us, and each kingdom hinges on our acceptance or our refusal of forgiveness.

Again, I didn't know what I was doing. My pity-pie heaped my unhappiness on others: "If only *he* would be more caring, that would fulfill my needs and I wouldn't be so miserable. If only *they* would listen to me and conform to my agenda and affirm my doings then I would be content. If only my parents hadn't been like they were, I wouldn't be so messed up. If only I hadn't been tempted into that "big mistake" in 1971, I would feel like something now. Poor little me! I've been put-down, walked on, ignored, but I'm still good and sweet—a sinner, yes, but not like that great mass of sinners out there who wouldn't know a martyr if they saw one..." In this frame of mind, I almost convinced myself I knew what I was doing.

When I looked myself straight in my self-pitying eyes, the part of me that had accepted some measure of forgiveness said hard words to me: "It's up to you; you can choose to be miserable and wait for happiness to fall in your lap and others to cater to your every need. Prepare for a long wait. Yes, those "others" are uncaring and hurt you and the world is disappointing and cruel, but what is your response? Will you struggle to know or will you wallow in self-pity? You can take responsibility for this mess you live with, take your forgiveness not only for yourself but for everyone around you, and take up your cross. No whining, no blaming, no judging. Admit you don't know and allow all those others in the boat with you. Even St. Paul saw through a glass darkly."

At this Easter may we all stand at the foot of the cross. "Father forgive me; Father forgive us. We don't know what we are doing." This confession makes all the difference. This confession frees us from our self-pity and lets us embrace our brokenness as well as our broken brothers. This confession grants us a grace to live here and redeem our places as best we can. The confession of not knowing is the beginning of knowing.

JULY 1986

You therefore must be perfect as your heavenly Father is perfect.
Matthew 5:48

Theologians tell us, dear God, that you are all powerful, all knowing, and ever present. In fancy words you are omnipotent, omniscient, and omnipresent. Then your son tells us we must be perfect as you are perfect. I've given it all a try.

Somehow the all-knowing has been the easiest one and I've given you a lot of help. I've known how my neighbors should raise their children, groom their bodies, run their finances, choose their mates, use the English language and how the preacher should preach, and what else, God? Oh, yes, the exact way to worship you—the right way with the right books and vestments. Lucky to have me around!

All powerful is a bit more difficult, God. But if I can have my way I can maneuver situations around and you will be surprised how, with my help, things will work out right. Influence and a bit of money will help us along, and coupled with our all-knowing, this is a winning combination. Events fall into place, children do as I wish, and my husband remains docile.

Omnipresent. God, this one is a bit wearing, but since you can do it, I will too. I'll be everywhere and be all things to all people. I'll be at the PTA, DAR, ECW, CHS, the grocery store, Aunt Betsy's for tea, and the annual Sippers-of-Sassafras-Tea-Soiree. If any of the above mentioned has a problem, I shall be there to solve it, not to mention being ever present for all my children, in-laws, and any stragglers under my roof. Move over, God, my ever-present presence may not leave much room for you. Sometimes I feel as if you aren't on my side anymore. I've given being perfect my best shot. Why do I feel so tired and frazzled?

"Dummy!" answers God. "Read what my son is saying. 'I am perfect in acceptance and forgiveness.' Read in context! Forget all those *Omnis* and relax you soul into the chaos of being real. I don't mean not to try to do right, but leave to me the grace to empower you in your search for perfection. In that search you will find your neighbor with his imperfections, those very imperfections which you find so distasteful in yourself, and you will be able to love him. As you love him in his humanity, you will be able to love yourself and forgive yourself. I am the ability to love. I am love. That's what I mean by being perfect."

OCTOBER 1985

> When pride cometh, then cometh shame: but with the lowly is wisdom.
>
> **Proverbs 11:2**

I went to a two-room school in Kirkwood where the classes went up to the recitation bench as their turn was called. Being in the lower grades I would listen in on the more advanced classes, feeling from time to time, some pride in my profound knowledge when I knew the answer when the higher-ups didn't. One day as the lesson in geography progressed and someone was locating Washington between Virginia and Maryland, I, despite the rules against the classes-not-at-the-bench responding, rose up and declared the fact that Washington was on the West Coast. Here for the whole school to see was my ignorance of the fact that there were two Washingtons. The laughter and to me the scorn burned itself indelibly into my childhood being, making me afraid to ask questions and afraid of wrong answers.

As I mull and muse about ignorance and knowledge, folly and wisdom and where to find the two noble ones, pride, as usual, is the cardinal obstacle. It's not that I fear ignorance, but it's the fear of being found out, exposed for all to see. And here comes the shame: I retreat into a pretense of knowing, smile illumined smiles, and haul my humiliated ego into a safe place where it can prop up the defenses it has built around itself. These defenses are many and reflect our unhealthy fear of each other and our lack of acceptance of each other with all of our ignorance and mistakes. Here we create a hostile environment to learning and free discussion, unrealistically expecting ourselves and others to know all the answers—and right answers too. When someone comes out with an honest blob of ignorance, we squirm with embarrassment. If the ignorance is ours, we redden with despair and batter away at our poor ego which will be quiet from now on in public but will tumble our pillows at night. How could I be so dumb? The shame of such pride thwarts the efforts to learn and leaves us with the pretense of knowledge or the deprecation of knowledge. "Who needs to know that junk anyway?"

My father used to say that everyone is dumb—they are just different dumb. We are ignorant. We need to quit pretending and say it. We know a few isolated facts out of the staggering and overwhelming knowledge of creation. We have a flyspeck of music, of history, of economics, of art. Even the most highly informed among us have more ignorance than knowledge. Unless we can tolerate this limitation in ourselves and extend it to others, we cannot outgrow the shame and sham of pretending to be wise. And as surely as the sun rises and you find yourself posturing in wisdom, you are showing the world your lack of it.

It is in humble acceptance of ourselves and others, in giving and receiving of our gifts, in forgiving and being forgiven, in leaving the heights and descending to servanthood that we lose our shame. "With the lowly is wisdom."

APRIL 1985

> But it is not the spiritual which is first but the physical, and then the spiritual...Just as we have borne the image of the man of dust, we shall also bear the image of the man of heaven. I tell you this brethren: flesh and blood cannot inherit the kingdom of God, nor does the perishable inherit the imperishable.
>
> **I Corinthians 15**

All will die. The man of dust, the descendants of Adam, must die. If he insists on not growing old, he must die young, This grim all-consuming fact has to be faced if he is to live with any degree of excellence in the only time that he has—the earthly now. No amount of paint, paste, powder, and the whole panoply of the pharmaceutical world can ward off the encroachment of the years. The dust can be rearranged, only to settle as mud in the wrong place. The lime can leach out and the teeth will come out one by one or in a group, if the dentist so ordains. The fair flowers that bloom on the cheeks wilt away and crow's feet are left in their lively beds. The bronze and pastels of a vigorous sod give way to the motley clays and the clotty bogs where enzymes get confused, drainage piped get clogged, and bacteria and mold find the immune fences broken down. Inside the fertile cranium, dust storms arise and this Adam, this crowning of creation, finds his unique gray dust gone with the wind, befilming his eyes and blocking his ears. He is reminded by each erosion that "dust thou art, and unto dust thou shalt return."

We know too well this man of dust and his foreordained end in earthly time. "But it is not the spiritual which is first, but the physical, and then the spiritual." These words of St. Paul set me mulling and musing about time and eternity and this place where we live out our days. We cannot escape our dusty apprenticeship. For the "right now" this physical self is the only self we have. We long for it to do right, to be nice and clean, not to blow its cool, and to stay as young as possible. If it is faithful, it spends a few minutes per week longing to bear the image of the man of heaven; but if it is honest it confesses to mostly doubt and an uneasy confusion. We are trapped in our small concept of time, of days and years, and eternity gets to be some far away floaty place where we grow wings and don't marry or give in marriage.

But what of Easter and resurrection and all this talk about eternal life? This physical man trapped by the clock—is he to live out his days only as the man of dust? This infinitesimal line from birth to death which we call *time*, is this contained in the timeless present which Christ calls eternal life? If so, this is eternity right now. We are living in the vastness of the eternal. Hear what the Man of Heaven says: "I am the Alpha and the Omega, the first and the last, the beginning and the end. Before Abraham was, I AM. I am the resurrection and the life; he who believes in me shall never die." In the dust of our existence, we are claimed by the Eternal.

"Such knowledge is too wonderful for me." Right now I am in eternity? Yes, we are new imperishable creations in Christ who has gone before us in the physical world and into death where we have yet to go. Who has one inkling what our spiritual image shall be or what eternity means? I don't know other than we shall bear the image of the Man of Heaven and that "we shall not count time by years." From the glimmers through the dark mirror, I am persuaded that in this eternity there is a mighty resurrection for all time—the past, the present, the future—when the man of dust will bear fully the image of the Man of Heaven.

And night shall be no more, they need no light or lamp or sun, for the Lord God will be their light, and they shall reign for ever and ever.

The Revelation

SEPTEMBER 1984

Till we all come in the unity of the faith, and the knowledge of the Son of God, unto a perfect man, unto the measure of the stature of fullness of Christ: That we henceforth be no more children...

Ephesians 4 KJV

Bob Wood wrote in his May *Woodwinds* "that most people are better at feeling guilty than at accepting pardon." Somehow that hit me, and I have mulled and mused about feeling guilty and "wrong" and unforgiven. After three months' reflection, I have arrived at the conclusion that I've been hiding behind this guilt, being a child, rather than accepting the gift of maturity that is mine to claim. Actually when I do not accept forgiveness and keep on harping on some past failure or foul-up, I am putting myself beyond God who promises that as far as the east is from the west he will remove our transgressions, and I refuse to accept such abundant pardon. Who do I think I am!

The gift of maturity "to the measure of the stature of the fullness of Christ..." now that is our promise. We are not to be guilt-ridden, breast-beaters. We are the body of Christ in the world, his called-out communion of forgiven sinners, the Church. And we are called to vigorous manhood—to the full measure of being Christ at this point in time and at this place in history. When I try to understand the totality of Christ in all and over all and our union with him, the knowledge is too wonderful for me. But from the sure promise of his indwelling gifts and his expectations of his people, I cannot fall back on the poor-old-guilty-me routine. I stand in thankful awe at the grace that makes me what I am and at the portion of the "measure of the fullness of Christ" that has been given me.

Grace Abounding

> *I am the resurrection and the life; he who believes in me, though he die, yet shall he live.*

These words of Christ are said at every Christian graveside. Yet they should be said at our tableside, at our bedside, and along the roadside. Life is death and resurrection.

As I mull and muse over Christ's words, over my own deaths and resurrections, the battle between life and death is eternally fought between that grim graveyard—my egocentric self—and the divine love and forgiveness that are resurrection and life. The path out of this struggle seems so clear and simple when I grasp it; yet, again and again, I fall away from such unfathomable love back into old patterns, old traps, old self-pities, and die once more.

I die because I have such a need to be right; I die and go to Hell before I say "I'm wrong; I'm sorry; I made a mistake;" and I justify myself at all cost. I live when I know we are all wrong—all sinners—and are made right through the love of Christ.

I die when I put up my facades of self-righteousness and judgment. Out of my desperate need for affirmation and love, I can't let you see how I truly am on the inside lest you reject me. I live when I am vulnerable and let you know me in weakness and confess my dependence on a strength that is a grace given me.

I die when I tread the dreary workaholic road. I strain every nerve and sinew to be the first and best and somehow prove my worth, all the while doing violence to myself and to my family with my eternal busyness. I live when I get my priorities right: the Kingdom of God first, my dear ones next, and then the world of my busy schedule.

I die when I manipulate people for my own needs, taking from them their freedom to find life. I live when I hold them in a open hand—my children in particular—and say, "Go with my love; find your life for yourself."

I live when I know that I will continue to live and die, make the same old mistakes, forget the "good news" and blunder around in the dark, and that I cannot change these destructive forces within me. But "Thanks be to God," the changing is God's business, not mine. When we come out of our graves, Christ is there, resurrected in his power and might, eager to empower us to live again. Our task is to follow him into life.

FEBRUARY 1984

> *The good which I want to do, I fail to do; but what I do is the wrong against my will; and if what I do is against my will, clearly it is no longer I who am the agent, but sin that has its lodging in me...But where sin was thus multiplied, grace immediately exceeded it...*
> **St. Paul**

Mull and muse as I will through the theological maze of will, free will, and sin, I can't find too many answers, only glimmers through a glass darkly. But it seems to me that it is perhaps better to have a big, bold sin than a little, narrow, picky one. Big sins are obvious and self-mortifying; little ones are devious and look for self-justification.

From grammar school days, I had a friend who was an alcoholic—much against his will—until he found help through the A.A. group that met in the parish hall here at Trinity. What a joy in this man! He was released from a big sin that had him, and he had a big, open testimony about his emancipation. He could laugh at himself, all the while exulting in this amazing grit in his powerless will.

It seems that big sins have more potential for the gifts of grace than small ones. Christ told the Pharisees as the prostitute anointed his feet with perfume: "...her great love proves that her many sins have been forgiven; where little has been forgiven, little love is shown."

Are we then to exult in big sins? Only to the point where we, like this poor woman, can accept forgiveness for ourselves; and then, as we forgive ourselves, we forgive others. This opens a whole new world. No longer do we ostracize, criticize, judge, gossip, or know the answers for other peoples' lives. We keep an eye on the good we fail to do, and every morning pick up the struggles anew, knowing that even though our sin multiplies, grace immeasurably exceeds it.

Grace Abounding

Our epistle readings for the past few Sundays have been from St. Paul who tells us not to rejoice in wrong. This makes me mull and muse about our reaction to uncovered sins since we Puritans seem sometimes to revel in these sinister matters, recognizing at a glance all these easy roads to perdition.

I was cradled on a good Baptist bench and from infancy was warned of every "not to": drinking, smoking, dancing, card playing, cussing, movie-going, Sabbath ball-playing, shorts, make-up, too much skin showing anywhere, and mixed bathing which was the two sexes swimming in the creek together. The hush-hush of all sins, which my young ears did not fathom, was some mysterious, unpardonable evil forever banishing one not only from God, but from any good standing anywhere—the sins of the lustful flesh. As we rocked on the front porch in our Sabbatical holiness, recounting our neighbors' failings, we did not know we were committing the unpardonable sin.

Jesus said the only sin that cannot be forgiven is the sin against the Holy Spirit when it claims us and we hear its call but harden ourselves and will not hear. We continue in our judgmental attitudes and refuse the Holy Spirit with its offer of the greatest gift of all, the ability to love and forgive. We choose to rejoice in the wrong.

Let's all confess: Haven't we all secretly delighted when we have heard of our neighbors' sins? I have. Then I held my shabby little ego up and patted it for being good. For shame! We have all lied, stolen, coveted, lusted, and dishonored our parents. Some of us have been caught, but most of us have hidden behind our masks of respectability. But these sins are small indeed when we look at our rejection of what we can become through the gifts of the Spirit. We can be Christ in the world!

Then if we are the Body of Christ, we are given the ability to love our neighbors. So, let's be about that. Let us no longer smirk at his indiscretions but lift him up in caring support and prayer so that he might find his way. "Let us not rejoice in wrong, but rejoice in the right," giving ourselves up to the Holy Spirit who will show us "the more excellent way."

Grace Abounding

For the foolishness of God is wiser than men...whoever of you imagines that he is wise with this world's wisdom must become a fool if he really is to be wise.

St. Paul, I Corinthians

The foolishness of God! These words have always jarred against my sentimental piety. Since I was taught that God is omnipotent and omniscient and sits on his throne and keeps score in a huge judgment-day book, how could anyone speak of his foolishness? How can this unreasonable statement from St. Paul make sense? In the same writing, he tells us we must become fools to be wise. Therefore, attempting to be wise, I deem myself a fool as I mull and muse over the untenable, the unreasonable, the paradoxical, that must be the key to a glimmer of understanding into God's foolishness.

Certainly, his most outrageous foolishness was in his invasion of history with a helpless baby. All the power for the creation of galaxies and constellations in incomprehensible and unending space was in his hands; and yet we ponder the unreasonable, the foolishness of God, as he confounded Hebraic wisdom, Greek philosophy, and Roman organizational might with the gift of a child. But the most untenable and paradoxical part of this foolishness was the reason for the gift: God loved us so much that he gave us this example of selfless love to suffer and die that we might know the depth of his passion to redeem us. With this mighty act of grace, reason is abandoned, mystery is embraced as we become little children and accept this unmerited gift of God's love.

Again, it is unreasonable that I, a mere speck in time and creation, have been encountered by the Eternal, the Holy, the Divine—call it what you will—that confronts me, turns me around, gives the whole world a new complexion, and assures me I'm all right and will continue to be all right. The temporal has been invaded by an unreasonable hope that surprises me with a joy, a giddiness, that I can only attribute to the foolishness of God. All my finite wisdom strains toward the understanding of this encounter; and once more, the rational surrenders to the irrational and the final recourse is the leap—unbelieving, yet believing—into faith.

Foolishness, faith, folly, wisdom, all converge at one point in history—the Cross of Christ—where we find revealed not only the foolishness of God but "Christ the power of God and the wisdom of God."

MARCH 1987

I have been taking a class in French after a forty-seven year hiatus, and I find I am learning more than "Bonjour, Monsieur." I am learning that sin is not original. It is humbling, in fact frightening, to have surface after all these years the cold fear of being found out far from Straight A material; and I am amazed at the multitude of excuses and whipping boys that can be summoned to one's aid. For me, I have found a new excuse—"I'm too old; my brain has rotted."

So why do I say sin is not original? Did not our mother Eve when she lost her innocence and was faced with her freedom—her knowledge of good and evil—try to avoid her responsibility of persuing the good? Down the eons, I can hear her: "The snake told me if I ate the fruit, I would be smart like the gods. The snake deceived me. If I had known the course would be so hard after I bit the apple I never would have signed up. Of course, Adam's responsible too. He could have warned me about getting in over my head, but he decided this idea of instant smarts was a good one; so when I plucked the forbidden fruit, he bit right in. That male chauvinist, ruling over me! Now I'm pregnant, he's all worked down from sweating his brow, and all he can do is blame me. I'm having a big test in Good/Evil 102 tomorrow. I think I'll be sick. God's not fair. You never know what's on his tests. Some of the questions he asks aren't even in the book. When I get all these babies, I'll teach them the easy way out: blame God, the snake, sour apples, scanty fig leaves, too new genes, or the Edenist!" Poor Eve. She never had an unhappy childhood to blame.

So what's original about sin? From Eve to us, this long line of excuses, cherished and unbroken, has kept us from honestly facing our fears and inadequacies. This dishonesty keeps us ever separated from our true selves, from the fulfillment of our potential, from being made in the image of God. This is the essence of evil. This is original sin.

The Lord God foreordained St. Paul to tell us how he deals with sin. "Where sin abounded, grace did much more abound." So surely when the Lord God was walking in the cool of evening East-of-Eden and came upon Eve wrestling with her lessons, he must have offered her his grace: "My daughter, I demand the discipline of true effort. I want your willingness to give of your best without excuses. I give you the opportunity to excel, but undergird you with the knowledge that you are eternally cherished even though you fail. I undergird you again with the knowledge that failure and suffering are often the parents of your true self. You will not always understand the lesson of good and evil, but in your openness to learn, I will come to you in unexpected ways. I will be that peace, that indwelling sense of worth, that affirms your efforts to grow. I will teach you the final lesson so you may choose the good over the evil and then you may embrace yourself and all those whom I have given you. Then, and only then, will I have made you into the Image of God."

OCTOBER 1990

Awake, my soul, stretch every nerve and press with vigor on: a heavenly race demands thy zeal, and an immortal crown.
Philip Doddridge 1775

This old Calvinistic hymn doesn't do my frayed psyche much good. If I must "stretch every nerve and press with vigor on," this may be the stretch that breaks this Nervous Nelly, leaving me totally unable to make the heavenly race. If the heavenly race demands my zeal, where does my zeal get its power and why would it be so presumptuous as to demand an immortal crown? Or maybe it's my soul demanding the crown. Mr. Doddridge, I need some mulling and musing time to think through your words as we hear Bishop Reynolds' call across the Diocese for *Total Ministry.*

We of the Diocese of Middle Tennessee have begun a "heavenly race," the goal being the involvement of each member of every parish, will *All* using their unique talents in ministry: no more sitting on the back benches, no more hiding lights under a bushel, no more letting the clergy do it or the ardent church workers, no more ignoring the world outside the safe wall of the institutionalized church, no more refusing Christ's all-prevailing voice—"Follow me." Awake, our souls, stretch every nerve.

In years past I have stretched my nerves with the Baptists who have taught me that each person was his own priest, responsible for his servanthood. Then the Presbyterians taught me of the "Sanctity of the Laity" with each person being ordained to be a minister and on an equal footing with the clergy. Now the Episcopalians have me into *Total Ministry,* and I'm searching with vigor to find the fine lines between Personal Priesthood, Sanctity of the Laity, and Total Ministry. But I shall press with vigor on.

Grace Abounding

And I press to some conclusions: After having stretched through *Everyone-Win-one, Every-Member-a-Minister,* and *All-on-the-Altar,* I am still faced with the unadorned call: "Follow me." My call to servanthood does not go away amid my protestations of worn ideas and failed programs. My effectual call to servanthood does depend on the empowering of my zeal by the Holy Spirit who ever goes before us and calls us to be his people. He calls to all across the Diocese. May our souls awake!

The victorious conclusion is Christ's words from the Revelation of John:

> *Hear, you who have ears to hear what the spirit says to churches! Here I stand knocking at the door; if anyone hears my voice and opens the door, I will come in and sit down to supper with him and he with me. To him who is victorious I will grant a place on my throne, as I myself was victorious and sat down with my father on his throne. Hear, you who have ears to hear, what the Spirit says to the churches*

Our *Total Ministry* is in direct proportion to how wide we open the door. Our victorious servanthood is our immortal crown.

JULY 1996

> *Today I say to you, unless you turn and become like children, you will never enter the kingdom of heaven. Whoever humbles himself like this child is the greatest in the kingdom of heaven.*
> **Matthew 18:3-4**

I have a child within me who has never grown up. Psychologist tell me I must nurture this inner child, heal its hurts, probe its psyche, and let it lead me into adulthood. To be child-honest, I don't want my child to grow up, but to turn me around, play through the distempers of the years, and show me the yellow brick road to this kingdom of heaven.

According to our master-teacher, to be great in this kingdom, my child must humble me. I must suffer this child to come unto me and lead me. Suffering with my child's teaching, I find too soon that I'm no good at being humble and honest. I have a wall of facades so wide, so high, so patched, so confused, so cherished, pretending at being grown-up, that my child is lost. I must find her to help me break down a long conviction of my worthlessness and get me on the road to the kingdom so we can become alive together. We need to play. I'm tired of playing adult and being dead-dull serious. My child needs to laugh, to laugh with all the other children, and above all, to laugh at myself. I need *leap-frog*, and *hop-scotch*, and *Ring around the Roses* since I can hardly hop or scotch anymore. Yet, my honest, liberated child encourages me into spontaneity and joy, which are my right in the kingdom of heaven.

So my child says to your child: "Little children, let us love one another." Let us know that we all hide behind our wall. We pretend to be wise and expose our foolishness; we pretend at goodness and are found to be empty fuss-budgets; we pretend at status in the world and our pride goes before our fall; we pretend to be humble and stumble on self-righteousness. This is our grown-up world.

Crying behind our walls, we must jump over them in a leap-frog of faith, knowing that we are cherished by the greatest love and acceptance of all time; and, clapping our hands in praise, we shall skip into the kingdom of our true inheritance. The offer of the kingdom of heaven is right now.

Abba Father, help us to hold hands with all our friends, near and far and everywhere, so we can dance and sing and be free. Since your kingdom is right now and forever, may we not be afraid to go through its gates and sing "Ring around the Roses" in a new and timeless place. There are no booger-bears there; there is no dark at the top of the stairs; and you, dear Father, will wipe away every tear from our eyes.

AUGUST 1997

> *A bastard shall not enter into the congregation of the Lord; even to the tenth generation none of his descendants shall enter the congregation of the Lord.*
>
> **Deuteronomy 23:2**

With the gift of Christ we were delivered from Moses' Old Testament God who banished bastards. This God would have a full time banishing job if he read the birth announcements in our local newspaper. This outcast list would demand that he set up a tedious bureaucracy for ten generations worth of "outside" children and post genealogy guards at the Sunday School doors to keep the little bastards out. Carefully conceived children could not be defiled.

Grace Abounding

Before I condemn the Mosaic Law too severely, I can recall in my time that the word "illegitimate" was something said behind the hand, and the stigma was ever new in our small judgmental world, giving us hours of delicious conjectures of clandestine matings and the progeny thereof. A child of such an assignation appeared at Kirkwood Church, and the mystery of her conception lay forever unsolved in hot beds of gossip.

Her mother was no doubt Mab, the fairy queen, and her father a Rhett Butler because Dolly Mae was a tiny version of Bonnie, the daughter of Scarlett and Rhett. As a toddler, she was a porcelain doll, tousled with cascades of dark curls and illuminated with great shining eyes the color of bluebird wings...whence this vision of delight, this ethereal outsider?

Two sisters, Mollie and Bess, who were reputed to be Indian, lived in almost total isolation in our community. Once a year they walked abroad, put on their long black dresses, pulled the door to on their cabin, and came to the big meetin' at our church. They were there every night, holding down the same bench on the back row and scanning the July congregation with the roving eyes of a suspicious lizard. Why they came this one time a year we did not know. Darkly mute, they sat without communication and evaporated into the night when the final sinner had been exhorted. To these two from God knows where, came Dolly Mae.

Suddenly Mollie and Bess's fortune did an upswing that confounded the neighborhood. There was food, there were clothes, there were repairs for their cabin, and we saw that they had two expressions—the second one brought on by the joy of having this little girl enter their bleak world.

The bastard's beginning was ever before us. Who is this child? What son or daughter of our pure society is hiding his sin? Who are Mollie and Bess to bring such doings among decent people? The mystery of Dolly Mae's parentage ran the gamut from movie stars to a liaison between a family doctor and a fourteen year old patient. For someone from somewhere supplied her with all she needed and the two crones with fuel, food, and clothing. Close neighbors watched their cabin for comings and goings, but, as far as we knew, no one solved the mystery of Dolly Mae.

Dolly Mae grew in stature and knowledge and was a delight to all who knew her. At length she joined the congregation of the Lord at

Kirkwood Church, and we gladly accepted her as a child of God, no longer an outcast, but an heir through hope.

Who are the true heirs, the legitimate ones of God? James writes, "Listen my beloved brothers. Has not God chosen those who are poor in the world to be rich in faith and heirs of the kingdom which he has promised to those who love him?" And St. Paul in Galatians—"There is neither Jew nor Greek, there is neither slave nor free, there is neither male nor female..." and I shall add neither legitimate or illegitimate... "for you are all one in Christ...heirs according to promise." Christ's gift of love poured into us makes us true sons and daughters and joint heirs with him. Bastards are of their own making. They refuse to surrender to this all encompassing love of Christ and choose to live in their joyless world of hatred, judgment, and exclusion.

May God be praised for his redemption of our illegitimacy and for the promised inheritance prepared for all who love him.